PREPARING FOR

ENGLISH FOR COMMERCE

Other business-related titles of interest include:

BRIEGER, N. and J. COMFORT
*Business Contacts**

BRIEGER, N. and J. COMFORT
*Technical Contacts**

BRIEGER, N. and J. COMFORT
*Social Contacts**

BRIEGER, N. and J. COMFORT
Business Issues

BRIEGER, N. and J. COMFORT
Early Business Contacts

BRIEGER, N. and J. COMFORT
*Secretarial Contacts**

DAVIES, S. *et al.*
Bilingual Handbooks of Business Correspondence and Communication

McGOVERN, J. and J. McGOVERN
Bank on Your English

PALSTRA, R.
*Telephone English**

PALSTRA, R.
Telex English

POTE, M. *et al.*
*A Case for Business English**

*includes audio cassette(s)

PREPARING FOR

ENGLISH FOR COMMERCE

DAVID DAVIES

Lecturer in EFL (ESP), State of Bahrain, Ministry of Health,
College of Health Sciences

DOUGLAS PICKETT

Senior Examinations Officer (Languages and EFL),
The London Chamber of Commerce and Industry Examinations Board

PRENTICE HALL

New York   London   Toronto   Sydney   Tokyo   Singapore

First published 1990 by
Prentice Hall International (UK) Ltd
66 Wood Lane End, Hemel Hempstead
Hertfordshire HP2 4RG
A division of
Simon Schuster International Group

Typeset in 10/12 pt Compugraphic Palacio
by MHL Typesetting Ltd, Coventry

Printed and bound in Great Britain
at The Camelot Press, Trowbridge, Wiltshire.

Library of Congress Cataloging-in-Publication Data

Davies, David
    Preparing for English for commerce / David Davies and Douglas Pickett
        p. cm.
    ISBN 0-13-697293-4 : $8.95
        1. English language — Business English — Examinations — Study guides.
    2. Commerce — Examinations — Study guides. I. Davies, David.
    II. Title.
PE1115.P47   1990
428'.0076 — dc20
                                                                            89-29488
                                                                                CIP

British Library Cataloguing in Publication Data

Davies, David
Preparing for English for commerce.
1. English language. Business English. Manuals
I. Title II. Pickett, Douglas
808'.066651021

ISBN 0-13-697293-4

1 2 3 4 5   94 93 92 91 90

Contents

Introduction

The London Chamber of Commerce and Industry (LCCI) examination 'English for Commerce' caters for tens of thousands of candidates annually, so a comprehensive textbook to help students prepare for it is long overdue.

However, this book appears at a time when there is a wealth of English textbooks on the market, most of them for general English but many of them also for business English.

It does not try to do what they all do — to lay a broad foundation of general or business English. Rather, it assumes that this foundation will have been laid and it concentrates on the narrower task of leading students from that point to the 'English for Commerce' examination at the First and Second Levels.

Nevertheless, to ensure that the basic common ground has been covered, it contains an element of revision and consolidation of the basic principles of writing English for business and other practical everyday purposes. In this respect, the material will also be very useful for students of business English, who may not be taking the examination. In addition, there is specific training in the forms and tasks of the examination using past examination material as the basis for exercises, exercises that afford genuine insight into how English is composed, understood and analysed.

Business English, and examinations in it, are not a world apart. There is a considerable overlap with general English though this overlap tends to diminish the more one specialises professionally and the higher one aims linguistically. Hence, at First and Second Level of 'English for Commerce' there is a good deal that will be familiar and accessible to the student of general English and what the examination provides is a systematic and measured transition to higher and more specialised types of English. Candidates who have successfully passed the Second Level will be able to address themselves to taking the specialised modules now being planned in the English of a variety of business specialisms — banking, travel and tourism, technology, insurance, shipping, etc.

Whatever wider purposes it may serve, however, the shape and content of the present textbook have been determined by the form and requirements of the examination and we need to examine these a little more closely.

'English for Commerce'

The examination was launched in 1977 and uses the following well-tried examining techniques:

1. Continuous writing tasks (essay, report, etc.).
2. Comprehension tasks.
3. Summarising tasks.
4. Letter-writing tasks.

There is nothing specifically business oriented about any of these but they are reliable and stable techniques for eliciting the candidates' language, knowledge and imagination on the basis of which examiners can judge whether their language is at the level to carry out day-to-day business tasks.

Fashions in teaching and examining come and go but whatever techniques are chosen, they all rely for their intrinsic validity on the fact that skills can be transferred from whatever tasks appear in the examination to tasks performed in real life. Provided there is sufficient analogy and common ground between the two such as make the possibility of transfer credible, employers and other users of examinations may have confidence in the qualifications presented to them. There are many more testing techniques than can possibly be crowded into one examination and therefore any examination will have to make a selection. Despite a tendency in recent years to ignore skill transfer and concentrate on extreme forms of face validity and 'authenticity', it remains true that the sort of tasks set for 'English for Commerce' test broad-spectrum capacities that underlie good written communication for any practical purpose, just as the standard driving test equips one to drive any sort of car on any sort of road in any kind of weather.

The pattern of defects

In 1987 I carried out a thorough analysis of examiners' reports over a three-year period* and was able to establish a pattern of candidate faults that is probably stable despite minor variations from year to year. These patterns for First and Second Levels are represented on the pie charts opposite.

What is immediately obvious from both charts is that formal *linguistic* defects like bad concord, bad syntax and mechanical inaccuracy account for just under 50 per cent of the defects while two varieties of *carelessness* account for some 26 per cent at First Level and 16 per cent at Second Level — the difference perhaps being accounted for by the fact that the experience of taking First Level improves this aspect of performance at Second Level.

All these five factors, which together account for over 60 per cent of the causes of failure, are things that can be taught and improved upon, as are most of the others. It is with this knowledge, and a determination to ensure that students can and will improve on all these fronts, that this book is offered to the teacher and the student.

* Now published in *A Guide to English for Commerce* LCCIEB, 1990.

CANDIDATES' FAULTS

First Level

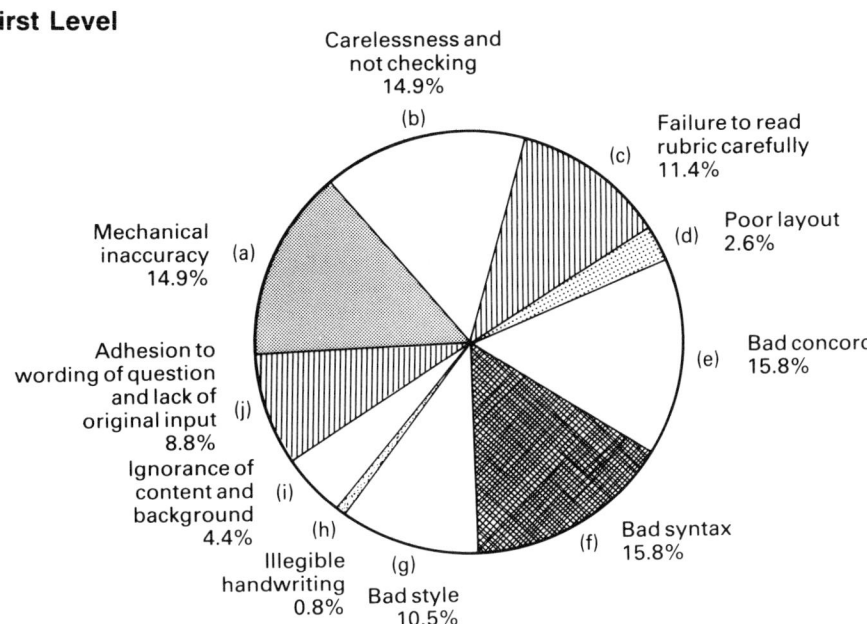

Second Level

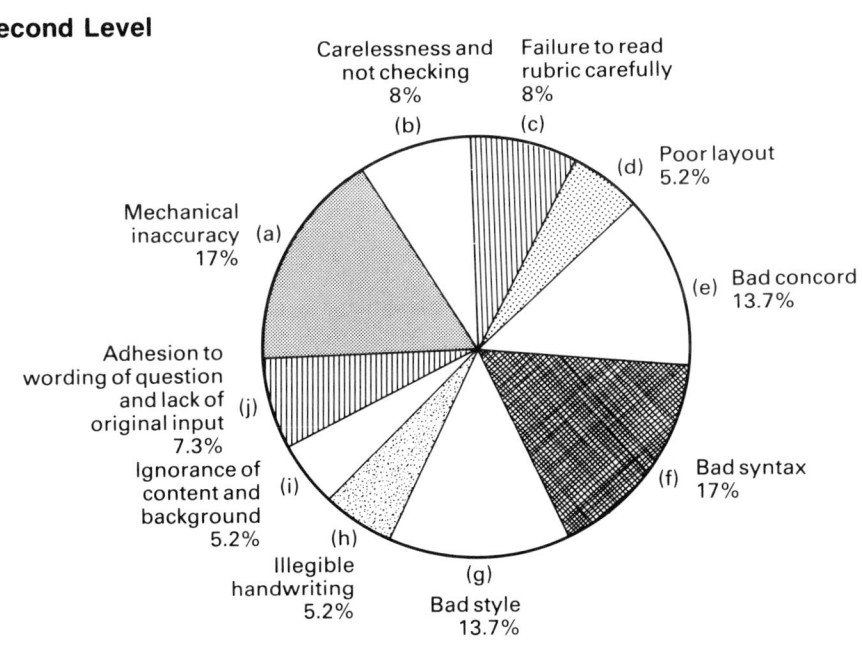

The book

A glance down the table of contents will show that the book closely follows the content of the examination but it also dives below the surface to analyse and exercise the skills that lead to good performance in the examination tasks.

Although the tasks are written ones, it is recognised that communication in writing has its roots in everyday communication in speech, just as business transactions have their roots in everyday human transactions. There is therefore an attempt throughout to base the units on oral classroom activity and to enliven it with group and pair work. Ultimately, however, the student has to be left alone to practise the techniques learned in class and to be applied in the examination.

There is, therefore, a wealth of holistic exercises close to the real-life examination which synthesise the skills analysed and practised separately in earlier units.

Though differing in linguistic standard, the First and Second Levels have two tasks in common — continuous writing and letter-writing — and are therefore part of a continuum across these skills. They are different in that the First Level has a comprehension passage whereas the Second Level offers a summary task. Both of these, however, are based on comprehension and analysis of an expository prose passage and only the ways of signalling comprehension differ. These two tasks therefore also have a great deal in common.

Because of this considerable overlap and continuity, both levels can be treated harmoniously within the covers of one book as representing 'foundation' and 'intermediate' levels of the same skills. It is strongly recommended that candidates take the First Level before they attempt the Second Level, unless they have a secure pass in some other well-established public examination using similar formats, e.g. Cambridge First Certificate. Nevertheless, it is recognised that students will be making the transition from general to business English at a variety of levels so by spanning both levels in one textbook, we provide teachers and students with the facility of finding a suitable starting point within the material offered.

It is expected, therefore, that according to the previous learning experience of students, some units will demand little attention while others will demand a lot.

On the basis of this, teachers should choose the right moment to introduce the book. Broadly, we might suggest three to six months before the examination, depending on what other books are being used, what other topics the course is covering and how many contact hours are available.

There are forty-two units in all, half dealing with the First Level and half with the Second Level; though insofar as the Second Level rests on skills acquired for the First Level, they all contribute to the Second Level and might therefore provide the textbook for a one-year (thirty-week?) Second Level course provided the right foundations have already been laid.

This book is envisaged as a *class* textbook — one which both teachers and students will use. Teachers will not, therefore, have to wrestle with a massive teacher's book. The authors assume teachers know their jobs and their students and do not want textbook writers looking over their shoulders. On the contrary, we should like to free them to expand, supplement or modify the basic menu from their own creative powers and there will be days when students will benefit most from reading the business press or discussing business issues or current affairs. The book is therefore to be used permissively rather than prescriptively. Its maximum benefits will accrue only to those who have a chance to talk to the teacher and other students in class; but the straightforward explanations and key to exercises will also make it useful for students working on their own.

The 'English for Commerce' examination, to the surprise of many, is open to native speakers as well as learners of English as a foreign or second language; but it should not be imagined that native speakers will therefore always sail through. In actual fact, the lists of prizewinners for the best results show that it is often the non-native speaker who scales the heights. Nevertheless, it is broadly true to say that native speakers should not fall down on purely linguistic faults of syntax and concord in the same way that the foreign learner might. However, they find the examination a difficult challenge in other ways and the registration and marking system makes no distinction between native and non-native speakers other than obliging non-native speakers to take short oral tests at Second and Third Levels. These are a relatively minor part of the examination and are not catered for in this textbook since it is quite rare for someone who is well prepared for the written papers to fail the oral examination. This lack of discrimination means that everyone is judged by the same criteria regardless of where they started and how they managed to satisfy those criteria. This makes sense in the increasingly homogeneous world of international business, where employers are interested in results, not origins, and in product rather than process.

It is hoped that this textbook will enable all those studying English for business purposes to attain the goals set by the examination and to participate more fully in the exciting and rewarding world of international business.

G.D. Pickett
1990

FIRST LEVEL

Letter

Unit 1 ADDRESS, DATE, SALUTATION AND CLOSE

Here are the beginnings and endings of three letters:

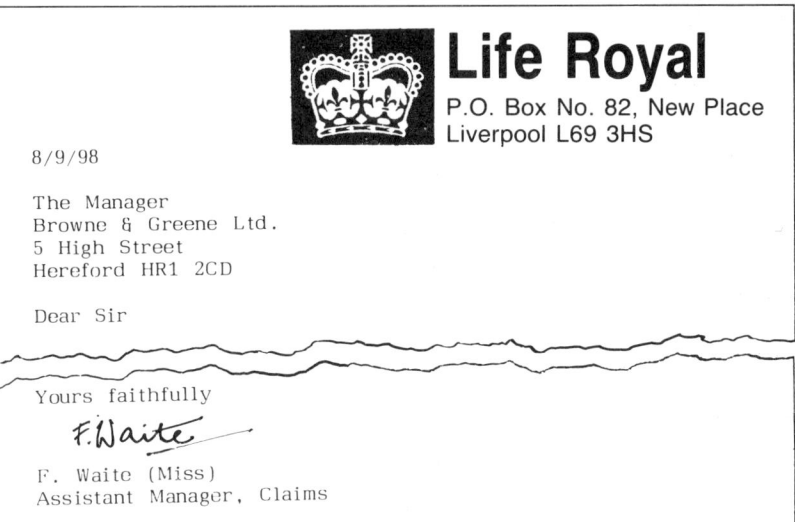

Life Royal
P.O. Box No. 82, New Place
Liverpool L69 3HS

8/9/98

The Manager
Browne & Greene Ltd.
5 High Street
Hereford HR1 2CD

Dear Sir

Yours faithfully

F. Waite

F. Waite (Miss)
Assistant Manager, Claims

2 Elm Avenue
Southend
SS4 7BD

Dr D. Black, Principal
Globe School of Languages
66 Grimshaw Gardens
Folkestone
Kent CT20 2PY

3/8/94

Dear Dr Black,

Yours sincerely

John White

John White

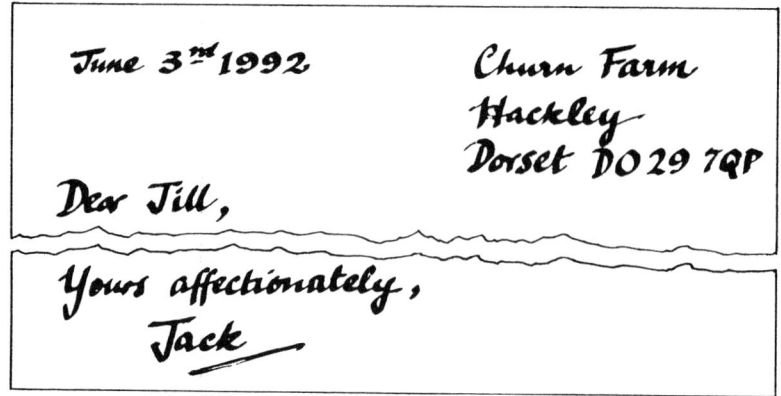

June 3rd 1992   Churn Farm
                                Hackley
                                Dorset DO 29 7QP

Dear Jill,

Yours affectionately,
    Jack

Information

As you can see, even the beginnings and endings of letters contain information about the following:

1.   When the letter was written and sent.
2.   Who wrote it.
3.   Where they can be contacted.
4.   Who the letter is written to.
5.   Where they are.

Exercise 1

Answer the following:

(a) Who lives at Churn Farm?
(b) Where does John White live?
(c) Who is the manager of Browne & Greene's?
(d) Where is the head office of Life Royal?
(e) Who is in charge of the Globe School of Languages?
(f) What is the job of F. Waite?
(g) Does she know the person she is writing to?
(h) Where is the Globe School?
(i) Are all three letters business letters?
(j) Which two writers know each other best?

Formality

The three letters are not the same. They use different forms of greeting and different types of presentation. They are written with different degrees of formality, depending on how well the writers know each other.

Exercise 2

Arrange the letters in order of formality:

(a) MOST FORMAL   (letter _____)
(b)   (letter _____)
(c) LEAST FORMAL   (letter _____)

Parts of a letter

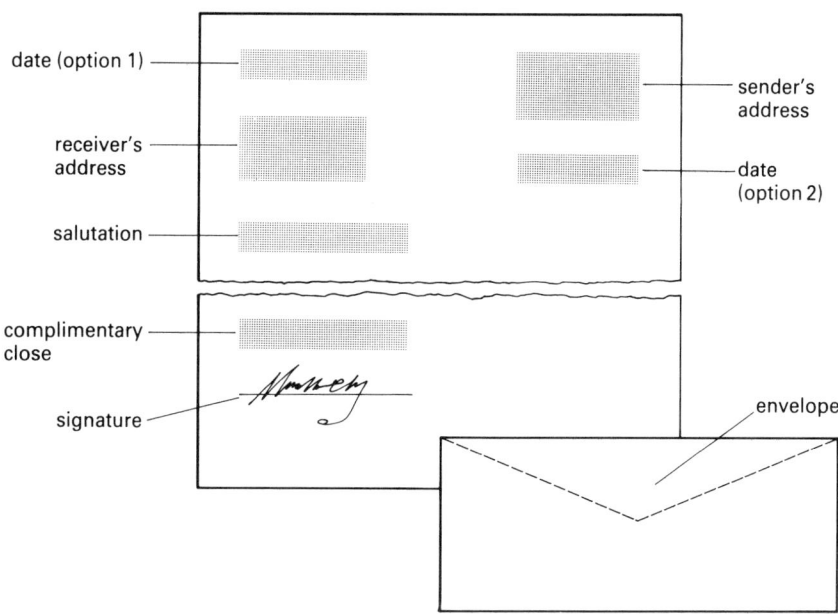

Envelope

Note that the envelope carries the receiver's address, as in the letter itself, written in the centre of the plain side. The sender's address may also be written on the envelope, in the corner or on the back, as long as the two are not confused.

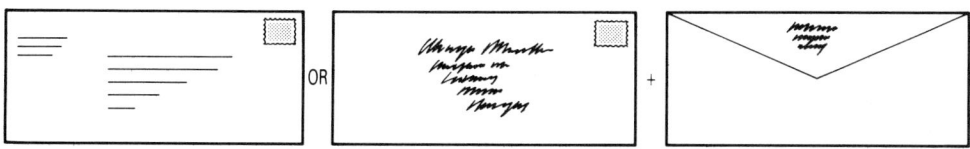

Exercise 3

Complete the following table using information from the three letters:

Tone	Salutation	Complimentary close
formal	(a) _____	(b) _____
semi-formal	(c) _____	(d) _____
personal	(e) _____	Yours sincerely*

*A variety of closes are possible in a personal letter, depending on the relationship between the speakers; some others are as follows:
'Love', 'Best wishes', 'Yours affectionately', 'Yours ever', etc.

Exercise 4

Correct the following:

(a) Dear Bill ...   Yours faithfully, Ben
(b) Dear Mr Willis ...   Yours faithfully, John Laws
(c) Dear Sir ...   Yours, Albert Bridge
(d) Dear Marge ...   Yours faithfully, Lill
(e) Dear Sir ...   Yours sincerely, J.J. Kale

Letter layouts

For Exercises 5–7, provide the following:

1. Date
2. Sender's address
3. Receiver's address
4. Salutation
5. Close
6. Signature
7. Addressed envelope

Lay them out as shown above.

Exercise 5

You are Ronald Wrigley of General Dealers Ltd, Mill Lane, London EC1 2BF. You are writing to the Station Master at British Rail, Little Chippings, Buckinghamshire MK18 9OL. Use today's date.

Exercise 6

You are Ben Beverley and you live at 29 Oak End Lane, Bradford BD5 4RG. You are writing to Miss Rosie Lee, The Nook Inn, Ingleton, Derby DE7 8ME. She is a very close friend.

Exercise 7

You are Walter Wimborne of 149 Great North Road, Motherwell ML2 2WA. You are writing to Arthur Pointer, who is the manager of Gerry's Building Supplies, Grimes Street, Gloucester GL2 6YH.

Dear Sir or Madam?

If you are not sure whether the receiver is male or female, the salutation 'Dear Sir or Madam' is used. Consider the following table:

Dear Sir or Madam	Man or woman, name not known
Dear Sir	Man, name not known
Dear Madam	Woman, name not known
Dear Miss Smith Dear Mrs Smith Dear Ms Smith }	Alternative salutations for women. If not sure, use 'Ms'

Exercise 8

Choose the correct salutation and complimentary close for the following:

(a) The Manager, Lady Fair Fashions Ltd
(b) The Secretary, Pitton Miners' Club
(c) Lobelia Jones, Gaunton Women's Guild
(d) The Foreman, Brick's Construction Co.
(e) Mrs Lydia Lang, Cromby & Son Solicitors

Exercise 9

Name (a)–(f).

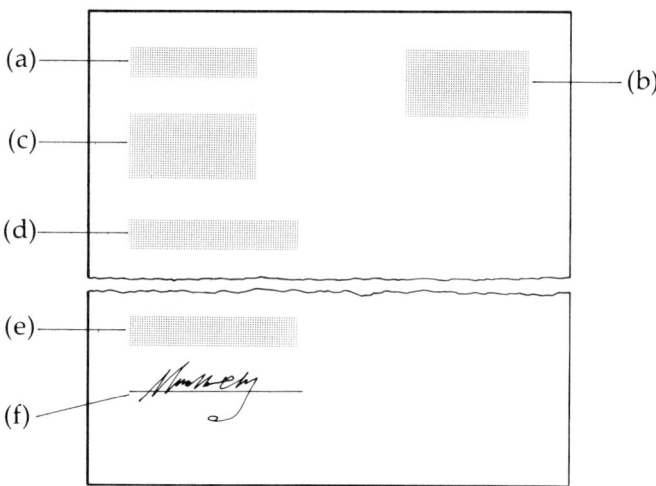

Unit 2   ADDRESSES

Part of the LCCI letter-writing task involves making up addresses, as in the following example. You will have to invent a suitable name and address for yourself, and one for the person you are writing to.

Letter question

> You are the secretary of a young people's club and you are writing to the Public Relations Officer of a manufacturing company . . .

Sample answer

```
                                        Dalton Youth Centre
                                        5 Thorpe Lane
                                        Huddersfield
                                        HD4 6AE

The Public Relations Officer
Wroughton Manufacturing Ltd
28-34 Lord Street
Huddersfield
HD2 8UJ
```

What does an address consist of?

1. The Public Relations Officer
2. Wroughton Manufacturing Ltd
3. 28–34 Lord Street
4. Huddersfield
5. HD2 8UJ

A business address consists of at least five parts — six if you add the country at the end, although this is not necessary if you are writing from within Britain.

Exercise 1

Put the parts of an address into the correct order:

> the number and street/the postcode/the addressee/the town or city/the name of the company

Company names

You can often tell something about a company or institution from the name, e.g:

> Worldwide Travel Ltd
> Federal Investment Trust
> Allied Building Society Plc
> Grimes & Sons Machine Tools Ltd
> Ladyfair Fashions Ltd

Exercise 2

Match the following institutions with the names:

(a) a young people's club   Adventure Safaris Ltd
(b) a shoe shop   The Farchester Echo
                                                In Step Ltd
(c) a travel agency
(d) an insurance company   Greys Instruments Ltd
(e) a local newspaper   Brite Interiors
(f) a decorating firm   Newfont Council
(g) a youth hostel
(h) a local authority   Prudent & Provident
(i) a sports club   Greenhill Lodge   Sandford Athletic
(j) a manufacturing firm   Oak End Community Centre

Exercise 3   Writing to the right person

For each of the companies, clubs, etc., in Exercise 2, decide which of the following will be the addressee:

> the warden/the editor/the secretary/the manager/the chief clerk

Postcode

In British addresses, a postcode is required. The British postcode usually consists of three parts (e.g. Oxford OX3 9BW):

1. One or two letters from the name of the town
   (a large city may have only one letter, and London addresses have area codes, e.g. N1 2AB, SE3 4CD, etc.).
2. One or two numbers showing the part of the town
   (the central areas may be 1 or 2; outer areas 12 or 13).
3. A number and two letters showing the exact location.

Exercise 4

Match the following towns with their postcodes:

Leicester	SE5 2RU
Swansea	SL6 3QL
Liverpool	TN3 7YD
London (South East)	SP9 5BE
Edinburgh	HP2 4RG
Birmingham	LE7 4RG
Tunbridge Wells	SA4 1EB
Southampton	B4 6DA
Slough	EH3 9YW
Hemel Hempstead	L17 4JG

Letterheads

Study the letterheads opposite and answer the exercises on page 12.

1

THE DICTIONARY OF ART

4 Little Essex Street London WC2R 3LF   Telephone 01-836 6633   Night line 01-836 3139

2

TURPIN
BARKER &
ARMSTRONG

CERTIFIED ACCOUNTANTS

The Old Town Jail, 14-18 London Road, Sevenoaks, Kent TN13 1AJ

Foreign and Commonwealth Office
London SW1A 2AH

4

3

Legal &
General

**Legal & General
Assurance Society Limited**

2 Montefiore Road
Hove
East Sussex
BN3 1SE

5

Kent
County
Council

PLANNING

Springfield
Maidstone
Kent   ME14 2LX

6

Mirror Group
Newspapers

Holborn Circus London EC1P 1DQ

7

The British Council

Promoting cultural, educational
and technical co-operation between
Britain and other countries

65 Davies Street
London W1Y 2AA

8

The British Bank of the Middle East

Falcon House
Curzon Street
LONDON
W1Y 8AA

10

SCHOOL OF ENGLISH
STUDIES FOLKESTONE

26 Grimston Gardens, Folkestone, Kent CT20 2PX, England
Telephone: 0303 850007 Fax: 0303 56544 Telex: 965415 SES G

9

SAVE &
PROSPER

Save & Prosper Group Ltd

Administration Centre
Hexagon House
28 Western Road
Romford RM1 3LB

Exercise 5

Which letterhead belongs to:

(a) a bank
(b) a government ministry
(c) a language teaching institution
(d) a book publisher
(e) a savings company
(f) a cultural organisation
(g) an insurance company
(h) a newspaper publisher
(i) a firm of accountants
(j) a local authority

Exercise 6   Understanding the postcode

Which of the organisations is located near:

(a) Tunbridge Wells
(b) Brighton
(c) Chatham

Exercise 7

Identify the street or road where you would find:

(a) The Dictionary of Art
(b) SES
(c) Save & Prosper
(d) MGN

Exercise 8

Find the name of the building occupied by:

(a) Turpin, Barker & Armstrong
(b) The British Bank of the Middle East
(c) Kent County Council
(d) Save & Prosper
(e) The Foreign and Commonwealth Office

Exercise 9   Practice

For each of the following you will need:

Your address

The name and address of the
   person you are writing to

The date

Salutation

Complimentary close

Signature

Write to:

1. Ann Smith, the secretary of a Leicester youth club.
2. An insurance company in Edinburgh.
3. Alf Roberts, a Liverpool sports club chairman.
4. A travel agency in Slough.
5. Basil Broome at his decorating firm in Hemel Hempstead.
6. A Birmingham manufacturing company.
7. A local newspaper in Tunbridge Wells.
8. Bryan Evans at his youth hostel near Swansea.

Note: Postcodes for these towns are shown in earlier exercises.

Unit 3 REASONS FOR WRITING ───────────────────

As secretary of a young people's club, write to an expert inviting him to address your members . . .

Oak End Community Centre
59 Oak End Lane
Leicester
LE2 7FG

2 November 1990

Professor Hans Stern
21 King Street
Cambridge
CB2 2RU

Dear Professor Stern,

I am writing to invite you to address the members of the Oak End Community Centre ...

Yours sincerely,

Ann Smith - HON. SEC.

Why are you writing?

When you write first, you will probably use the first sentence of your letter to say why you are writing. There are several ways of doing this:

I am writing to   ask   (a) _____
                  confirm (b) _____
                  complain (c) _____
                  inform   (d) _____
                  thank   (e) _____

Here is a slightly more 'polite' formulation:

I would like to   inquire (f) _____
                  apply   (g) _____
                  request (h) _____
                  invite   (i) _____
                  apologise (j) _____

Exercise 1   Which word comes next?

From the list below, choose the correct word to follow (a)–(j) opposite:

     about   that   you   for

Exercise 2

For each of the ten verbs ((a)–(j) opposite), choose a suitable complement from the following:

(a)   ... for the position advertised ...
(b)   ... for the misunderstanding ...
(c)   ... you for the high quality of services ...
(d)   ... you that arrangements have been made ...
(e)   ... you to visit our establishment ...
(f)   ... for some information on certain matters ...
(g)   ... the dates which we agreed ...
(h)   ... about the offer advertised ...
(i)   ... about the low standard of services ...
(j)   ... your assistance in certain matters ...

Exercise 3   'On behalf of ...'

If you are writing as a secretary or organiser, you may wish to write 'on behalf of' your members. Practise this opening by thinking of a name for each of the following:

On behalf of the _____ Society
                   _____ Club
                   _____ Group
                   _____ Organisation
                   _____ Association
                   _____ Institute

Exercise 4

If you write first, you will probably expect some kind of reply to your letter. In that case, the closing sentence will be to that effect, e.g:

     I look forward to hearing from you.

If you expect more than a letter, for example a visit or extra information, what might you write in place of 'hearing'?

I look forward to (a) _____ you next Thursday
                       (b) _____ your brochure
                       (c) _____ your factory
                       (d) _____ your representative
                       (e) _____

Replying

When you are writing in answer you will probably use the first sentence of your letter to acknowledge the one you have received. There are several ways of doing this, perhaps the most common being:

Thank you for your letter.

Exercise 5

Think of some other forms of written communication which could replace 'letter' in the above sentence:

Thank you for your (a) _____
                      (b) _____
                      (c) _____
                      (d) _____
                      (e) _____
                      (f) _____
                      (g) _____

Parts of speech

Note the different forms used in this example:

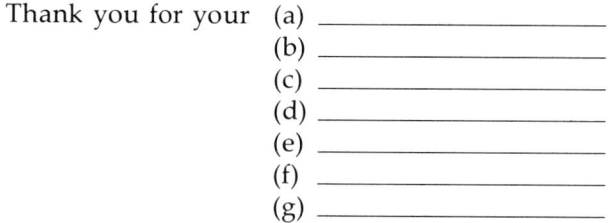

```
Dear Professor Stern,

I am writing to invite you ...
```

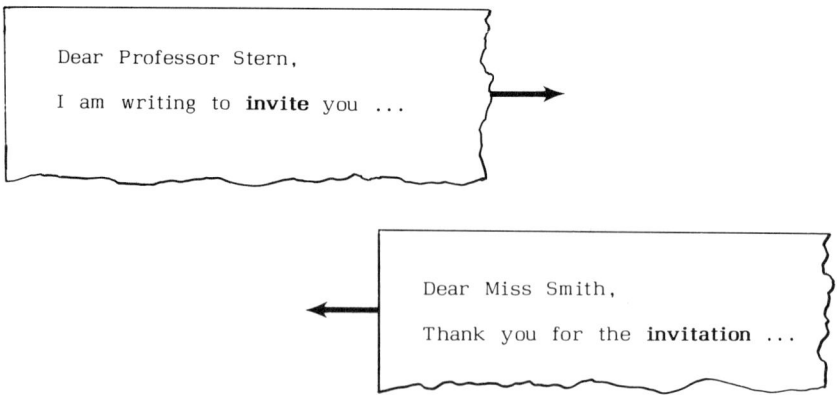

```
Dear Miss Smith,

Thank you for the invitation ...
```

Exercise 6

Complete the following table:

Verb	Noun
e.g. invite	invitation
(a) explain	_____
(b) advise	_____
(c) apply	_____
(d) thank	_____
(e) confirm	_____
(f) request	_____
(g) warn	_____
(h) inform	_____
(i) inquire	_____
(j) quote	_____

Tone

As we saw in Unit 1, letters can be formal or informal in tone. They can also be friendly or unfriendly! Instead of 'thank you for your letter', we might use a more impersonal and less friendly beginning:

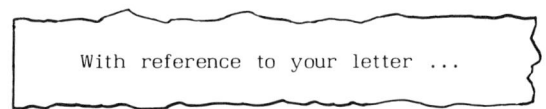

With reference to your letter ...

Exercise 7

Use 'thank you for' and 'with reference to' to reply to the following, e.g.:

I am writing to warn you ...
With reference to your warning ...

(a) I wish to complain ... _____
(b) I would like to apply ... _____
(c) I am writing to request ... _____
(d) I would like to inquire ... _____
(e) I suggest ... _____
(f) I enclose the information ... _____
(g) We have pleasure in inviting you ... _____
(h) This is to confirm ... _____
(i) I would like to explain ... _____
(j) Please be advised ... _____

Restating purpose

Another method is to restate the purpose of the original letter. This helps the reader by making it unnecessary to look up the original. It would be particularly useful if you were sending a copy to someone who did not see the original letter, e.g.:

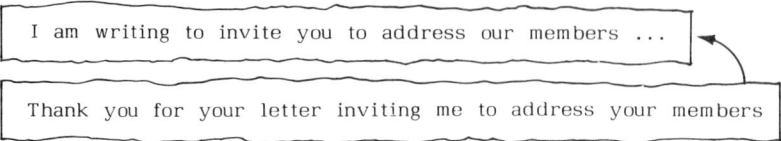

I am writing to invite you to address our members ...

Thank you for your letter inviting me to address your members

Exercise 8

Use the above formula to answer the following prompts:

(a) I am writing to confirm the arrangements for the fair ...
(b) I would like to inform you of my opinions on the subject ...
(c) I would like to inquire about the facilities you provide ...
(d) This is to advise you that your book is ready for collection ...
(e) You are cordially invited to the reception for Professor H. Stern ...

Date of letter

All letters **must** bear a date. This is usually in the top right-hand corner under the sender's address, but in typed letters which are blocked on the left it may be above the receiver's address. As the examination is done in manuscript, it is best to use the first method. Dates can be expressed in a variety of ways: 2 November 1990; 2.11.90; 2 Nov. '90; November 11th 1990; November 11 1990. In the United States it is sometimes the practice to write the number of the month first, e.g. 11.2.90 or 3.25.90, which can be confusing. We recommend candidates stick to the first convention which is now most widespread.

Date of receipt

Sometimes for reference purposes it helps to mention the date of the letter which you are answering, e.g.:

                                                                2 November 1990

Dear Professor Stern,

I am writing to invite you to address the members of the Oak End Community Centre at a time to your convenience.

Yours sincerely,   Ann Smith

```
                                              7 November 1990

Dear Miss Smith,

Thank you for your letter of 2nd November inviting me to address your
members.
```

Exercise 9

Answer the following, using the example given above. Invent an appropriate date
and address for the reply.

(a)
```
                                              10 October 1991

Dear Sir,

I wish to apply for the post of beverage operative, and attach my c.v.
and references.
                    Yours faithfully,    Earle Grey
                                         Earle Grey
```

(b)
```
                                              6 June 1992

Dear Mr Shelley,

You are cordially invited to the annual Lord Byron Evening on 5 August,
starting at 7 p.m. (dress informal).

Yours sincerely,
                  S. T. Coleridge
S. T. Coleridge (Hon. Sec?)
```

(c)
```
                                              3 March 1993

Dear Captain Cook,

This is to confirm your travel arrangements as discussed at our meeting on
28 February.

Yours sincerely, Emily Wood
pp Global Travel Inc.
```

Note: It is only the date at the head of the letter that you need to refer to.

Exercise 10

For each of the prompts given, write *both* an original letter *and* a reply. The original letter should consist of:

Sender's address
Name or title of the addressee
Receiver's address
Date
Salutation
Reason for writing
Brief message (body of the letter)
Complimentary close
Signature
Addressed envelope

```
                                    Hatch Dining Club
                                    Community Centre
                                    Hatch End
                                    Herts HE8 7GT
The Proprietor
Le Gourmet
101 Picadilly
London WC1 2ED
                                    5/8/93
Dear Sir,

I am writing to complain about the food in your
restaurant.  After a recent visit, most of our
group were ill with food poisoning.  We shall
not be returning.

Yours faithfully

Albrecht Colon
Albrecht Colon
Hon. Sec.
```

```
The Proprietor
Le Gourmet
   101 Picadilly
      London WC1 2ED
```

The reply should consist of:

Addresses in reverse
Date *1 week after the original letter*
Salutation
Opening sentence, stating *date and purpose* of the original body of the letter (a brief message)
Complimentary close
Signature
Addressed envelope

```
                                    Le Gourmet
                                    101 Picadilly
                                    London WC1 2ED
Albrecht Colon, Hon. Sec.
Hatch Dining Club
Community Centre
Hatch End
Herts HE8 7GT
                                    12/8/93
Dear Mr Colon,

With reference to your letter of complaint dated
5/8/93, it is my duty to apologise to your
members for the inconvenience caused.  Should
any of your group change their minds about
eating at Le Gourmet, they will be my personal
guests.

Yours sincerely,

Pierre Du Pont
Pierre Du Pont
Proprietor
```

```
Albrech Colon, Hon. Sec.
Hatch Dining Club
Community Centre
Hatch End
Herts HE8 7GT
```

(a) You stayed in a hotel where the service was bad. You are writing on January 17th, 1990.
(b) A building firm did some excellent work on your house. The date is 15/6/89.
(c) 2/7/91   You want to know what services a home-help agency can provide.
(d) 5/5/92   You have made a provisional booking to stay with a family in a holiday resort. You now wish to make a firm booking.
(e) 12/12/93   You want to know if a local company manufactures the items you need for your small business.

Unit 4   LETTERS OF REQUEST

Making requests

We often have to write asking for things, rather like this:

```
Dear Sir,

Please send an application form for the King's Club.   Kindly include
details of fees and any other relevant information.

Yours faithfully,
```

The language is quite polite, but we can create an even more polite tone by using the forms WOULD, COULD and SHOULD:

```
I should be grateful if you would send an application form for the King's
Club.   In addition it would be helpful if you could include details of fees
and any other relevant information.
```

What we have called 'polite' forms are related to the verbs WILL, CAN, SHALL and MAY:

will — would
can   — could
shall — should
may   — might

Exercise 1   Using polite forms

The following letter sounds rather direct and demanding, as if written from a
superior to an inferior. Improve the tone of the letter by transforming the verbs
in capitals into polite forms:

```
Dear Mr Smith,

We SHALL be grateful if you CAN explain the delay in the shipment
expected on May 1st.  You MAY call us on the above number to save time,
otherwise it WILL be appreciated if you CAN reply by return.

Yours sincerely,

Al Packer   Al Packer.
```

WOULD and COULD

It is important to note that although WOULD and COULD can often replace each
other without any change in the meaning of the sentence, they are not completely
interchangeable.
   You might write

> EITHER: Would you please inform me of the price?
>   OR: Could you please inform me of the price?

and

> EITHER: I would be grateful if you could reply to my home address.
>   OR: I would be grateful if you would reply to my home address.

However, to distinguish cases where WOULD and COULD are not
interchangeable, remember the meanings of WILL and CAN:

> WILL expresses willingness, volition, wanting to do something whether
>   or not it is possible.
> CAN expresses ability or possibility, independent of will.

   Thus we might WANT to do something, but be UNABLE to do it. Conversely,
we might BE ABLE to do a thing but not WANT to. Consider the following:

> "Would you go to the moon?" "I would if I could."
> "Could you lend me £50?" "I could but I wouldn't."

   In letters, WOULD is often used where a refusal is not expected, and to give
one might cause offence.
   If COULD is used, the writer gives the addressee a chance to refuse on the
grounds of inability. It is therefore a less demanding form of request (and may
be more successful as a result!)

Look at the following examples:

Would
1. I should be grateful if you would return the questionnaire.
2. We would appreciate it if you would inform Mr Smith.
3. If you would be prepared to speak, please let us know.
4. Would you please give your name to the receptionist on arrival?
5. Perhaps you would be so kind as to return the sample.

Could
6. I should be grateful if you could reply by return of post.
7. If you could possibly let me have the details before my departure, I should very much appreciate it.
8. We would appreciate it if you could see your way to giving us a discount.
9. We would very much welcome a visit if you could manage one before April.
10. Perhaps you could send the package by airmail to avoid further delay.

Note: WOULD. In 3, 4 and 5 the result depends on the goodwill of the addressee. This probably applies in 1 and 2, but by using WOULD rather than COULD we remove the option for refusal on the grounds of inability to meet the request. COULD. In examples 6–10 the action requested involves a time deadline, expense or other inconvenience, so a gentle suggestion is more polite than a direct request. It gives the addressee a chance to refuse without causing offence.

Exercise 2

Fill the gaps using WOULD, COULD or both where it is possible in the following:

   I should be grateful if . . .

(a) you _____ be kind enough to inform us.
(b) they _____ provide the information by Tuesday.
(c) you _____ send a price list.
(d) you _____ be able to assist in this matter.
(e) she _____ meet the deadline as agreed.
(f) you _____ agree to join the project.
(g) they _____ be so helpful as to send it at once.
(h) he _____ give the matter his full attention.

Note: Where WOULD is the second alternative it seems to imply slight irritation that what COULD be done may not have been done and therefore a more forceful request is made.

Polite formulations of 'please'

Kindly							write
			good kind	enough			send return reply
Please	be	so	helpful obliging	as		to	refer to reconsider

e.g.

> Kindly inform us of your arrival.
> Please be good enough to remit the money soon.
> Please be so obliging as to let us have your new address.

Exercise 3

Use a different formulation of 'please' for each of the following, e.g.:

> _____ by return of post.
> Please be so kind as to answer by return of post.

(a) _____ the bill.
(b) _____ a stamped addressed envelope.
(c) _____ me of your arrival time.
(d) _____ notify the local police.
(e) _____ the damaged goods.
(f) _____ me at the office.
(g) _____ our agent in Frankfurt.
(h) _____ the outstanding amounts.
(i) _____ us on your mailing list.
(j) _____ before the next meeting.

Note: It is *incorrect* to use expressions like the above in relation to your own actions,
e.g:

> *I am kindly sending you the book.
> *I am being so good as to return your invoice.

Other forms of request

		appreciate welcome				your	early prompt speedy	advice answer assistance co-operation reply
I We	should would	be	most very	grateful	for			
					if	you	would could	advise answer assist co-operate reply

Your	early prompt	advice answer assistance co-operation reply	would be	appreciated welcomed helpful advisable

Note: 'Your co-operation would be appreciated' is often a hidden threat to those who do not co-operate, and the use of 'prompt' has a menacing overtone in a request. Hence 'Your prompt response would be appreciated' implies the recipient is usually slow to respond, whereas 'Thank you for your prompt action' is highly complimentary. The indefinite article is often preferred to 'Your' as being less pointed e.g. An early reply ..., Prompt cooperation ..., etc.

Exercise 4

Practise the above formulae using the following:

(a) help (noun)   (b) help (verb)
(c) co-operate   (d) co-operation
(e) suggestion   (f) suggest
(g) inform   (h) information
(i) notification   (j) notify

Exercise 5

Write the following letter:

You wish to spend a holiday abroad but, with limited funds, an inexpensive holiday is essential. Write a letter of about 100 words to a travel agency requesting the necessary information.

Unit 5 ADDITIONAL REQUESTS AND REPLYING TO REQUESTS

Additional requests

When writing to ask for more than one thing it may be necessary to list your requirements. There are two points to note:

1. It is better to use a different variant of 'please' each time.
2. The following items will be useful:

   also   as well as   further   additional   besides

Exercise 1

Fill the gaps, using each of the above items once only:

Please send the shipment as arranged. We would ____(a)____ be grateful for your help in extending our product range. Kindly send a ____(b)____ set of brochures on your latest series. If possible, ____(c)____ the brochures, we shall require an ____(d)____ copy of the current price list, ____(e)____ details of the updated specification.

Asking for a reply

We have already seen this ending:

   I look forward to hearing from you.

In letters of request we may require a quick reply. There are several ways of asking for this, some more polite than others:

(a) I look forward to hearing from you as soon as possible.
(b) Please give the matter your urgent attention.
(c) Your prompt reply would be appreciated.
(d) We look forward to hearing from you at your earliest convenience.
(e) Kindly treat this as a matter of urgency.
(f) We require your reply at once.

Exercise 2

Rearrange (a)–(f) above in order of politeness, from 1 (most) to 6 (least). You may discuss the ordering in pairs.

Note: Look again at the more insistent and less polite of the above examples. It is worth noting that this sort of pressuring for an early reply may be resented by the recipient and have the *opposite effect!*

Answering requests

We may wish to refer to the request in our reply, as follows:

> With reference to your request . . .
> As requested . . .
> In accordance with your request . . .

Complying with requests

When complying we may wish to indicate the fact in our reply:

We are pleased to	attach dispatch enclose remit send			NOUN PHRASE
	confirm			VERB PHRASE
	inform advise	you	that	
We have pleasure in	advising informing			
	confirming			
	sending remitting enclosing dispatching attaching			NOUN PHRASE

Also:

Please find enclosed	X	
		is enclosed

Exercise 3

Write the opening lines of ten letters complying with the following requests and referring to what you have enclosed, e.g.:

> In accordance with your request for information about our cleaning services, we have pleasure in enclosing our current brochure.

1. Please send us information about your cleaning services.
2. Kindly provide us with details of your charges.
3. I should be grateful to receive your current catalogue.
4. It would be most helpful if you could send the brochure.
5. We would welcome your views on this matter.
6. Could you please send me your price list and prospectus?
7. I should be glad to receive your quotation for this job.
8. Perhaps you could let me have a copy of the statistics.
9. If you could send the parcel soon, I would be most grateful.
10. We would be interested in receiving the details of your courses.

Turning down requests

If we have been unable to comply with a request, we will **not** begin:

> As requested ...
> In accordance with your request ...

but perhaps:

> With reference to your request ...

and continue with a phrase indicating polite and reluctant refusal:

We regret I am afraid	(to inform you)	(that)	we are out of stock we are unable to help the product is unavailable etc.
Unfortunately Regretfully Sadly			

Exercise 4

Write the opening lines of five letters apologising for not meeting the following requests:

(a) We would be grateful if you could send your 1995 catalogue.

(b) Please include samples of your current wallpaper designs.
(c) We would welcome your advice on this difficult matter.
(d) It would be most informative if you could include a copy of the statement.
(e) Please be so kind as to include a free sample.

Offering further assistance

Whether meeting or politely refusing requests, it is common to end the letter of reply as follows:

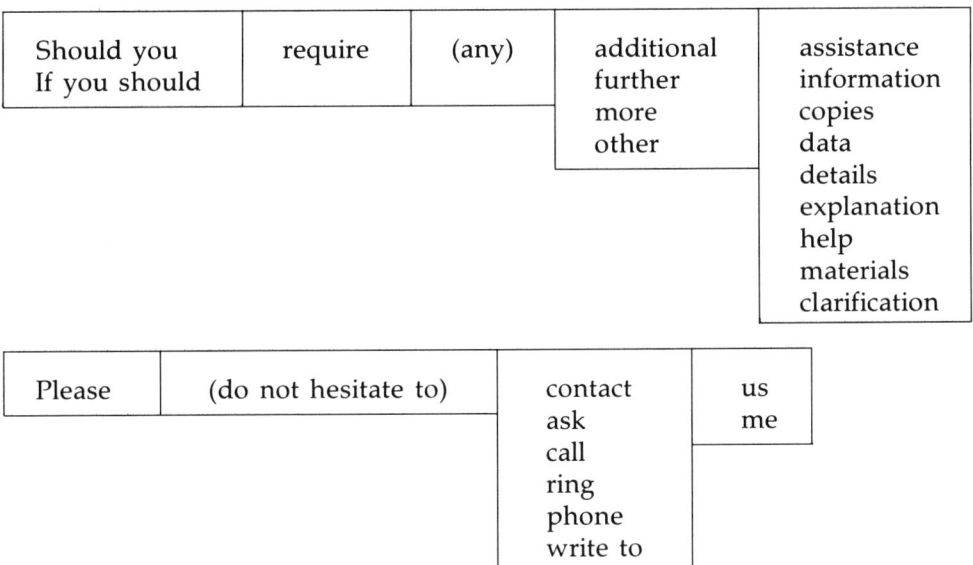

This helps to maintain good communication and friendly relations.

Encouraging further interest

If you have had to turn down the request, but do not wish to discourage the inquirer, you might write:

We regret to inform you . . .

However, if we can
| help |
| assist |
| be of assistance |
in any other way, please do not hesistate to contact us.

Thanks again

Whether meeting or turning down requests, especially *where no further correspondence is expected*, in place of:

I/We look forward to hearing from you

it is common to conclude with:

Thank you again for your interest

Exercise 5

For each of the requests in Exercises 3 and 4, write a short letter including the following:

(a) reference to the request
(b) statement of compliance or regret
(c) reference to enclosure (if any)
(d) concluding sentence

E.g.: In accordance with your request for information about our cleaning services, we have pleasure in enclosing our current brochure.
    Should you require any further information, please do not hesitate to contact us.

Pair work

Exercise 6

A should write a simple letter of request and B reply COMPLYING with the request. (Remember to include ENCLOSURES.)

Exercise 7

B should write a simple letter of request and A reply TURNING DOWN the request (without regret!).

Exercise 8

A should write a letter with TWO OR MORE requests, B reply UNABLE TO COMPLY (regretfully).

Exercise 9

B should write a letter with SEVERAL requests, and A reply COMPLYING WITH SOME BUT NOT WITH OTHERS, either regretfully or otherwise. (ENCLOSURES as appropriate.)

Unit 6 FURTHER DETAILS

Question A

> As the representative of a group of young people, write a letter of about 100 words to the Public Relations Officer of a large manufacturing firm, asking him whether he can arrange for your group to visit the firm's main factory, which is within easy reach of your town. Be careful to give a sensible reason or reasons for your visit; state the probable number of persons in your group and suggest some alternative dates.

As in this typical question, the First Level Letter usually involves giving (or requesting) details, often as a member of the public writing to an organisation. Details can be placed under the general headings of time, place, purpose and quantity.

Time

Dates and times
See First Level Letter Unit 3 for writing dates.
   When giving further details you may need to give both day and date, like this:

>   on Tuesday, January 17th . . . or January 17 . . . or 17 January . . .

N.B. The omission of the ordinal 'th' is increasingly common even in speech.

Perhaps followed by a time:

>   either: . . . at 6 o'clock
>   or: . . . at 6 p.m. (never 'at 6 o'clock p.m.')

Remember that 'a.m.' means in the morning and 'p.m.' means after noon. An alternative to this is the '24-hour clock', which is never used with 'o'clock' or 'a.m./p.m.', e.g.:

>   . . . at 1800 hours

Exercise 1

Not forgetting noon, midday and midnight, transform the dates and times given below: e.g.

>   1800, Tue 17/1

becomes

>   On Tuesday, January 17th, at 6 p.m.

(a) 1430, Sat 31/3   (b) 0935, Thu 4/4   (c) 1200, Wed 6/7
(d) 2400, Sun 19/10   (e) 1915, Mon 31/1

Time prepositions
When giving details of time, prepositions are very important:

> in   on   at   for   since   by   from   to   until   after   before   etc.

TIME WHEN

> *at*   an exact time; at noon, at lunchtime, at 8 o'clock
> *on*   on a day or date; on Tuesday, on March 1st, on your birthday, on
> > an occasion
>
> *in*
>
> (a) DURING a period: in April, in winter, in the football season
> (b) AFTER a period: in ten minutes, in a short time, in five years

TIME PERIOD

> *for* a period of time: for three months, for five minutes, for years
> *since* a specific point in the past: since dinner, since noon, since we last
> > met, since October 10th.
> *until* X, where X marks the end of a continuous period, past and future:
> > until next time, until this evening, until Monday week, until he died
> *by* and *before*, where the deadline falls within a period that ends with the
> > point stated: by next week, before the next meeting
> *after* and *from*, where a period starts beyond a certain point: after tomorrow,
> > from next month
> *from—to*, *between—and*, defining the limits of a period: from 1 to 6 p.m.,
> > from May to September, between sunrise and sunset, etc.

TIME FREQUENCY

> *on* + *(days)*   On Mondays, on weekdays, on alternate Sundays
> > Also: on the hour (every hour)
> *every*   Every spring, every (other) Saturday, every (second) year
> _____*ly*   Daily, weekly, annually (i.e. yearly), monthly, hourly
> > *Note:* On a daily (etc.) basis
> > But: On an annual basis

Exercise 2

Complete the following sentences with appropriate expressions of time:

(a) We would like to hire the hall _____
(b) I suggest we hold tennis matches _____
(c) If possible, the visit would take place _____
(d) I should like to stay _____
(e) We were there _____
(f) This would take no longer than _____

(g) The dates I have in mind are _____

(h) If it is convenient, we could meet _____

(i) Please drop in any _____ (not 'time'!)

(j) We require your answer at the latest _____

(k) The paper needs to be published _____

(l) Can you let me know _____

(m) He was injured for a few weeks _____

(n) I can only wait for an answer _____

(o) The salesman normally calls _____

(p) We would require the use of your hall only _____

(q) They will be on holiday _____

(r) Deliveries take place _____

(s) We are not in a position to wait _____

(t) The grounds are open to the public _____

Place

Having established when the action is to take place, the next question might well be 'where?'

Venue (= place to come to)
> *at* is most common: at the sports club, at the hostel, at the factory
> *in* is sometimes used: in the lecture hall, in the clubhouse (where the interior of a building is specified)

Transport
> *by* when referring to a medium of transport (route or vehicle) in general: by air, by sea, by car (BUT on land, on foot)
> *on* if the vehicle is open, or has decks: on a ship, on a horse, on a bus, on a Jumbo jet, on a camel
> *in* if it is enclosed: in a car, in a light aircraft

Journeys
> *from ... to*, or *between ... and*: rather like periods of time
> *via (by way of)*: He went from London to Sydney via Bahrain

Locations (static)
> *in* countries and cities: in England, in Paris

Direction (motion towards)
> *to*: go to Paris, welcome to LA, pay *a* visit (NOUN) to Fez
> But: visit (VERB) Fez

Exercise 3

Add the appropriate preposition (if any is required):

(a) We spent our holiday _____ in Japan.
(b) I must have left my camera _____ the SS Oceanic.
(c) We met when sailing _____ Malta _____ Cadiz.
(d) The meeting will be held _____ the Oak End Youth Centre.
(e) We would like to visit _____ your museum.
(f) If possible, we would like to spend a week _____ the hostel.
(g) The matches will be held _____ the Sandford United ground.
(h) We would be pleased to welcome your party _____ Grimms & Co.
(i) I intend to travel _____ road.
(j) Next year we are going on holiday _____ Blackpool.

Purpose

Reasons
It is often necessary, especially when making requests, to give reasons. Here are
some ways of expressing them:

(a) in order to do, e.g.:
    We require the use of the hall in order to hold a seminar
(b) with a view to doing, e.g.:
    We would like to borrow the hall with a view to holding a table tennis
    tournament
(c) for the purpose(s) of doing, e.g.:
    We request access to your hall for the purpose of holding judo classes
(d) for _____ (ADJECTIVE) purposes, e.g.:
    We would appreciate the use of your hall for social purposes

Exercise 4

Complete the following sentences by supplying an appropriate reason:

(a) We wish to hire the hall _____
(b) I would like a copy of your travel brochure _____
(c) We would appreciate a tour of your factory _____
(d) If possible we would stay at Hilltop Lodge _____
(e) I would like to take the Orient Express _____
(f) You are invited to Sandford United _____
(g) She has notified all the relevant offices _____
(h) I am writing to the Daily Echo _____
(i) We should like to see the documents _____
(j) Could you please provide a sample _____

Intention and need

I We	intend plan hope would like need have	to	start go leave return reply etc.	as soon as possible shortly immediately etc.
	must			

In a well-written request the writer will build up a sentence or paragraph expressing all these aspects of the request clearly and neatly. See if you can do this in the following exercise:

Exercise 5

Write an expression of intention or need for each of the following verbs, e.g. report:

> We must report/We intend to report
> We hope to report/We need to report

(a) arrive   (b) depart   (c) travel   (d) stay   (e) play
(f) speak   (g) meet   (h) go   (i) race   (f) walk

Add to each an expression of PLACE, e.g.:

> We must report to the office

Now add an expression of TIME, e.g.:

> We must report to the office by noon

Finally, add a REASON, e.g.:

> We must report to the office by noon in order to submit our sales figures.

This exercise gives the basic order for expression information in sentences of this type:

> Place — Time — Purpose

Quantity

Groups

Many First Level Letter questions assume a secretarial function, making arrangements on behalf of groups. When giving details of group numbers, the following formulae are useful:

There are _____ of us
                (people) in our party
                (members)
                        etc.

a group of _____ (people)
party   etc.

The group numbers _____ (people, etc.)
        comprises
        consists of
        is made up of

Be careful *not* to use these wrong forms:

        *The team is consist of ...
        *The team comprises of ...

Exercise 6

Using the above formulae, make statements about each of the following concerning numbers of members:

(a) Sandford Athletic
(b) The Oak End Communty Centre
(c) The board of directors of Grimms & Co.
(d) The Adventure Safari group
(e) The residents of Greenhill Lodge
(f) The staff of Brite Interiors

Groups: singular or plural?

You can treat organisations and bodies as singular or plural, depending on whether you are emphasising their unity as a body or individuality as members, e.g.:

1. Sandford Athletic consists of a hundred members.
    Sandford Athletic were at their best last Saturday.
2. The Adventure Safari Group comprises five travel companies.
    The Adventure Safari Group were collected from the airport.

It follows that when making them plural we use 'who' as the relative pronoun because we are thinking of the people in the oranisation, whereas with a singular we use 'which' as we are thinking of a thing or abstraction.

Value
You may be asked to state details of cost and value, for example in question B.

Question B

> When you were arranging with a tourist agency for a holiday abroad, you insured your luggage with the insurance company recommended by them. During your holiday one of your cases was stolen and it was not recovered. Write a letter of about 100 words to the insurance company, giving essential details of your holiday, insurance policy, the theft and estimated value of contents to ensure the return of the appropriate claim form.

Some useful expressions are:

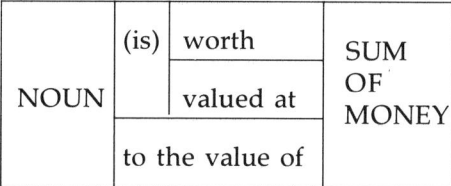

NOUN	(is)	worth	SUM OF MONEY
		valued at	
		to the value of	

e.g. My watch is worth $200.
The ring was valued at $1000.
I lost cash to the value of 88,000 lire.

Exercise 7

Answer the following question:

What items might have been in the suitcase?

The suitcase contained . . .

(a) two suits
(b) a camera
(c) ——————
(d) ——————
(e) ——————

Add a VALUE to each item, e.g.:

Two suits worth $300 each,
a camera valued at $1000,
etc.

Serial numbers
As with addresses, it is sometimes necessary to invent reference numbers.

Exercise 8

Write down documents and appropriate serial numbers:

cheque	no. 45 67 79
passport	no. CB 98 76 54 P
policy	no. RL/134/CV/8201

_____	_____
_____	_____

Further practice

Exercise 9

Write the letter to the insurance company, as specified in question B above, giving all relevant details.

Exercise 10

Write the letter to the Public Relations Officer of the factory, as specified in question A.

Remember that the 'English for Commerce' examination gives credit to students who fill out the situation with appropriate details from their own imagination. They must at least give the amount of detail specifically requested by the rubric, otherwise they lose marks. However, absolute accuracy and realism of detail is not expected.

Unit 7   REVIEW

Exercise 1

Fill the gaps in these fragments of letters:

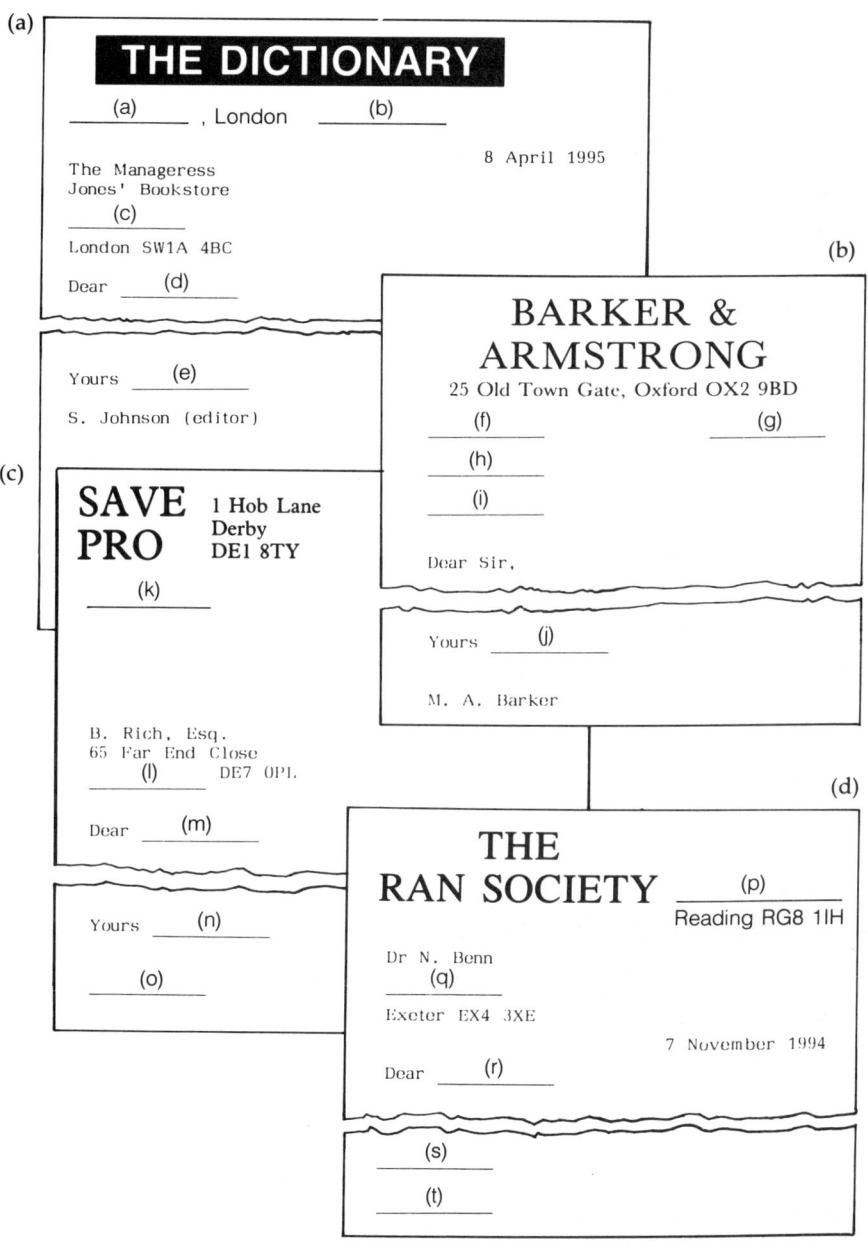

(a)

THE DICTIONARY

_____(a)_____ , London _____(b)_____

8 April 1995

The Manageress
Jones' Bookstore
_____(c)_____

London SW1A 4BC

Dear _____(d)_____

Yours _____(e)_____

S. Johnson (editor)

(b)

BARKER & ARMSTRONG

25 Old Town Gate, Oxford OX2 9BD

_____(f)_____   _____(g)_____

_____(h)_____

_____(i)_____

Dear Sir,

Yours _____(j)_____

M. A. Barker

(c)

SAVE PRO
1 Hob Lane
Derby
DE1 8TY

_____(k)_____

B. Rich, Esq.
65 Far End Close
_____(l)_____   DE7 0PL

Dear _____(m)_____

Yours _____(n)_____

_____(o)_____

(d)

THE RAN SOCIETY
_____(p)_____
Reading RG8 1IH

Dr N. Benn
_____(q)_____

Exeter EX4 3XE

7 November 1994

Dear _____(r)_____

_____(s)_____

_____(t)_____

Exercise 2

Fill the gaps in the following letters:

(a)

UNIVERSITY PRESS
3 Old Narrow Lane Cambridge CB1 1BC

Mr J. Smith
59 Newhouse Close
Enfield EN34 8UZ

4 July 1996

Dear Mr Smith,

Thank you _____(a)_____ _____(b)_____ letter dated _____(c)_____ . With

_____(d)_____ to your _____(e)_____ for the post of assistant editor. I

_____(f)_____ to _____(g)_____ you that the post has already been filled.

_____(h)_____ you again _____(i)_____ your interest.

Yours _____(j)_____ ,

C. Bligh

C. Bligh
Editor

(b)

ℭℊ **Beauty Products Ltd**
5 Cannery Row Crewe CW3 6ET

The Manageress
Chi-She Fashions
89 Lower End Street
Manchester M27 9UG

7 March 1995

Dear _____(k)_____ ,

I am _____(l)_____ to _____(m)_____ you of our new 'NOVA' product range. I

_____(n)_____ our current catalogue for your information. Should you require

_____(o)_____ information, _____(p)_____ call our Marketing Division.

We look _____(q)_____ to _____(r)_____ your order form at your _____(s)_____

_____(t)_____ .

Yours faithfully,

Lillian Bell

Lillian Bell
Sales Director

Exercise 3

Reply to the following letters:

(a)

Mir   5 Lion Chambers   Halifax   HX2 9KN
News

The Secretary
Todmorden Athletic
69 Blackburn Road
Halifax HX14 6YF   11 November 1994

Dear Sir or Madam

We are starting a weekly feature on sports clubs in the Halifax area, and we
would like to include your club in our column. We should therefore be
most grateful if you would write to us with details of your membership,
sporting activities and any other information you think may be of interest to
our readers.

I look forward to hearing from you.

Yours faithfully

A. Briggs

A. Briggs
Assistant Editor

(b)

The British Bank

1–3 High Street
Leeds LS1 01O

1 April 1993

Mr F. Jones
44 Roman Avenue
York YO5 9JK

Dear Mr Jones

Owing to an extensive computer failure at our Head Office recently, I regret
to inform you that we have lost all records of your accounts.

We would therefore be extremely grateful if you could write us at your
earliest convenience, giving full details of all your business with us,
including details of last known balances, standing orders and any other
relevant information.

We apologise for the inconvenience.

Yours sincerely

P. Bancroft

P. Bancroft
Manager

Exercise 4

Transform the verbs into their polite forms:

Dear Sir,

I <u>will</u> be grateful if you <u>can</u> explain the incident at the Polo Club last Saturday, although I <u>shall</u> be surprised if there <u>can</u> be an acceptable explanation.   You <u>may</u> also consider writing to the committee to ask if they <u>will</u> consider a hearing, since otherwise your membership <u>can</u> be revoked.

Yours faithfully,

C.P. Bagshot

C. P. Bagshot, Col. (ret'd.)

Exercise 5   Pair work

Form pairs. A and B each select two different letters from the following, which are taken from past 'English for Commerce' question papers. Note the details asked for, shown in *italic* type, and make sure you provide them.

> Write the letters and 'send' them to your partner.
> Answer the two letters you receive.
> Correct and discuss each other's work.

(a) Write a letter of about 100 words to a firm of painters and decorators, *complaining* about the unsatisfactory way in which a piece of work was recently carried out at your place of residence. Be careful to set out in full the *reasons* for your dissatisfaction and ask what *steps* the firm intends to take to deal with your complaint.

(b) As a secretary of a sports club, write a letter of about 100 words to a secretary of a similar club to explore the possibility of arranging *matches or contests* between the members of your respective clubs next season. You should *confine* your choice of games or sports to those of which you have some knowledge. It may be useful to refer to the *situation* and *amenities* of your sports ground, and you should certainly give a wide choice of *dates*.

(c) On behalf of a group of young people, write a letter of about 100 words to the warden of a youth hostel, either at home or abroad, where your group spent an enjoyable fortnight last year. Thank him for his *hospitality* on that occasion and ask him whether he can *accommodate* your group for a *fortnight next summer*. Mention the *number of persons* in the party and give a choice of suitable *dates*.

(d) Write a letter of about 100 words to the editor of your local newspaper, giving your *views on some topic or problem* which is of particular interest or concern to the *young people* of your *town or district*.

Reading

Unit 1   UNDERSTANDING VOCABULARY

The 'English for Commerce' examination question on reading comprehension features text on a wide range of topics, for which it is important to develop a wide and flexible vocabulary. This can be achieved by understanding the relationships between words both in meaning and form.

Read and answer the vocabulary questions which follow:

Text A

The motor car, which has now superseded the railway train as the principal means of transport in many countries, is altogether unfavourable to reading. In general, people consume more time moving about than they did, and they consume it under conditions which, even for people with good eyes, must make reading difficult, if not impossible.

Moreover, the cinema, the radio and television with all their delights have appeared one after another as further distractions to divert people from time that might otherwise be given to the pleasure of reading. All these things must make it difficult for successive generations to acquire the habit of reading and, if that habit be acquired, to maintain it.

Exercise 1

Find words in the text which mean the same as:

(a) alternatively   _____
(b) circumstances   _____
(c) completely   _____
(d) gain   _____
(e) main   _____
(f) method   _____
(g) pleasures   _____
(h) spend   _____
(i) sustain   _____
(j) taken the place of _____

Exercise 2

Find words in the text which mean the opposite of:

(a) attractions _____
(b) easy   _____
(c) particular   _____
(d) lose   _____
(e) few   _____
(f) less   _____
(g) neglect   _____
(h) pain   _____
(i) partially   _____
(j) preceding   _____

Exercise 3

Explain in a single word or short phrase what is meant by:

(a) superseded   (line 1) _____
(b) principal   (line 1) _____
(c) distractions   (line 6) _____
(d) divert   (line 6) _____
(e) successive   (line 7) _____

Exercise 4   Word formation noun—verb

Note how nouns are formed from verbs (or are sometimes identical with them, at least in written form, e.g. delight/delight) and vice versa.
    Complete the table (use a dictionary if necessary).

	Verb	Noun
	sustain	sustenance
	divert	diversion
	distract	distraction
(a)	appear	
(b)	consume	
(c)	divert	
(d)	acquire	
(e)		delight
(f)	maintain	
(g)		encroachment
(h)	supersede	
(i)		pleasure
(j)	give	

Exercise 5   Vocabulary extension

The first paragraph of the text refers to means of transport. How many of these can you add to the diagram below?

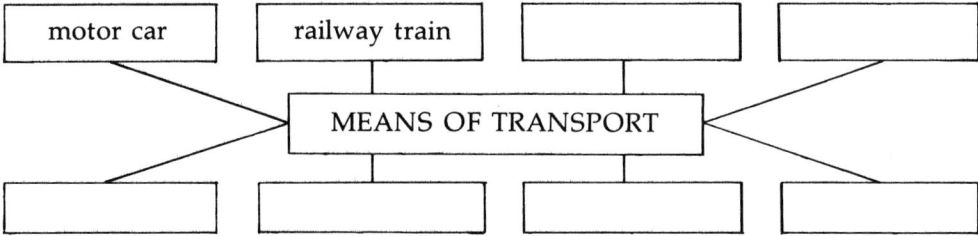

Exercise 6

Read the following paragraph, and underline all the words you do not know:

Text B

They came on deck one morning to see a grim waste of slushy, floating ice and floes around them. As the steam-heated ship was insulated against cold, they were snug enough in their cabins but, on deck, they wore duffle coats, helmets and fur-lined gloves. However, they had not come 57 degrees south as sightseers, for there was work to be done. As George was a laboratory technician, he looked after the store of scientific equipment, and took care of the jars of plankton (the minute living organisms of the ocean). Since Roy worked as an ordinary seaman, one of his more chilly jobs was to chip ice off the deck.

Exercise 7

Here is the same paragraph again. *Without looking at the original,* fill the gaps with words you *do* know. Each gap may require more than one word.

They came _____ one morning to see a _____ waste of _____ , floating ice and _____ around them. As the steam-heated ship was _____ against cold, they were _____ enough in their cabins but, on deck, they wore _____ coats, helmets and _____ gloves. However, they had not come 57 degrees south as _____ , for there was work to be done. As George was a _____ technician, he looked after the store of scientific equipment, and took care of the jars of _____ (the minute living _____ of the ocean). Since Roy worked as an ordinary seaman, one of his more _____ jobs was to _____ ice off the deck.

Exercise 8   Headings and related words

In Exercise 5 you were asked to add to the list of means of transport. 'Means of transport' is a heading under which the other items belong; it is called a 'generic' term because it covers numerous things *of the same kind.*

Find vocabulary items in text C which fit in the same way under the following headings:

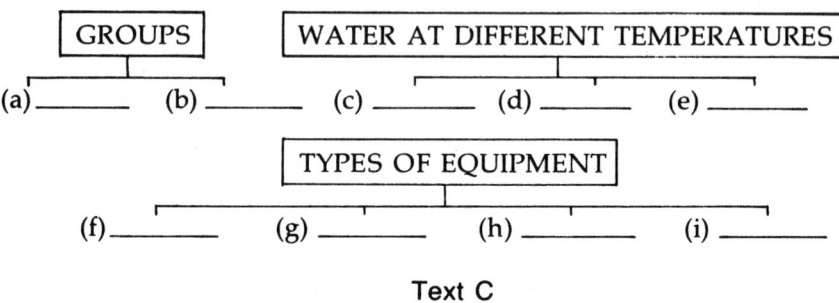

Text C

They came on deck one morning to see a grim waste of slush, floating ice and floes around them. As the steam-heated ship was insulated against cold they were snug enough in their cabins but, on deck, they wore duffle coats, helmets and fur-lined gloves. However, they had not come 57 degrees south as sightseers, for there was work to be done. As George was a laboratory technician, he looked after the store of scientific equipment, and took care of the jars of plankton (the minute living organisms of the ocean). Since Roy worked as an ordinary seaman, one of his more chilly jobs was to chip ice off the deck.

Both were on duty when the ship's apparatus for obtaining samples of water and plankton (at various depths) was put into action. For this there were four machines on the upper deck, two for taking water and plankton, one for lowering nets, and the fourth for taking the temperature of the water at different depths.

When the party landed at desolate Macquarrie Island, where a party of Australian scientists were stationed, they found crowds of penguins and had great fun with these sociable natives of Antarctica.

Exercise 9

Provide the missing heading(s) and related items from the text for the words given:

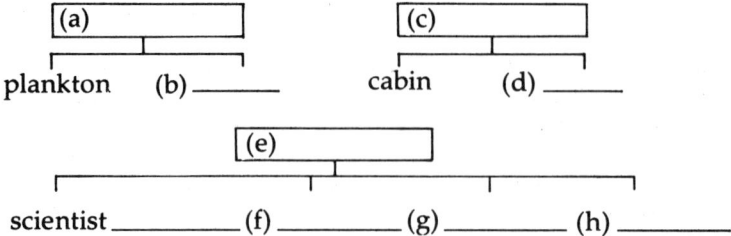

Exercise 10

Explain in a single word or short phrase what is meant by:

(a) grim   (line 1)   ——————————————
(b) insulated   (line 2)   ——————————————
(c) minute   (line 6)   ——————————————
(d) desolate   (line 13) ——————————————
(e) sociable   (line 15) ——————————————

Note: Make sure your definition belongs to the same part of speech as the word you are defining, e.g. a noun should be explained by another noun or a noun phrase, **not** a verb or adjective.

Exercise 11   Vocabulary extension

Think of as many words as you can which could be used in text C in place of the following:

grim,	desolate,	————,	————,	————,
minute,	small,	————,	————,	————,
look after,	take care of,	————,	————,	————,
stationed,	————,	————,	————,	————,
snug,	————,	————,	————,	————,

Exercise 12

Context is the essential clue to a word's meaning. In this exercise we shall reverse the process by seeking a context to match the word. Take note of the grammatical information: parts of speech, possessive endings, etc.

Fill the gaps in Text D by replacing these words:

beginning	bulletins	carrier	century
Continent	engage	exploit	extremely
famous	financiers	networks	news
newspaper	organised	pigeon's	pigeons
result	situation	telegraph	transactions

Text D

At the ____(a)____ of the nineteenth ____(b)____, businessmen decided to ____(c)____ the ____(d)____ sense of direction. The ____(e)____ London banker, Nathan Rothschild, had ____(f)____ of the military ____(g)____ brought to him by ____(h)____ from the ____(i)____ during the Napoleonic Wars. As a ____(j)____ of these on-the-spot ____(k)____ he was able to ____(l)____ in ____(m)____ profitable ____(n)____ on the Stock Exchange. Other ____(o)____ imitated his example. In the eighteen-forties the German ____(p)____-man, Reuter, ____(q)____ a regular ____(r)____ pigeon run to bridge the gap between the German and the Franco-Belgian ____(s)____ ____(t)____.

Exercise 13 Pair work

In pairs compare and discuss your answers.

Note: IN THE EXAMINATION do not be discouraged if at first sight there are a lot of words you do not know. Read the passage again and again and many of the words will become clearer, because the context limits them to only a narrow range of meaning; e.g. SNUG (Text B), in contrast to the suggestion of COLD and DISCOMFORT on deck, must have to do with WARMTH and COMFORT, so you can make a good guess at its meaning.

Exercise 14

Paying careful attention to grammatical information and context, fill the gaps in text E by replacing the following words:

along	as	certain	completely
during	first	ingenious	new
return	safely	same	since
so	still	that	themselves
thus	before	whose	yet

Text E

_____(a)_____ the nineteenth century, _____(b)_____ many years of communication were _____(c)_____ revolutionized, man _____(d)_____ had to rely on one creature _____(e)_____ cleverness and endurance no nineteenth-century machine could match. _____(f)_____ dependable, steerable flying-machines had not as
5 _____(g)_____ been built, the _____(h)_____ practical air-mail was a carrier pigeon service. This use of birds was not _____(i)_____ ; the tendency of _____(j)_____ birds to fly back to the _____(k)_____ place had been discovered in antiquity and had given rise to _____(l)_____ postal systems. _____(m)_____ sailors on Egyptian and Greek vessels used to take pigeons _____(n)_____ with them and, on the
10 _____(o)_____ trip, release them _____(p)_____ they were nearing home, _____(q)_____ that their relatives might know _____(r)_____ the longest part of the voyage was _____(s)_____ over and that the voyagers _____(t)_____ would soon be home.

Exercise 15 Pair work

In pairs compare and discuss your answers.

Unit 2 UNDERSTANDING REFERENCE

A given item is **not** repeated every time it is featured in a text e.g.:

*John said that John was going to back to John's house

We would normally read the following:

John said that he was going back to his house

Words, phrases and sentences can thus be replaced by words (pro-forms) which refer *backwards* and *forwards* to concepts expressed elsewhere in the text. They stand in place of them.

Pronouns

In the example above, *he* and *his* are *pronouns. They* stand in place of a noun and do *its* work. *He* and *his* are used to *refer to* John. Consider the following table:

Personal pronouns		Possessive pronouns		Reflexive pronouns
subject	object	determiner (or adjective)	true pronoun	
I	me	my	mine	myself
you	you	your	yours	yourself yourselves (pl)
he	him	his	his	himself
she	her	her	hers	herself
it	it	its	its	itself
we	us	our	ours	ourselves
they	them	their	theirs	themselves

Read and answer the questions which follow:

Text A

People who are in the habit of using a motor car whenever *they* want to move half a mile become physically lazy and lose the power of enjoying a vigorous walk. *Those* who travel by train through a country at ninety miles an hour do not see much of the life of *that* country, *its* animals and plants, as *they* flash past.

Exercise 1

What do the following refer to?

(a) they (line 1) _____

(b) Those (line 2) _____

(c) that country (line 4) _____

(d) its (line 4) _____

(e) they (line 4) _____

This, that, these, those (demonstratives)

These are similar to pronouns, and act both as NOUNS and ADJECTIVES but give more emphasis and a sense of distance.

Read and answer the questions that follow:

Text B

It was only **this** spring, after two years of hesitation, **that I** did buy something. **That** cost **me** five hundred pounds, and I bought **it** only because I needed a suitable gift for **my** wife on the twenty-fifth anniversary of **our** wedding.

Exercise 2

In text B, to what do the following refer?:

(a) this (line 1) _____

(b) that (line 1) _____

(c) That (line 1) _____

(d) I (line 1) _____

(e) me (line 2) _____

(f) it (line 2) _____

(g) my (line 2) _____

(h) our (line 3) _____

Such, thus

If a thing or an action has been described, the entire description can be replaced using 'such' or 'thus':

The car is a sleek racer. I dream of such a car.
'such' = a sleek racer

He ran as fast as he could, thus eluding his pursuers.
'thus' = by running as fast as he could

One

This refers to a single item from a class or group of things:

He offered the pistols and I selected one.
'one' = a pistol

Some

Similar to ONE, but for plural items from a class:

She offered me apples, so I chose some.
'some' = apples

So

This is used where an action, state or condition is restated:

They asked me to leave and I did so.
'so' = leave

I am happy living here and will remain so.
'so' = happy

Another/others

Like ONE and SOME, these are singular and plural pronouns referring to alternatives from a class:

He offered me one pistol but I took another.
'another' = pistol

She offered me bad apples so I bought others.
'others' = apples

Read and answer the questions which follow:

Text C

Propaganda is the name generally given to the various methods by **which** powerful groups try to influence other people's beliefs and actions. The purpose of **such** propaganda is usually to persuade people to do or think things **which they** would not do or think if left to **themselves**.

5 The more intelligent a person is, the more **he** will think out **his** own courses of action. Then **he** will not need propaganda to make **him** do things and, if people attempt to influence **him** by propaganda, **he** will resist **it** unless **they** want **him** to do something sensible.

Of course, propaganda is not always bad. **Thus** some advertisements are of great
10 use in informing **us** about goods or new developments in air travel. Most people would not call **this** propaganda bad, becuase the idea seems to **them** a sensible **one**.

Note: Despite the apparent grammatical inconsistency, there is a tendency in English to use 'they, them, their' to refer to single persons when they could be either male or female. This is usual when referring to sexually unmarked pronouns like 'anybody, somebody, nobody, everybody', e.g:

> Has anybody hurt themselves?
> Nobody likes to lose their job.

This also avoids offending feminist sentiment, as does the rather clumsy 'Nobody likes to lose his or her job'. The most usual form in both grammar and style is the *unmarked* form 'Nobody likes to lose his job'. Examiners will accept all three variants as appropriate.

Exercise 3

In text C, to what do the following refer?:

(a) such (line 2) _____
(b) they (line 3) _____
(c) themselves (line 4) _____
(d) he, his, him (lines 5–7) _____
(e) it (line 7) _____
(f) they (line 7) _____
(g) thus (line 9) _____
(h) this (line 11) _____
(i) them (line 11) _____
(j) one (line 11) _____

Which

Note in text C the use of *which*:

> ... the methods by which powerful groups try to influence others ...
> = by these methods

> ... persuade people to do things which they would not do ...
> = things

See also: that   who, whom and whose   when   where   whence   whereby

Read and answer the questions which follow:

Text D

The coalminer in *his* underground calling was constantly exposed to the dangers of a highly flammable gas called 'fire damp', and was liable to be killed without

a moment's notice by a fearful explosion when using a naked flame. Over the years, countless miners had lost *their* lives in *this* way.
5   However, for some years a young Cornishman, named Humphrey Davy, the son of a wood carver in Penzance, *who* had risen to the rank of Professor of Chemistry of the Royal Institution, had been experimenting with *this* dangerous gas. As a result of repeated experiments *he* had made certain astonishing discoveries, *which* led to *his* invention, in 1815, of the first safety lamp, one of the most beneficial inventions
10 *that* have ever been given to mankind. *It* enabled the most dangerous mines to be worked with comparative safety.

Exercise 4

In text D to what do the following refer?:

(a) his (line 1) _____
(b) their (line 4) _____
(c) this (line 4) _____
(d) who (line 6) _____
(e) this (line 7) _____
(f) he (line 8) _____
(g) which (line 8) _____
(h) his (line 9) _____
(i) that (line 10) _____
(j) it (line 10) _____

Text E

Some people have such a passion for reading that *they* will acquire *the habit* and maintain *it* against all obstacles. There are *others* with the inclination and capacity to get *that pleasure*, but *who* must find *it* increasingly difficult under modern conditions to indulge the inclination and cultivate the capacity. If *they* do not do
5   *so*, *they* lose one of the greatest resources and most precious recreations of life.

Exercise 5

In text E, to what do the following refer?:

(a) they (line 1) _____
(b) the habit (line 1) _____
(c) it (line 2) _____
(d) others (line 2) _____
(e) that pleasure (line 3) _____
(f) who (line 3) _____

(g) it (line 3) _____

(h) they (line 4) _____

(i) so (line 5) _____

(j) they (line 5) _____

Exercise 6

Fill the gaps in the text with appropriate reference words:

Text F

_____(a)_____ is the early bird _____(b)_____ catches the worm.' If
_____(c)_____ is repeated often enough _____(d)_____ may induce a person
to get up early, although if left to _____(e)_____ _____(f)_____ might not do
_____(g)_____ . Among the groups _____(h)_____ most successfully exploit the
5 constant repetition of a piece of advice in a short, catchy phrase for
_____(i)_____ own profit are advertisers. In _____(j)_____ way _____(k)_____
often persuade people to buy things _____(l)_____ do not really want. If
_____(m)_____ propaganda finds _____(n)_____ way into newspapers
_____(o)_____ has a very good chance of influencing people, because
10 _____(p)_____ always seem ready to believe what _____(q)_____ read.

Exercise 7

Fill the gaps in the text with appropriate reference words:

Text G

Greed is a great evil, and _____(a)_____ is _____(b)_____ _____(c)_____ is
now endangering the future of _____(d)_____ world. Poor countries have to
exploit _____(e)_____ resources in order to pay off _____(f)_____ foreign debts
and improve conditions for _____(g)_____ people. Multinational corporations
5 take advantage of _____(h)_____ situation for _____(i)_____ own gain. Tropical
rain forest is cleared for mining or fuel, and although _____(j)_____ importance
to the earth's ecology is much greater than _____(k)_____ commercial value, short-
term profits are placed before the well-being of _____(l)_____ . _____(m)_____ ,
if forest clearance continues at _____(n)_____ present rate, _____(o)_____
10 _____(p)_____ remain will be gone by the end of _____(q)_____ century, and
_____(r)_____ , the inhabitants of the earth, may _____(s)_____ face extinction
as _____(t)_____ environment is destroyed.

Unit 3 SKIMMING AND SCANNING

We read in different ways, according to our purpose in reading.

Skimming

In order to quickly gain an impression of the subject matter and style of a text, whether page- or book-length, we read quickly, without pausing to study the details. This is skim reading or skimming.

Scanning

When we are studying a text in detail, looking for specific information, we read the relevant sections more slowly and carefully, although perhaps not word by word, until we find the information we are seeking. This is known as scanning the text.

In the 'English for Commerce' examination, you are given a reading text of approximately 300 words for comprehension. Before attempting to answer the questions you should do the following:

1. Skim the text, to gain an impression of the subject matter and style.
2. Read the questions carefully.
3. Read the text carefully, aiming for a good general understanding of its contents, but not worrying if a few words are not understood.
4. Take each question in turn, making sure you understand exactly what is being asked.
5. Scan the text for the answer to the question.

Before reading the first text, prepare to look for the following information:

1. What is the subject of the text?
2. Is the style technical, with specialised vocabulary, or of more general interest?
3. Is the content fact, fiction or opinion — or a mixture?

Text A

Advantages and Disadvantages of Speed in Modern Life

In the nineteenth century Charles Dickens, the most famous English novelist of his time, wrote in a state of great excitement about a stage-coach, pulled along by a team of horses, that could cover more than twenty miles of road within sixty minutes. To us in the twentieth century, in which man is able to move and to
5 communicate with such rapidity, the speed of the stage-coach seems no speed at all. Aeroplanes fly many hundreds of miles in an hour; express trains can achieve over five times the speed of the stage-coach. Even without moving, we can communicate within seconds with people on the other side of the globe.
    The advantages of these increased speeds are numerous. For instance,
10 businessmen travelling from Europe to the Far East can now reach their destination

within twenty-four hours, instead of the four or five weeks their journey would once have taken. Fruit, vegetables and other perishable goods can now safely be sent to far-distant places. Members of a family separated from each other by vast distances can have a conversation with each other as easily as if they were all sitting
15   in the same room.

  Not all the effects of speed, however, are beneficial. People who are in the habit of using a motor car whenever they want to move half a mile become physically lazy and lose the power of enjoying a vigorous walk. Those who travel by train through a country at ninety miles an hour do not see much of the life of that country,
20   its people, animals and plants, as they flash past. They become so anxious about moving quickly from one place to another that they are no longer able to relax and enjoy a leisurely journey. People are made restless by speedy travel; the pace of their whole way of living is increased; and, amid the noise of machinery, their nerves are tormented and their peace of mind is destroyed.

Exercise 1   Skimming I

(a) What is the general subject of the text?:
   (i)   Speed in the nineteenth century
   (ii)   The speed of life
   (iii) Speed in the twentieth century

(b) Describe the content of the passage:
   (i)   Purely factual
   (ii)   A mixture of fact and opinion
   (iii) Purely opinion

(c) What is the author's attitude to speed?:
   (i)   All in favour
   (ii)   Partly for, partly against
   (iii) Completely against

For the second stage of the skimming operation, aim to find out what topic is dealt with in each paragraph. This will facilitate scanning for further detail, because the reader will have gained an idea of where in the text information is located. This part of the exercise concerns the *topic structure*, and to help us determine the topic structure we can skim the *topic sentences*. These usually, although not always, occur at the beginning of each paragraph:

Exercise 2   Skimming II

(a) In which paragraph does the author discuss the disadvantages of speed?:
   #1   #2   #3   none
(b) In which paragraph does the author discuss speed past and present?:
   #1   #2   #3   none
(c) In which paragraph does the author discuss the future of speed?:
   #1   #2   #3   none

(d) In which paragraph does the author discuss the advantages of speed?:
#1   #2   #3   none
(e) In which paragraph does the author discuss Charles Dickens?:
#1   #2   #3   none

As a result of the above skimming exercises, you should have formed an idea of where in the text the author deals with each of the topics. Try to use that information when scanning for specific details. *Make sure you understand the question first!*

Exercise 3   Scanning I

Find the sentence which deals with:

(a) the performance of trains and aircraft
(b) communication between relations
(c) how people on trains miss the scenery
(d) transport of foodstuffs
(e) the range and power of telecommunications

Exercise 4   Scanning II

Answer in your own words:

(a) What was the occupation of Charles Dickens?
(b) What achievement of the stage-coach excited him?
(c) How has faster travel benefited businessmen?
(d) What happens to people who habitually use the car?
(e) What psychological harm does fast travel cause?

Skim the text of Text B below:

Text B

The Attraction of Christie's Auction Sale Rooms

I often wonder why so many people who have a liking for and some knowledge of antiques should regard Christie's as something remote and even unapproachable by ordinary mortals. Sometimes they don't believe me when I try to convince them that their attitude is mistaken.

5   If neither your dress nor your manners are clearly unacceptable, you simply go through the main door, pass the enquiry desk unchallenged and proceed up the wide stairway. You will then see the auction rooms in front of you. For a small sum of money you buy a catalogue of the day's sale. You then either inspect the items or, if it is a forthcoming sale that interests you, walk round the rooms in which the

10   objects for those future sales are on display. At no cost whatever, you can view many rare and valuable objects, such as fine porcelain, pictures, furniture, silver and jewellery.

If you are interested in the day's sale, either with the hope of buying something within your means or merely to see how such a sale is conducted, you just take
15   a seat. Sales begin at eleven o'clock precisely. At a second or two before the hour, the auctioneer mounts the rostrum, and, as the clock strikes, the first lot is announced.
All sorts of people are in the room: dealers from all over the world, collectors and those who are merely interested. I am nearly always one of the last-named group, though I am a collector in a very humble way. It was only this spring, after
20   two years of non-bidding, that I did buy something. That cost me five hundred pounds, and I bought it only because I needed a suitable gift for my wife on the twenty-fifth anniversary of our wedding.
Why do I go to Christie's whenever I have a few hours to spare? I love beautiful things and Christie's gives me the chance to see them, and even handle some
25   of them, at the closest quarters. I have both a passionate interest in my fellow human beings and an incredible curiousity, so I like to watch faces and reactions.

Exercise 5

Answer the following:

(a) What is the subject of the text?:
   (i)   The attraction of Christie's
   (ii)   The attraction of auctions
   (iii) The attraction of sale rooms

(b) Describe the style of the passage:
   (i)   scientific and technical
   (ii)   objective history
   (iii) a personal account

Exercise 6

State in which paragraph the author discusses:

(a) the start of the sale*
(b) the reasons for his interest in Christie's
(c) other people's views of Christie's
(d) the types of people who attend the sales
(e) what to do before the sale*

Note: The topic sentence is not the first sentence of these paragraphs.

Exercise 7

Find the sentence which deals with:

(a) buying a catalogue
(b) why the author bought something
(c) his interest in other people
(d) the fact that to inspect items is free
(e) the fact that you should be properly dressed
(f) the arrival of the auctioneer
(g) that the author is a collector
(h) the author's love of beautiful things

Exercise 8

Answer the following:

(a) On what occasion did the author become a collector?
(b) At what time does the sale commence?
(c) To which of the three groups of people in the room does the author say he usually belongs?
(d) The people whose attitude to Christie's surprises the author reveal two qualities. What are they?
     (i)
     (ii)
(e) State briefly the three qualities of the author that prompt his frequent visits to Christie's, according to the last paragraph.
     (i)
     (ii)
     (iii)

Unit 4   DISCOURSE MARKERS ————————————————

In order to understand a text, we have to follow the logic of the argument which the author develops. The logic is indicated by discourse markers which show the following links between ideas:

Addition and reinforcement

A new point *confirms expectations* and *strengthens* what has gone before; e.g.:

> He was an able manager and he was popular.

Both 'able' and 'popular' are points in the manager's favour. Other markers in this category are:

> also   in addition   as well as   moreover   furthermore   too   besides
> (either) or   (neither) nor   both . . . and

Exercise 1

Fill the gaps using appropriate discourse markers:

(a) _____ to shorthand, she was qualified in bookkeeping.
(b) The office was ill-equipped _____ undermanned.
(c) The new job pays a higher salary _____ being closer to home.
(d) They will disagree; _____ they will be quite correct.
(e) The company was inefficient. It was unprofitable _____ .
(f) He told me the reason why he left and many more things _____ .
(g) 'They _____ serve who only stand and wait.'
(h) I rely on your discretion and _____ I do not want any statement to the press.
(i) He doesn't like sport, _____ anything that attracts crowds.
(j) The manager wasn't fair and he wasn't honest _____ .

Note: Some items typically occur at the *beginning* of a sentence, e.g.: Moreover. Others typically occur at the *end*, e.g.: too.

Contrast and disjunction

Where the new point goes *against expectations* created by what went before; e.g.:

> The antique is old *but* it is beautiful.

Others in this category are:

> but however yet on the other hand although nevertheless whereas
> while instead still though

Exercise 2

Fill the gaps using contrastive discourse markers:

(a) _____ he worked very hard, he did not pass the exam.
(b) I never met him _____ I feel I know him well.
(c) He applied for the job _____ the board did not recommend him.
(d) Might is right. _____ , the pen is mightier than the sword.
(e) We warned them of the dangers. _____ , they went ahead.
(f) The climate is fine here, _____ there the computers overheated.
(g) The offer was on the table. _____ the talks fell through at the eleventh hour.
(h) My wife loves Hong Kong, _____ I prefer Singapore.
(i) He lost half a fortune, _____ he managed to save his life.
(j) The company lost heavily. That did not affect its staff _____ .

Cause

Where an explanation of why is given — the reason for or the cause of something, e.g.:

> They lost their jobs *because* they were bad workers.

Others like this are:

> since as for due to owing to thanks to

Exercise 3

Fill the gaps using appropriate cause markers:

(a) _____ unforeseen circumstances, the flight has been delayed.
(b) _____ so few people have arrived, we will cancel the party.
(c) He left by the back door, _____ he had no idea they were waiting in the lobby.
(d) She lost the opportunity _____ her own indecisiveness.
(e) The heavy loss was _____ careless speculation on the stock market.
(f) Beware the Ides of March, _____ your days are numbered.

Result

Gives the result, conclusion or consequence of an action or logical process, e.g.:

> He left the drawer open *so* she looked inside it.
> A horse is a quadruped *so* it has four legs.

Other markers are:

> therefore   thus   as a result   consequently   hence

Exercise 4

Fill the gaps using the above items:

(a) _____ of his comments, the director was fired.
(b) The Saxons yielded the high ground and _____ lost the battle.
(c) The figures are unavailable, _____ we have had to postpone the presentation.
(d) You have broken the law, _____ I have no choice but to pass sentence.
(e) The chemicals leaked from the container, _____ causing the fire.

Condition

Gives the circumstances under which, and only under which, something will happen, e.g.:

> I will sign only *if* you delete the penalty clause.
> *Unless* he gets oxygen quickly, he will die.

Similar items are:

> when   where   provided   providing   unless   whether

Exercise 5

Fill the gaps in the following sentences:

(a) You should not dive _____ you have been properly trained.
(b) A dictionary may be used _____ necessary.
(c) You may join the group _____ you pay the membership fee.
(d) _____ he goes or stays she will be in danger.
(e) Pull the trigger only _____ you are certain the suspect is armed.
(f) '_____ winter comes, can spring be far behind?'
(g) _____ you are not out of your room by noon, you will be charged for another day.

Purpose

Explains the reason for an action and the purpose behind it, e.g.:

One must work hard *in order* to succeed.

Similar items are:

to   so as to   so that   with a view to   intending   with the intention of

Exercise 6

Fill the gaps using the above items:

(a) He took out insurance _____ his property would be secure.
(b) The tools are laid out neatly _____ make the job easier.
(c) Sugar Ray Smith took up boxing _____ escape from poverty.
(d) She went to the airport _____ meeting her husband.
(e) He opened the safe _____ to put the jewels inside.
(f) They gave a big party _____ impressing the new director.

Exercise 7

Choose the correct continuation for the following from the two alternatives offered:

(a) They needed help with the financial report, however . . .
    the accountant was helping them.
    the accountant was unavailable.
(b) If the rain does not stop . . .
    we will be able to sunbathe.
    the match will be postponed.
(c) Lord Cars have closed their assembly plant, consequently . . .
    local unemployment has risen.
    productivity has fallen in recent years.
(d) Coal reserves are depleted due to . . .
    the introduction of nuclear power stations.
    long-term mining.
(e) The introduction of electronic funds transfer will mean instant payments, as
    well as . . .
    removing the need to carry cash.
    delays only when the machines fail.
(f) The police carry guns in order to . . .
    encourage the growing use of firearms by criminals.
    protect society against rising violence.

(g) The firm expanded rapidly last year because . . .
    it received a large refund of taxes.
    the bottom fell out of the market.
(h) The factory will have to close down unless . . .
    a wealthy buyer can be found.
    it continues to make a loss.
(i) The office was on holiday last Friday, therefore . . .
    more work was done than in the previous week.
    nobody answered the telephone.
(j) The robber went to prison, still . . .
    the money was restored to its rightful owner.
    he was a rich man on his release seven years later.

Exercise 8   Pair work

In the following extract, you are given a choice of two discourse markers each
time one is used. Choose the correct item and try to explain why to your partner
or teacher:

Propaganda is not always bad. (a) *Consequently/On the other hand* all sorts of
propaganda is used to stir up hatred against other people. For propaganda seen as
this some facts are distorted, (b) *while/thus* others are concealed (c) *and/but* even
deliberate lies are told. (d) *So/If* such propaganda finds its way into newspapers, it has
a very good chance of effectively influencing people (e) *because/although* newspapers
are (f) *as/so* widely read. (g) *Moreover/Nevertheless*, people always seem ready to
believe what they see in print.

Exercise 9

The discourse markers have been omitted from the following text. They are the
following words:

although	and	and	however
if	if	moreover	otherwise
on the other hand	therefore		

Fill the gaps with the missing discourse markers:

Text A

The first thing necessary to the pleasure of reading is that when people are young they
should acquire the habit of reading. This is becoming more and more difficult. Railways
helped to change people's habits by enabling them to move about much more.

_____(a)_____ , railways have this compensating advantage — that, _____(b)_____ they take people away from home, a long railway journey affords a first-rate opportunity for reading. Their coming was not, _____(c)_____ , an unmixed disadvantage. _____(d)_____ , the motor car, which has now superseded the railway train as the principal means of transport in many countries, is altogether unfavourable to reading. In general, people consume more time moving about than they did, _____(e)_____ they consume it under conditions which, even for people with good eyes, must make reading difficult, _____(f)_____ not impossible.

_____(g)_____ , the cinema, the radio and television with all their delights have appeared one after another as further distractions to divert people from time that might _____(h)_____ be given to the pleasure of reading. All these things must make it difficult for successive generations to acquire the habit of reading _____(i)_____ , _____(j)_____ that habit is acquired, to maintain it.

Exercise 10

As we have seen, discourse markers provide the logical links between ideas in a text. Because of this, we can use them to re-order information.

Use the clues given by the discourse markers to reorganise this jumbled paragraph:

(a) as no one had thought of using wood,
(b) As a result only sixty per cent of the produce of each mine was raised above the ground.
(c) Before the commencement of the nineteenth century there were two great difficulties which interfered with the operations of the miner.
(d) coal itself was used for the purpose.
(e) In the first place the roof of the mine had to be propped, and,

Exercise 11

Supply the missing discourse markers:

Text B

They came on deck one morning to see a grim waste of slushy, floating ice and floes around them. _____(a)_____ the steam-heated ship was insulated against cold they were snug enough in their cabins _____(b)_____ , on deck, they wore duffle coats, helmets and fur-lined gloves. _____(c)_____ , they had not come 57 degrees south as sightseers, for there was work to be done. _____(d)_____ George was a laboratory technician, he looked after the store of scientific equipment, and took care of the jars of plankton (the minute living organisms of the ocean). _____(e)_____ Roy worked as an ordinary seaman, one of his more chilly jobs was to chip ice off the deck.

Text C

_____(f)_____ dependable, steerable flying-machines had not as yet been built, the first practical air-mail was a carrier pigeon service. This use of birds was not new; the tendency of certain birds to fly back to the same place had been discovered in antiquity _____(g)_____ had given rise to ingenious postal systems. _____(h)_____ sailors on Egyptian and Greek vessels used to take pigeons along with them and, on the return trip, release them as they were nearing home, _____(i)_____ their relatives might know that the longest part of the voyage was safety over _____(j)_____ that the voyagers themselves would soon be home.

Unit 5   PREDICTION

As we have seen in previous units, reading is a complex process involving the following:

1. Recognising or guessing the meanings of words.
2. Linking reference words to the concepts they replace.
3. Reading quickly for general understanding or slowly for detail.
4. Following the linking of ideas through discourse markers.

Prediction, guessing what is coming next, is important for fast and efficient reading. As each piece of information is read and understood, it helps the reader prepare for the next. The better the reader predicts the development of the text, the faster comprehension takes place.

The title

The prediction process begins with the title. Given the titles below, which of the sentences given would you expect to follow?

Exercise 1

Choose the correct opening sentence:

Title: (a) Pigeon Post

(i)   Culture shock might be called an occupational disease of people who travel abroad.
(ii) During the nineteenth century man still had to rely on one creature whose cleverness no machine could match.

(iii) When you glance at a map of Indonesia, you will know the location of Indonesia.

Title: (b) The Popularity of Television

(i) In the nineteenth century Charles Dickens wrote in a state of great excitement about a stage-coach travelling at twenty miles per hour.
(ii) Propaganda is the name generally given to the various methods by which powerful groups try to influence other persons' beliefs and actions.
(iii) Where there is a television set a great deal of time is spent in viewing.

Title: (c) What's in a Brand Name?

(i) The purpose of advertising is to ensure that your product is known to the buying public.
(ii) Paying with plastic means you no longer have to carry cash everywhere you go.
(iii) Some years ago, two boys took part in an Antarctic voyage.

The opening sentence

The topic sentence was introduced in Unit 3. In skimming exercises, it tells us what each paragraph is likely to consist of. The opening sentence of a text is a particularly important topic sentence, sometimes referred to as the thesis sentence.

Exercise 2

Which of the alternatives given do you think is most likely to follow these opening sentences:

(a) During the nineteenth century, when many means of communication were completely revolutionised, man still had to rely on one creature whose cleverness and endurance no nineteenth-century machine could match.
    (i) a description of nineteenth-century machines
    (ii) the history of the creature's use
    (iii) the competition between creature and machine

(b) Where there is a television set a great deal of time is spent in viewing.
    (i) arguments in favour of the cinema
    (ii) an analysis of propaganda
    (iii) an explanation for the supremacy of television

(c) The purpose of advertising is to ensure that your product is known to the buying public.
    (i) a discussion of advertising methods
    (ii) a discussion of household names
    (iii) an attack on advertisers

Exercise 3 Predicting from topic sentences

Below are five complete or partial topic sentences. Say what you think each paragraph might contain.

(a) Coal has been used for domestic purposes from a very early period.

_____

(b) Before the commencement of the nineteenth century there were two great difficulties which interfered with the operations of the miner.

_____

(c) Soon afterwards a much more important discovery was made.

_____

(d) However, for some years a young Cornishman had been experimenting with this dangerous gas.

_____

(e) The Davy lamp

_____

Reading comprehension practice

Read the text and do the exercises which follow:

How Sir Humphrey Davy Helped Coal Miners

Coal has been used for domestic purposes from a very early period. However, by the beginning of the nineteenth century it had already become very important industrially for its use in the smelting of iron. The urgent need for an ever greater supply of coal led to new contrivances for ensuring its economical production.
5   Before the commencement of the nineteenth century there were two great difficulties which interfered with the operations of the miner. In the first place, the roof of the mine had necessarily to be propped and, as no one had thought of using wood, coal itself was employed for the purpose. As a result, only sixty per cent of the produce of each mine was raised above the ground. About the
10   beginning of the nineteenth century, timber struts were gradually substituted for the pillars of coal, and it became possible consequently to raise from the mine all the coal won by the miner.
     Soon afterwards a much more important discovery was made. The coal miner in his underground calling was constantly exposed to the dangers of a highly
15   inflammable gas called 'fire damp', and was liable to be killed without a moment's notice by a fearful explosion when using a naked flame. Over the years, countless miners had lost their lives in this way.
     However, for some years a young Cornishman, named Humphrey Davy, the son of a wood carver in Penzance, who had risen to the rank of Professor of Chemistry
20   of the Royal Institutiuon, had been experimenting with this dangerous gas. As a result of repeated experiments he had made certain astonishing discoveries, which led to his invention, in 1815, of the first safety lamp, one of the most beneficial inventions that have ever been given to mankind. It enabled the most dangerous mines to be worked with comparative safety.

Exercise 4

Some items have been excluded from the final paragraph of the text. Fill the gaps:

25   The Davy lamp, _____(a)_____ _____(b)_____ has always since been known,
       consists _____(c)_____ a hollow cylinder of wire gauze _____(d)_____ surrounds
       the naked flame from an oil burner. The presence of an explosive gas is indicated
       _____(e)_____ the burning of the fire damp in the interior of the gauze cylinder,
       the heat from _____(f)_____ is conducted away _____(g)_____ sufficient rapidity
30   to prevent the flame inside the cylinder _____(h)_____ spreading _____(i)_____
       the gas _____(j)_____ the mine.

Exercise 5

Find words in the passage which mean the same as:

(a) surprising   _____
(b) speed   _____
(c) innumerable   _____
(d) beginning   _____
(e) devices   _____

Exercise 6

Explain in a single word or short phrase what is meant by the following as they
are used in the passage:

(a) economical   (line 4)   _____
(b) substituted   (line 10) _____
(c) calling   (line 14) _____
(d) exposed   (line 14) _____
(e) inflammable (line 15) _____

Exercise 7   Scanning for detail

(a) For what domestic purpose is coal generally used?
(b) For what important industrial purpose was it used at the beginning of the
     nineteenth century?
(c) Why was it necessary to prop the roof of a mine?
(d) What was originally used for this purpose?
(e) How did this affect coal production?
(f) What better method of propping the roof was later introduced?

(g) How did this affect coal production?
(h) To what dangerous substance were miners exposed?
(i) Why was it dangerous?
(j) What was the occupation of Davy's father?
(k) In what town did he live?
(l) To what position had Davy risen?
(m) With what had he been experimenting?
(n) What did he invent as a result of his experiments?
(o) In what year?
(p) What was the beneficial result of Davy's discovery?

Exercise 8   True or false?

(a) Coal has been in domestic use since the beginning of the nineteenth century.
(b) Coal was used for smelting iron before the beginning of the nineteenth century.
(c) Wood was used as a pit prop before the beginning of the nineteenth century.
(d) Coal was used as a pit prop before the beginning of the nineteenth century.
(e) Most of the coal produced in the nineteenth century was used for pit props.
(f) Coal miners were exposed to gas in the nineteenth century.
(g) Coal miners were killed by the damp in the nineteenth century.
(h) Nobody knows how many miners died in explosions in the nineteenth century.
(i) Humphrey Davy was a wood carver in the early nineteenth century.
(j) The Davy lamp produces light without the use of a flame.

Unit 6 INFERENCE

In reading a text, we make inferences, or assumptions about what the author wants us to understand, based on the language used. It may be only one word that carries the clue, so we need to read in detail.

The author's viewpoint

By using words like, for example, 'luckily' or 'unfortunately', the author reveals a viewpoint on what is being discussed. These words show us whether the author expects us to be, for example, pleased, surprised or disappointed by what we are being told.

Exercise 1

Add more words of this type to the list, expressing, for example, certainty, conviction, reality or lack of it, regret, relief, surprise, predictability:

luckily
unfortunately
of course

_____

_____

_____

Exercise 2

Now use each of these words to compose sentences.

Word value

The choice of words tells us much about what we are expected to infer from a text. When discussing, for example, the size of an object, the author can choose from a range of words of varying effect. Thus, an item could be 'big', 'huge' or 'gigantic'; on the other hand it could be 'small', 'tiny' or 'microscopic'.

Exercise 3

Think of stronger equivalents for each of the words in the following table, e.g.:

small — microscopic

good		bad	
hot		cold	
large		small	
loud		quiet	
tall		old	

pretty		ugly	
funny		silly	
unusual		difficult	
unpleasant		frightened	
expensive		valuable	

Inference and comprehension practice

Read the text and do the exercises which follow:

How the Iron Trade Developed in Great Britain

Iron, the most useful of all metals, presents greater difficulties than any other metal
to the manufacturer, and was _____(a)_____ one of the last minerals which were
applied to the service of man. Centuries elapsed before the rich mines of England
were even slightly worked. The Romans established iron works in Gloucestershire,
5   but the British did not imitate the example of their earliest conquerors, and the little
iron which was used in this country was imported from abroad.
    _____(b)_____ some progress was made in the southern counties, for the
smelters _____(c)_____ sought after ores in those places where wood, then the
only available fuel, was to be found in abundance. However, the prosperity of
10 the trade involved its own ruin. Iron could not be made without large quantities
of fuel. The wood gradually disappeared in the operations of the smelter. Indeed,

the country gentlemen hesitated to sell their trees for fuel when the increase of shipping was creating a growing demand for timber. Nor were the country gentlemen motivated in this respect by purely selfish reasons. Parliament itself regarded the
15 constant destruction of timber with such disfavour that it seriously contemplated the suppression of the iron trade as the only practicable remedy.
_____(d)_____ , so crucial a remedy was not necessary. At the commencement of the seventeenth century, Dudley had improved the feasibility of smelting iron with coal, but the prejudice and ignorance of the workpeople had prevented the
20 adoption of his invention. In the middle of the eighteenth century, attention was again drawn to his process and the possibility of substituting coal for wood was _____(e)_____ established at Darby's works in Coalbrookdale. The impetus which was thus given to the iron trade was _____(f)_____ . At that time the total iron production of the country amounted to only 18,000 tons a year, four-fifths of it being
25 imported from Sweden. Yet by 1802 Great Britain possessed 169 blast-furnaces, and produced 170,000 tons of iron annually. So rapid was the progress of the iron trade in the course of the nineteenth century, that in 1870 6,000,000 tons of iron were produced from British ores.

Inference exercises

Exercise 4

Six words which indicate the author's viewpoint have been omitted from the text; they are the following:

conclusively	extraordinary	fortunately
naturally	probably	undoubtedly

Fill gaps (a)–(f) with the missing items.

Exercise 5

From the options given, choose the word which best expresses the author's opinion about the following:

(a) The workpeople	enlightened	reasonable	backward
(b) The gentlemen	selfless	pragmatic	grasping
(c) Dudley	antiquated	ordinary	progressive
(d) The suppression of the iron trade	essential	reasonable	excessive
(e) The iron trade's chief enemy	government	gentry	workforce

Exercise 6

State which word or phrase in the text tells us that:

(a) Parliament's view was very important.
(b) Coalbrookdale made a big difference to the trade.
(c) There are large deposits of iron in England.
(d) English iron deposits were not at all used before the Romans.
(e) Iron production was surprisingly low at the time of Coalbrookdale.

Exercise 7

Use *your own words* to summarise the author's opinions on the following:

(a) The usefulness of iron.
(b) Iron in manufacturing.
(c) When the mines of England began to be worked.
(d) The comparison of Roman and ancient British attitudes to mining.
(e) The availability of wood in southern England.
(f) The dependence of the iron trade on wood.
(g) The reluctance of country gentlemen to sell wood for fuel.
(h) Parliament's attitude to the iron trade.
(i) The idea of suppressing the iron trade.
(j) The effect of Dudley's process.

Comprehension exercises

Exercise 8

Find a word in the text which means the same as:

(a) wood   (b) copy
(c) completely   (d) practicality
(e) wealth   (f) passed
(g) plenty   (h) considered
(i) set up   (j) disapproval

Exercise 9

Explain in a single word or short phrase what is meant by the following as they are used in the text. Remember to make your explanation the same part of speech as the thing explained:

(a) motivated (line 14) _____
(b) crucial   (line 17) _____
(c) remedy   (line 17) _____
(d) prejudice (line 19) _____
(e) impetus   (line 22) _____

Exercise 10

To what do the following refer?

(a) one   (line 2) _____
(b) their   (line 5) _____
(c) this   (line 6) _____
(d) those   (line 8) _____
(e) its   (line 10) _____
(f) their   (line 12) _____
(g) this   (line 14) _____
(h) it   (line 15) _____
(i) his   (line 20) _____
(j) thus   (line 23) _____
(k) that   (line 23) _____
(l) the country (line 24) _____

Exercise 11   Scanning for detail

(a) To whom does the phrase 'their earliest conquerors' refer?
(b) Where was the iron used by the British originally obtained?
(c) In what region of Britain was progress in iron smelting made?
(d) Why did the prosperity of the trade involve its own ruin?
(e) Why did the country gentlemen hesitate to sell their wood for fuel?
(f) What was Parliament's attitude to the iron trade?
(g) For what reason?
(h) Why was Parliament's proposed remedy unnecessary?
(i) Why was no further progress in iron smelting made at this time?
(j) When was Dudley's process finally adopted?

Unit 7 REVIEW ─────────────────────────────────

Read the following passages carefully and then answer the questions in the exercises, *using your own words where possible.* Your answers should be written concisely in complete sentences, unless you are otherwise instructed.

Text A
Saturday is Match Day

Exercise 1 Prediction

Do you think the text will be about:

(a) accidental fires
(b) weekend activities
(c) a popular sport

Many aspects of the modern age began in Britain — railways, industry, seaside resorts, weekend holidays and organised sports. Of the latter, perhaps the most successful has been the game of association football, or soccer as it is now more widely known.

5   Different ideas have been put forward as to the earliest origins of the game. It seems likely that it began as a ritual battle between rival villages, the object of which was to win and keep possession of an inflated pig's bladder. The game has since evolved into one of great elegance and skill, and is not, as some might think, simply a matter of twenty-two men trying to kick a ball into a net.

10   Until the 1950s, when the players were mainly working men from the local community who held ordinary jobs by day and trained in the evenings for the Saturday match, the maximum wage per game was fixed at a modest twenty pounds. However, those days are long gone, and nowadays soccer is a major international business. Outstanding players enjoy the status of celebrities, and are

15   transferred from club to club for multi-million pound fees.

Every Saturday, world-wide, millions of devoted supporters crowd through the gates of their local stadium to watch their heroes in action. Of course, there is nothing new in this, for in ancient Greece and Rome thousands filled the amphitheatres to watch games and contests. But why, one may ask, do so many football

20   enthusiasts choose to risk the discomfort of crowds and bad weather when they could watch the big match live on television in the comfort of their own homes? The answer, we are told, is that there is no substitute for the atmosphere of the stadium, where the roar of the crowd is medicine against the stresses of the working week for football fans around the globe.

Exercise 2

Find a word in the text which means the same as:

(a) aim   _____   (b) competing   _____
(c) developed _____   (d) limited   _____
(e) loyal   _____   (f) replacement _____

Exercise 3

Find TWO words in the text which mean the same as:

sporting arena   (a) _____   (b) _____
supporters   (c) _____   (d) _____
contests   (e) _____   (f) _____

Exercise 4

Explain in a single word or short phrase what is meant by the following words as they are used in the text:

(a) ritual   (line 6) _____
(b) inflated   (line 7) _____
(c) elegance   (line 8) _____
(d) status   (line 14) _____
(e) celebrities (line 14) _____

Exercise 5

To what do the following words refer?:

(a) it   (line 3) _____   (b) it   (line 5) _____
(c) which   (line 6) _____   (d) one   (line 8) _____
(e) those days (line 13) _____   (f) their (line 17) _____
(g) this   (line 18) _____   (h) they (line 20) _____

Exercise 6 Scanning for detail

(a) By which name is the sport in question best known?
(b) How did the game probably originate?
(c) Where did the game originate?
(d) What was the forerunner of the modern ball?
(e) When did the players start earning a lot of money?

Exercise 7   Inference

Say whether the following statements are true or false:

(a) The distant origins of soccer are well known.
(b) Something is known about the more recent history of the game.
(c) The game's popularity is mainly restricted to Britain.
(d) The author regards soccer as merely kicking a ball into a net.
(e) Soccer players have always been rich and famous.
(f) In the author's opinion it is better to watch the match on television than to go to the stadium.

Text B
The Cashless Society

Exercise 8   Prediction I

Do you think the text is about:

(a) a financial organisation
(b) credit cards
(c) poor people

> 'Buy now and pay later' is the promise offered by the credit card companies, and it might appear an irresistible offer to the unwary.

Exercise 9   Prediction II

Having read the opening sentence, do you think the author will continue by:

(d) arguing in favour of credit cards
(e) presenting a balanced argument, for and against
(f) arguing against credit cards

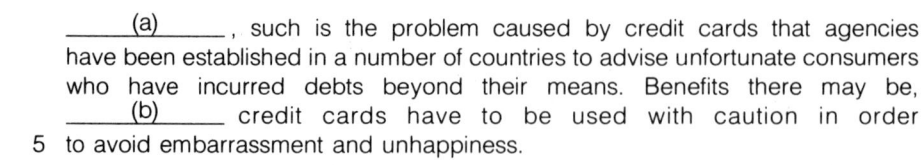

      ___(a)___ , such is the problem caused by credit cards that agencies have been established in a number of countries to advise unfortunate consumers who have incurred debts beyond their means. Benefits there may be, ___(b)___ credit cards have to be used with caution in order
5 to avoid embarrassment and unhappiness.

Exercise 10   Prediction III

The author will now:

(g) point out the benefits of credit cards
(h) list some more disadvantages of credit cards
(i) argue in favour of cash

Of course, paying with plastic means you no longer have to carry large amounts of cash everywhere you go, which can be an advantage _____(c)_____ is undoubtedly safer in these times of rising crime. _____(d)_____ , there is nothing more annoying than having to wait in a supermarket queue while someone pays
10 for a handful of groceries by credit card. _____(e)_____ , new developments to the credit card are afoot which will put an end to problems such as overspending and waiting in queues.

Exercise 11   Prediction IV

The author will now:

(j) argue in favour of cash
(k) explain the new developments
(l) list more advantages of credit cards

In the present system, all card transactions are processed by hand. The shop assistant transfers details from the card to a voucher by means of a press machine.
15 The voucher is then signed and sent to the bank, which takes several days to clear the amount. This time-wasting will soon be eliminated with the arrival of the 'smart card'.
    The brown magnetic strip on the 'smart' credit card contains coded information about the card-holder and his or her hand account details. By means of a
20 card-reading device linked to the cash register, the shop assistant adds the price of goods purchased to the information on the card, all of which is beamed directly to the bank's computers. The sum is then instantly deducted from the card-holder's bank balance. _____(f)_____ the cashless society, once a remote fantasy, is gradually becoming a reality.

Exercise 12

Find a word in the text which means the same as:

(a) dream   (b) incautious
(c) prudence   (d) removed
(e) tempting

Exercise 13

Explain *in your own words* the meaning of the following as they are used in the text:

(a) consumers   (line 2) _____
(b) means   (line 6) _____
(c) afoot   (line 11) _____
(d) transactions (line 13) _____
(e) device   (line 20) _____

Exercise 14

Replace the following in gaps (a)–(f):

    and   but   however   however   on the other hand   thus

Exercise 15   Scanning for detail

(a) What kind of agencies have been set up?
(b) Why?
(c) What is the main advantage of not carrying cash, according to the author?
(d) What is the main disadvantage of the present credit card payment system?
(e) How are the details of credit card payments currently transmitted to banks?
(f) What is the distinguishing feature of the 'smart card'?
(g) How can the information contained by the card be read?
(h) What is the role of computers in 'smart card' transactions?

Exercise 16   Inference

Say which of the options is correct:

(a) The author is *sceptical/enthusiastic* about credit cards.
(b) The author feels they are *more/less secure* than cash.
(c) The author says delays due to credit card payment are *inevitable/intolerable*.
(d) The author feels the time currently taken to process transactions is *minimal/excessive*.
(e) The 'smart card' will be *more/less acceptable* to the author than the present system.

Writing

Unit 1   CHOOSING A TOPIC

In a First Level Writing question, you are given a list of topics like this:

Write about 200 words on one of the following topics:

1. The importance of oil.
2. Bargain hunting.
3. Helping with the harvest.
4. Ships on the river or in harbour.
5. How improved communications are making the world seem smaller.
6. The repair of roads.

Knowledge

In order to write 200 words comfortably, and at the same time develop a good argument, it is best to choose a subject which you know about or have experience of.

Exercise 1

Decide which of titles 1–6 you would advise the following candidates to attempt:

(a) Someone who lives near a coastal port.
(b) A person experienced in international travel.
(c) Someone who does a lot of driving.
(d) A person who enjoys shopping.
(e) Someone who has lived in a farming area.
(f) A person who works in a heavy industry.

Note: You should make clear in your own mind and in the opening paragraph of your writing the scope and limitations of the title, e.g. that OIL in 1. means *petroleum* not edible oils.

Ideas

Of course, even if you do not fit into any of the above categories, you should still know something about or have an opinion on at least one of the topics. You should then choose the one which gives you most ideas.

Exercise 2

State under which of titles 1–6 you might discuss:

(a) Pitchforks and balers.
(b) Dredgers and tugs.
(c) Trains and TV sets.
(d) Delays and diversions.
(e) Paraffin and diesel.
(f) Sales and reductions.

Plan: vocabulary and shape

Having selected your topic on the basis of knowledge, experience, opinions or ideas, you should note down all the points and vocabulary you can think of under the heading you have chosen. This will give you an idea of the final shape your writing will take and provide the basis for a plan:

Exercise 3

Add as many items as you can to the following:

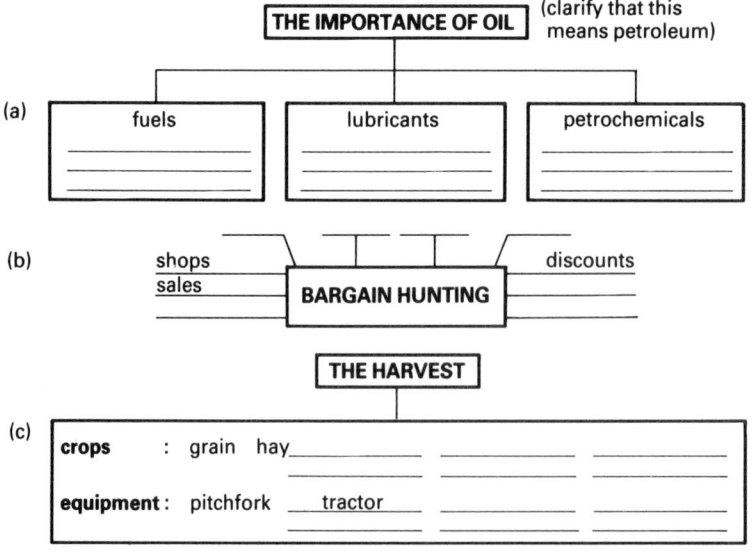

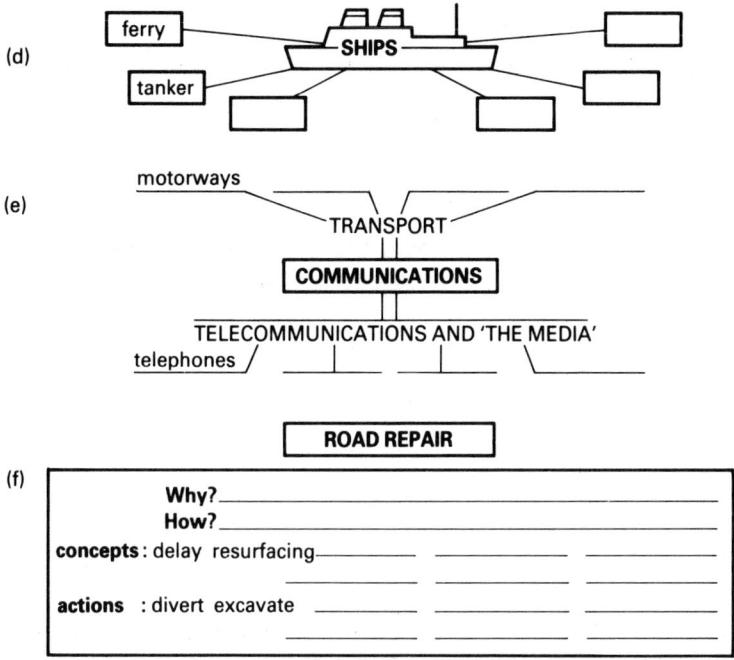

(d)

(e)

(f)

Outline: Vocabulary and ordering

Noting down vocabulary items helps you remember what you know about the subject you have chosen. The next step is to decide on the outline of your passage. Below we shall consider three simple patterns.

Pattern 1
For giving information about a series of items:

Type	Description	Function
Item 1	_____	_____
Item 2	_____	_____
etc.	etc.	etc.

Exercise 4

Add notes on description and function to the ship types from Exercise 3:

Ships

Type	Description	Function
tanker freighter liner ferry dredger tug yacht	large, long	bulk liquid carrier/to carry liquid in bulk

Exercise 5

Using your notes from Exercise 4, and following Pattern 1 above, write a simple paragraph on ships:

> **Ships in the Harbour**
>
> There are ships of many varieties in the harbour near my home. Tankers are large, long vessels, used for carrying liquids in bulk. _____
>
> _____
>
> _____

Exercise 6

Complete the following table with notes on oil:

Oil

Type	Item	Function
fuel petrochemicals	paraffin petrol diesel lubricant plastics etc.	

Exercise 7

Write two simple paragraphs based on Pattern 1 and your notes from Exercise 6:

The Importance of Oil

Oil from petroleum is of great importance to the contemporary world. It is used in a variety of forms. Paraffin is a fuel oil widely used in aviation and as a household fuel. _____

_____

In addition to fuels, petrochemicals derived from petroleum play a major role in the modern world. Plastics now replace many natural materials. _____

_____

Exercise 8

Complete the following table with notes on the effects of modern communications:

Communications

Class	Type	Effect	Advantages	Disadvantages
Transport	cars motorways trains jet aircraft			
Telecommuni- cations and other media	telex telephone television computer links facsimile (fax) newspapers the mail			

Exercise 9

Write two simple paragraphs, combining Pattern 1 with your notes from Exercise 8. Follow closely the wording used in Exercise 7:

How Improved Communications are Making the World Seem Smaller

Communications have had a revolutionary effect on the contemporary world. ____

_____

In addition to transport _____

_____

Pattern 2
For describing the steps in a process, or the sequence of events in a story:

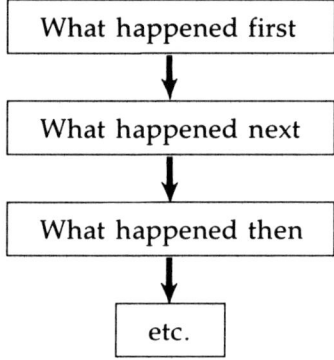

Exercise 10

Most people have had experience of bargain hunting. Think of an incident from your own experience, and make notes using the following table:

The Story of How I Found a Bargain

Step	What happened
1. 2. 3. etc.	(for example) It was the annual sale. I had seen _____ in a certain shop. I got up early and went into town. _____

Exercise 11

Using your notes from Exercise 10, and Pattern 2, write a paragraph on how you found a bargain:

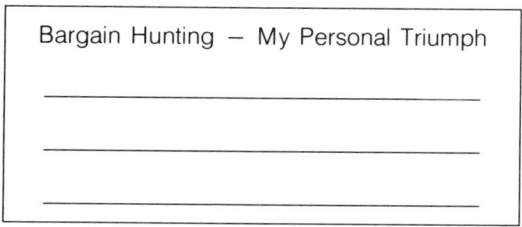

Pattern 3
For presenting a balanced argument, giving points for and against a particular subject:

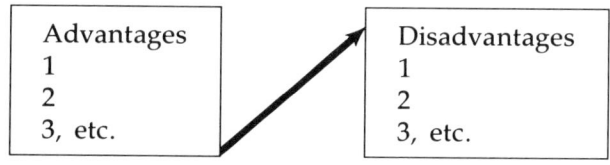

Exercise 12

Outline the arguments for and against road repairs using Pattern 3:

For	**Against**
smooth surface	long delays

Exercise 13

Complete the two simple paragraphs on the next page, one outlining the advantages and the other the disadvantages of road repairs:

The Repair of Roads

In my opinion, road repairs are a necessary evil. Since traffic moves at such high speed today, a smooth road surface is necessary for safety. Also _____

In addition _____

Furthermore   _____

   On the other hand, road repairs add to the stress of modern life. Long delays add to one's travelling time. Also _____

In addition _____

Finally _____

Exercise 14

Look again at the beginning of the unit. Choose from the writing questions 1—6 the one which you know most about, and, using the methods practised in this unit, attempt a complete answer.

Note: The 'English for Commerce' examination gives credit not only for correct language but also for *good planning* and *shaping* of what you write. Provided what you write is not obviously nonsense or self-contradictory, you will *not* be penalised for inaccurate facts or defective knowledge.

Unit 2 SENTENCE, PARAGRAPH, TEXT

Your written work should consist of three different levels of organisation:

1. The sentence.
2. The paragraph.
3. The complete text.

The sentence

The sentence is the basic unit of composition, and there are two important rules to remember:

1. A sentence must begin with a capital letter and end with a full stop.
2. A sentence will always have a main finite verb and a subject (explicit or implicit).

If you are in doubt about the accuracy of a sentence which you are writing, keep it short and simple. Short sentences can be very effective, whereas the longer the sentence, the more the likelihood of grammatical error increases.

Exercise 1

Disregarding the requirement for an initial capital and a final full stop, decide which of the following are NOT complete sentences:

(a) railways helped to change people's habits by enabling them to move about much more
(b) gentlemen themselves regarded the destruction of trees with disfavour
(c) neither your dress nor your manners clearly unacceptable
(d) sales at eleven o'clock precisely
(e) the Davy lamp, as it has always been known
(f) 'the early bird that catches the worm'
(g) in propaganda some facts distorted, while others concealed
(h) two boys in Antarctica
(i) these adventurous boys then aged sixteen
(j) since Roy worked as an ordinary seaman

Exercise 2

Correct the incomplete sentences in Exercise 1, adding capital letters, full stops or further information as necessary.

Exercise 3

Divide the following into complete sentences, adding punctuation as necessary:

when I was doing my homework last night I was stuck on some questions first I asked my father the date of Waterloo he said he couldn't remember then I asked him the formula for pi he answered he had no idea I said I hoped he didn't mind my asking he replied that if one never asks one never learns

Exercise 4

Repeat the procedure for the following:

there are a number of factors which should be taken into account when buying a dog the first is breed or type some dogs are bred for domestic life as pets whereas others are suited only for an outdoor existence the foxhound is a good example of a dog which is almost impossible to house train if left at home alone it will destroy clothing furniture and any other items it can get its teeth into its proper place is running with the pack

The paragraph

The purpose of the paragraph is to enable each new point and its supporting arguments to be presented separately, or to group closely related points.

Exercise 5

Rearrange the following sentences into three paragraphs about Adult Education courses:

(a) Patrick Bailey will present the first session on the creative use of filters.
(b) There will also be a special session on window boxes.
(c) Finally, we regret to announce that basketweaving has been suspended from the programme.
(d) The Adult Education Centre is pleased to announce that gardening classes are available for all levels.
(e) There has been insufficient interest to justify the hire of a tutor this year.
(f) These will focus on herbaceous borders, rockeries and hardy annuals.
(g) In addition to gardening, photography courses will resume this autumn.

Paragraph 1: _____

Paragraph 2: _____

Paragraph 3: _____

Exercise 6   Pair work

Compare your paragraphs and discuss any differences in ordering.

Writing questions

Write about 200 words on the following topics:

1. Good salesmanship.
2. Safety on the roads.
3. An industry that interests you.
4. Lonely occupations.
5. Craftsmanship today.

Paragraph structure

As we shall see in subsequent units, paragraphs can be used to express arguments in a number of ways. Some of these are as follows:

Giving examples (see Unit 3)
Making generalisations (see Unit 4)
Contrasting points (see Unit 5)
Describing a process (see Unit 6)
Telling a story (narrative) (see Unit 7)

Exercise 7

Below are the opening sentences of paragraphs on four of the writing question topics. Try to decide which of the above list of paragraph types is being constructed: then add one or more appropriate sentence(s) to complete the sense of the paragraph:

(a)

Safety on the Roads

The modern family car is built with a strong passenger compartment and front and rear seatbelts. Nevertheless _____

(b)

Lonely Occupations

Although we live in an age of mass production, there are still a number of occupations which can be thought of as lonely. One which springs readily to mind _____

(c)

An Industry that Interests Me

One industry that interests me is the advertising industry. My first experience

_____

(d)

Craftsmanship Today

Unfortunately, craftsmanship today is a thing of the past. The vast majority of former craftsmen _____

The complete text

A complete text should have a TITLE, a BEGINNING, a MIDDLE and an END. Consider the following example:

Title	*Obstacles to the Habit of Reading in Modern Times*
Paragraph 1 *Introduction*	I think that modern conditions are seriously endangering the pleasure of reading. _____
(supporting arguments)	_____
Paragraph 2 (point plus supporting arguments)	_____ _____
Paragraph 3 (point plus supporting arguments)	_____ _____
Conclusion	_____ All these things must make it difficult to acquire the habit of reading, and, if that habit is acquired, to maintain it.

Title
Note that in all examples so far, the title has used the same wording as the question. You are advised to follow this method in the First Level Examination. This serves two purposes: (a) to focus the attention of the writer on the question in hand, and (b) to ensure that the text passage has a title, which is obligatory!

Beginning
In the example above, the author opens the passage by stating his opinion on the subject. This is a good place to start. You should use the opening sentence (sometimes called the thesis statement) to set the tone of what is to follow, and, as with the title, to show that you understand what the question requires.

Middle
Between the opening and the final sentences, you should present your argument in structured paragraphs, as we shall continue to practise in this section.

End
In the example above, the author ends by 'pointing' to all the arguments he has presented in the intervening paragraphs, and also restating his opening point in a slightly modified form. This is a good method to bear in mind.

Exercise 8

Provide a TITLE, and OPENING SENTENCE and a CLOSING SENTENCE for the following:

(a) _____

(b) _____

> Some organisations prefer the 'hard sell', whereby the buyer is not given a chance to consider his or her decision. Psychology is indeed widely used to influence the customer.
>
> However, in my view the most ethical approach is for the representative to gain a thorough knowledge of his product, in order to answer all questions honestly. A satisfied customer is after all more likely to become a regular customer.

(c) _____

Exercise 9

Rewrite the following notes (and any you might wish to add) in paragraph form.
  A title, opening sentence and closing sentence are provided below:

  mass production — robots and automation
  small businesses — cost effectiveness
  lost skills — pride in handiwork
  beauty — uniqueness

Craftsmanship Today

Craftsmanship today is, alas, very much a thing of the past. _____

_____

_____

Nevertheless, the fact remains that nowadays craftsmanship is strictly for the enthusiast.

Exercise 10

Answer in full one of the writing questions 1–5 above.

Unit 3 GIVING EXAMPLES

One of the most important techniques in writing involves supporting your arguments with examples:

TEXT A

Advantages and Disadvantages of Speed in Modern Life

In the twentieth century, man is able to move and to communicate with great rapidity. Aeroplanes fly many hundreds of miles in an hour; some express trains are nearly as fast. Even without moving we can communicate within seconds with people on the other side of the globe.

The advantages of these increased speeds are numerous. For instance, business-men travel around the globe in hours instead of the weeks it once took. In addition, fruit and vegetables can now safely be sent to far-distant places.

Not all the effects of speed, however, are beneficial, such as the tendency of car-users to become physically lazy. Also, those who travel by train do not see much of the countryside as it flashes past.

Exercise 1

Analyse the text by isolating the three main statements and identifying the examples given by the author in support of them:

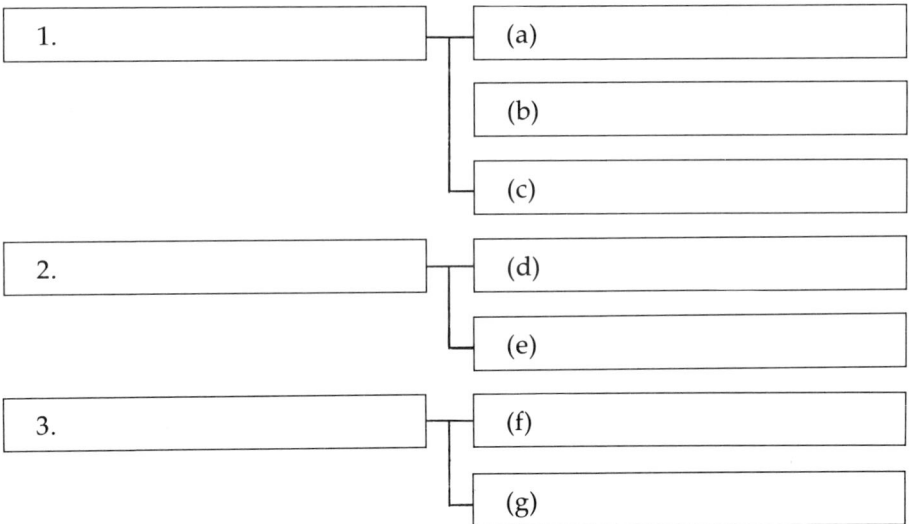

Writing questions

1. Steel.
2. Hire purchase.
3. The cultivation of a crop which is important for your country.
4. Dangers of drug addiction.
5. The difficulties experienced in doing a particular job either at home or at work.
6. Self-service stores.

Exercise 2

Think of examples for each of the following:

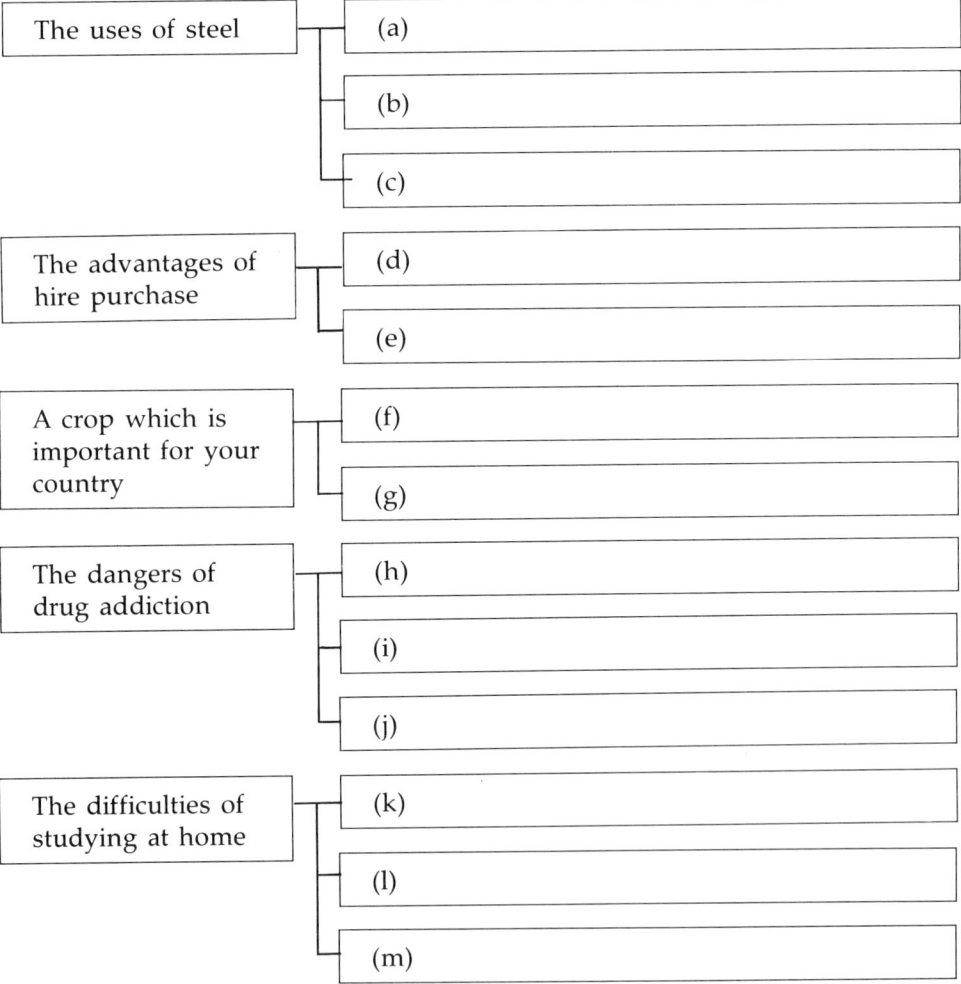

The uses of steel	(a)
	(b)
	(c)

| The advantages of hire purchase | (d) |
| | (e) |

| A crop which is important for your country | (f) |
| | (g) |

The dangers of drug addiction	(h)
	(i)
	(j)

The difficulties of studying at home	(k)
	(l)
	(m)

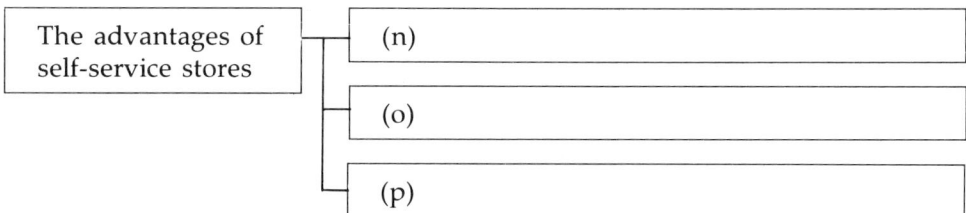

The advantages of self-service stores	(n)
	(o)
	(p)

Introducing examples

Look again at text A. Note how the examples are introduced.

New sentence followed by discourse marker

The advantages of these increased speeds are numerous. For instance ...

Others are:

FIRST MENTION	For	instance	(of this) is
	An One	example illustration	
SUBSEQUENT EXAMPLES	Another A further		
	Also In addition Moreover Furthermore		

Exercise 3

Using some of the discourse markers above, and your own examples from Exercise 2, complete the following paragraphs:

(a) The uses of steel are numerous. _____

_____

_____

(b) Hire purchase offers several advantages. _____

_____

_____

(c) Drug addiction is a great social evil which has many dangers. _____

_____

_____

New sentence and no discourse marker to follow

In the twentieth century man is able to move and to communicate with great rapidity. Aeroplanes . . .

Exercise 4

Add examples as new sentences without discourse markers:

(a) _____ is an important crop for a number of reasons. _____

_____

(b) I have experienced many different difficulties in my career so far. _____

_____

Same sentence and discourse marker

Not all the effects of speed are beneficial, such as the tendency . . .

Others are:

,	such as for example for instance		
		,	x	for instance for example

Be careful to use the comma correctly.

Note: If you want to list two or more points in the same sentence, remember the rule:

_____1_____ and _____2_____.

OR _____1_____ , _____2_____ and

_____3_____.

Exercise 5

Add two or more examples using discourse markers but without starting a new sentence:

(a) Hire purchase does, however, have its disadvantages, _____

_____

(b) There are however certain difficulties associated with the cultivation of this crop, _____

_____

Same sentence and no discourse marker

Aeroplanes fly many hundreds of miles in an hour; express trains . . .

Another punctuation mark used for examples is the dash ' − ', e.g.:

There are many high speed express trains − the Japanese 'bullet train', the British Advanced Passenger Train, the TGV in France.

Punctuating complex lists

Normally commas are enough to separate the items in a list of examples, but sometimes, where they are more complex, we need to use colons and semi-colons as well as commas, e.g.:

My uncle, Lord Stanley, the Commander in Chief of the Armed Forces, gave a dinner party.

We refer here to only one person, Lord Stanley, but if he was included in a list along with other people, we would need to separate all that is said about him from what is said about the others. So:

Those present at the dinner party were: Frederick, Prince of Wales; my uncle, Lord Stanley, the Commander in Chief of the Armed Forces; my parents, Lord and Lady Buxton; my nanny, Sarah Grip; and two visitors from India, Ranjit Singh and the Maharajah of Baroda.

How many people were at the dinner party? Fifteen or seven?

Exercise 6

Use commas, semi-colons and colons to separate the following items in a list-type paragraph:

In the toolshed
    an old, rickety lawn-mower
    five rusty nails
    a thick, heavy hammer
    a tube of Join, the best glue available
    a spade
    a fork borrowed from my neighbour, Joe Payne

Exercise 7

Repeat the procedure for the following:

In the lift
    Fred, the lift attendant
    two salesmen
    the Managing Director, Roger Clive
    his secretary, Ruth Wedge
    Harry, the Chief Accountant
    Harry's dog, Rover

Exercise 8

Write two paragraphs giving examples of (a) the advantages and (b) the disadvantages of self-service stores.

Exercise 9

Attempt a complete answer to one of the writing questions 1–6 above.

Unit 4   GENERALISATION AND GENERIC TERMS ————————

Consider the following:

> It is important for *the retailer or assistant* to be enthusiastic about shopkeeping if he is to be successful and happy in his work. *Most people* in retailing have a preference for dealing with the goods of a particular trade, *usually* that in which they have practical experience.

To which 'retailer or assistant' do you think the author is referring? Normally the definite article 'the' denotes a particular individual, and the indefinite article 'a' is used where the subject is not specific. Here, however, 'the retailer' implies all retailers, and is thus used to make a *generalisation*. Such use of 'the' is called *generic* because it refers to all individuals of a kind (Latin *genus*).

Similarly, while it is difficult to say exactly *how many* people in retailing have a preference for dealing with the goods of a particular trade, it is fairly safe to say 'most people'. In order to make a more categorical statement the author could have said:

> *All* retailers prefer to deal with the goods of a particular trade, and it is *always* the one in which they have practical experience.

Alternatively, a more cautious statement would be:

> *Some* retailers prefer to deal with the goods of a particular trade, *often* that in which they have practical experience.

Thus we can identify two important elements in a generalisation:

1. *How many* are involved in the generalisation:

> *Some* girls   *Most* retailers   *All* trees, etc.

2. *To what extent* the generalisation holds:

> often   usually   always

Note: It is safest to stick to cautious generalisations in speaking and writing since categorical generalisations like 'all Cretans are liars' are so easy to disprove — you only have to find one truthful Cretan and the statement is itself a lie!

Exercise 1

Discuss and place the following items on the scale 100%−zero:

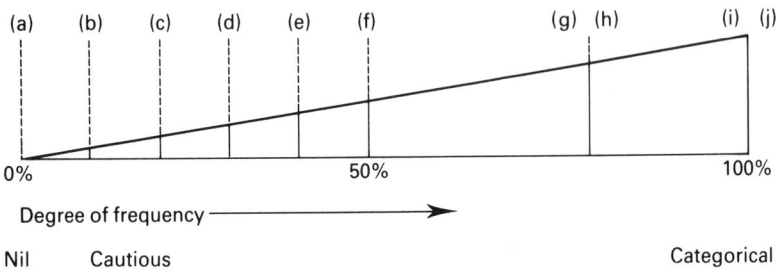

some/all/no(ne)/many/a few/the majority/a minority/almost all/few/most

Exercise 2

Discuss and place the following items on the scale:

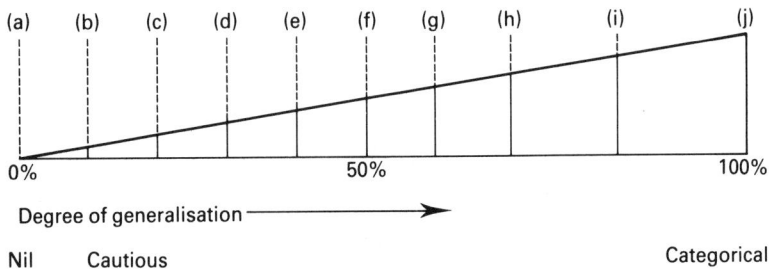

always/usually/normally/without fail/rarely/never/occasionally/seldom/frequently/sometimes

Visualising generalisations

Consider the following diagrams. Each represents a degree of generalisation. *The shaded area represents the cases involved.* In Exercises 3 and 4 you are asked to relate statements of generalisation to the equivalent diagram.

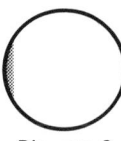
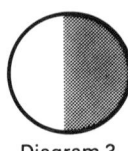
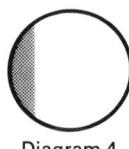

Diagram 1   Diagram 2   Diagram 3   Diagram 4   Diagram 5

Exercise 3

Choose the diagram which matches the following statements:

(a) Few retailers enjoy a monopoly.
(b) Most retailers close on Sundays in Britain.
(c) Retailers are, after all, only human.
(d) Retailers sometimes become millionaires.
(e) Many retailers live on the premises.
(f) A few retailers go bankrupt.
(g) Some retailers never make an adequate living.
(h) A lot of retailers open several shops.
(i) The majority of retailers face competition.
(j) The average retailer is a family man hoping to build a family business.
(k) The vast bulk of retailers sell up eventually.
(l) A minority of retailers strike it rich.

Exercise 4

Match the following statements with the diagrams:

(a) People occasionally marry their cousins.
(b) The disease is usually fatal.
(c) The leaves invariably fall in the autumn.
(d) The species is seldom seen.
(e) Fortune-tellers are often wrong.
(f) It always rains on Sundays.
(g) He frequently loses money.
(h) You can fool some of the people all of the time.
(i) His forecasts are hardly ever right.

Introducing generalisations

In general, farms are inherited.
Generally, football supporters are law-abiding citizens.
As a rule, university graduates have no difficulty in finding employment.
On the whole, pop music appeals to the young.
By and large, the firm has had a successful year.
Broadly speaking, the north is rich and the south is poor.

Discussing tendencies

More and more farms are being sold to property developers.
Increasingly, football supporters are juvenile delinquents.
Fewer and fewer graduates are finding jobs these days.

Women *tend to* live longer than men.
Gradually, the town is taking over the countryside.
In diminishing proportions, women are paid less than men.
To an ever greater extent, the ozone layer is being eroded.

General—particular

It is often necessary or useful to extend or qualify a generalisation by emphasising cases in which it particularly holds true, e.g.:

Most retailers prefer to deal with the goods of a particular trade, *especially* when they have practical experience in that trade.

Note: Cautious generalisations and statements of tendency cannot be disproved by quoting one exception, or even a few. Precise statistical data is required for that. In thoughtful writing counter-examples are often introduced to show that the writer has tested his generalisation against the facts and still found it to be more or less correct, e.g.:

It is true that this year only twenty retailers earned more than £40,000 per year *but by and large* it is still correct to say that retailing is a safe way to achieve a comfortable income.

Generalising about actions/behaviour

Consider the following:

A direct selling business *will* tell its agents in the field what they can do. It *will* also tell them what they must not do. A retail store *will* tell its buyers what it wants them to do. It *will* also tell them what it does not want them to do. And the sole trader *will* make up his policies as he goes along.

In this example, generalisations are being made on the basis of *predictable behaviour;* any direct selling or retail business *will* do these things; all sole traders *will* behave in this way. The underlying meaning is 'usually, in most cases' rather than 'all or always'.

Writing questions

Write about 200 words on the following topics:

1. Over-population in under-developed countries.
2. The benefits of a study of commerce.
3. Living a healthy life.
4. Breeding wild animals in captivity.

Exercise 5   Over-population

What generalisations can you make about the effects of over-population in under-developed countries? E.g.:

Over-population usually creates unemployment.

Discuss and make generalisations about the following in relation to over-population:

food   _____
wealth   _____
housing   _____
health   _____
birth rate   _____
crime   _____
sanitation   _____
disease   _____
education   _____
women   _____

Exercise 6

Use your generalisations as the basis of a composition.

Exercise 7   The benefits of studying commerce

Discuss and complete the following statements. Note that there are no absolutely correct answers: they depend on opinion and experience:

(a) _____ who study commerce learn something from it.
(b) _____ students enjoy it very much.
(c) _____ go on to enjoy great success.
(d) _____ actually become millionaires.
(e) _____ eventually chair multinational corporations.
(f) A study of commerce _____ involves reading.
(g) The subject is _____ taught in colleges.
(h) Good results can _____ be achieved through self-study.
(i) Practical experience is _____ a useful preparation for a study of commerce.
(j) Students _____ find commerce challenging.

Exercise 8

Base your composition on these generalisations, providing supporting arguments from your own experience.

Exercise 9   A healthy life

Discuss and make generalisations about the following in relation to a healthy life:

smoking _____
fatty foods _____
exercise _____
happiness _____
alcohol _____
sleep _____
work _____
recreation _____
heredity _____
stress _____

Exercise 10

Use the above as the basis of a composition.

Exercise 11   Breeding wild animals in captivity

Discuss and complete the following statements, adding particular examples to support your generalisations:

(a) _____ animals are threatened with extinction.
(b) _____ animals cannot be bred in captivity.
(c) _____ species are being wiped out by ivory poachers.
(d) _____ zoo parks accurately reproduce a natural environment.
(e) _____ animals would die out without the efforts of captive breeders.
(f) The natural habitat of _____ species is being destroyed.
(g) _____ species are already extinct.
(h) _____ zoos are inhumane places.
(i) _____ successes have been achieved through captive breeding.
(j) _____ animals now only survive in zoos.

Unit 5 CONTRASTING INFORMATION ⸻

Contrast is an important device in developing a balanced argument. Here are some examples of contrast:

> Since trains offer good opportunities for reading, their coming was not an unmixed disadvantage. *On the other hand,* the motor car is altogether unfavourable to reading.

> Progress was made in the southern counties where wood was to be found in abundance. *However,* the wood gradually disappeared in the operations of the smelter.

> In 1750 the total iron production amounted to only 18,000 tons a year. *Yet* by 1802 Great Britain produced 170,000 tons annually.

> Before the electronic age there was nothing to do in the evenings but read, *whereas* nowadays there are countless distractions.

In presenting contrasting arguments, there are three main options open to the writer:

1. In separate paragraphs:

```
┌─────────────────────────────────┐
│                                 │
│  (Arguments for)                │
│                                 │
└─────────────────────────────────┘
┌─────────────────────────────────┐
│  On the other hand ...          │
│  (Arguments against)            │
└─────────────────────────────────┘
```

2. In opposing sentences:

```
┌──────────────────────┐   ┌──────────────────────────┐
│  (Argument A)        │   │  However ... (Argument B) │
└──────────────────────┘   └──────────────────────────┘
┌──────────────────────┐   ┌──────────────────────────┐
│  (Argument C)        │   │  Yet ... (Argument D)     │
└──────────────────────┘   └──────────────────────────┘
```

Contrast markers used at the beginning of sentences:

> On the other hand
> However
> Yet
> Nevertheless
> In contrast
> Conversely
> But

3. In the same sentence:

EITHER:

1	2	3
(Argument A)	, whereas ...	(Argument B) .

OR:

1	2	3
Although ... (Argument A)	,	(Argument B) .

Contrast markers used within sentences:

although	while
whereas	but (mid-sentence only)

Writing questions

Write about 200 words on the following topics:

1. Fishing.
2. Credit cards.
3. Television as a medium of advertising.
4. Arguments for and against a business career.

Exercise 1

Here are several points on the subject of fishing. Your task is as follows:

(a) To rearrange the points under the four headings given below.
(b) To rewrite the information in four paragraphs.

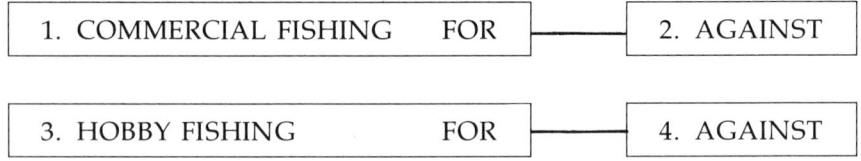

1. COMMERCIAL FISHING FOR	2. AGAINST

3. HOBBY FISHING FOR	4. AGAINST

Arguments:

   (i) Undersize fish are sometimes taken by anglers.
  (ii) Factory fishing methods are inhumane.
 (iii) The riverbank is a refreshing change from the city.
 (iv) The sea offers vast resources of protein.
  (v) Anglers press to keep rivers free of pollution.
 (vi) Fish are a source of much-needed nutrition.
(vii) Angling endangers other wildlife, e.g. swans.
(viii) Many species have been fished to extinction.
 (ix) People who fish for fun don't need to fish for food.

(x) Seals and dolphins are endangered by careless fishing.
(xi) Anglers stock rivers.
(xii) The sea's resources are not unlimited.
(xiii) Angling is a source of pleasure to millions.
(xiv) The sea is a vast unexplored universe.
(xv) Weekend fishermen disturb the environment.
(xvi) What is the point of getting cold and wet and going home empty-handed?

Exercise 2

Below is a list of arguments for and against credit cards. Your task is to do the following:

(a) Add to the list *by discussing in groups if possible.*
(b) Arrange the arguments in contrasting pairs, as in the diagram.
(c) Rewrite the list of arguments as a composition of two or more paragraphs.
(d) Add an introduction and a conclusion.

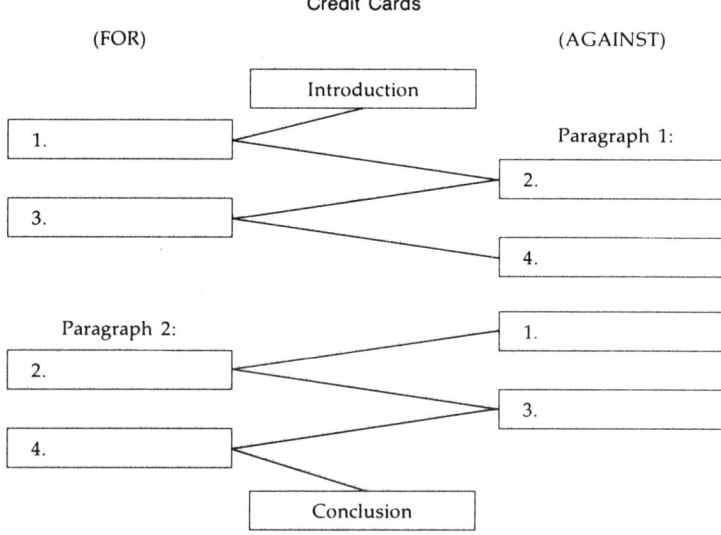

Arguments:
(i) Buy now pay later.
(ii) More consumer credit control.
(iii) People get into trouble through debt.
(iv) Plastic is safer than cash.
(v) Credit information can infringe civil liberties.
(vi) Instant credit encourages an unrealistic sense of wealth.
(vii) _____
(viii) _____
(ix) _____

Exercise 3   Television as a medium of advertising

(a) In groups (where possible), discuss the subject of television as a medium of advertising. Here are some headings which might be useful pointers in your discussions (or deliberations):

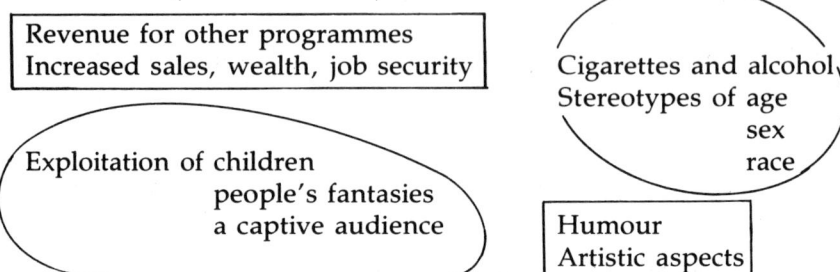

Revenue for other programmes
Increased sales, wealth, job security

Cigarettes and alcohol
Stereotypes of age
                      sex
                      race

Exploitation of children
            people's fantasies
            a captive audience

Humour
Artistic aspects

(b) List the points which arise in the appropriate box. Try to arrange them in contrasting pairs:

Television Advertising

For	Against
_____	_____
_____	_____
_____	_____

(c) Write a composition with the title *Television as a Medium of Advertising*. Try as far as possible to practise contrasting two points within the same sentence, e.g.:

> Television is a welcome escape from mundane reality into glittering fantasy, but this fact enables advertisers to exploit people's dreams in pushing their products.

Exercise 4   The advantages and disadvantages of a business career

(a) Taking this as your title, make a list of *arguments* based on your opinions.
(b) Decide on a suitable organisation for your arguments, subdividing them into *several paragraphs* as necessary.
(c) Write a composition of about *200 words*, not forgetting an *introduction and a conclusion*.

Unit 6   PROCESS

Here is an extract from an LCCI First Level Reading passage:

> You simply go through the main door, pass the enquiry desk unchallenged and proceed up the wide stairway. You will then see the auction rooms in front of you. For a small sum of money you buy a catalogue of the day's sale. You then inspect the items. If you are interested in the day's sale, you just take a seat.

Exercise 1

Note the seven main steps in the process which is being described:

1. _____
2. _____
3. _____
4. _____
5. _____
6. _____
7. _____

Describing a process

In Unit 1 of this section, we saw a simple method for describing the steps in a process, or sequence of events, as follows:

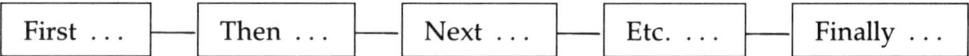

We could perhaps describe this arrangement as a *serial* ordering of the steps in the process.

Another possibility is *numerical* ordering:

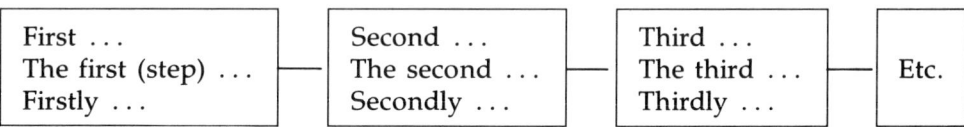

A further possibility is *chronological* ordering:

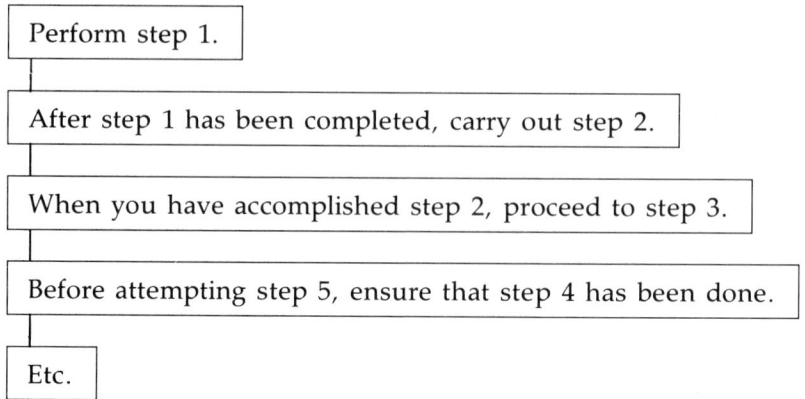

Note how the sequence of steps in the process is indicated by discourse markers:

after   before   when   during   while   once (= after)   by the time

Exercise 2

Note the synonyms for 'do' in the example above:

do   perform   complete   accomplish   carry out

Add more synonyms to the list:

_____   _____   _____   _____

Writing exercises

Write about 200 words on the following topics:
1. Hitch-hiking.
2. Hire purchase.
3. Fire in an office.
4. Keeping a city clean and tidy.

Exercise 3

Organise the following information into a three-paragraph explanation of hitch-hiking. Organise your paragraphs as follows:

1. Planning the trip.
2. Setting out.
3. En route.

Remember TITLE, INTRODUCTION and CONCLUSION.

Simple guide to hitch-hiking
1. Decide where you want to go.
2. Get a map and select the best route.
3. Choose roads with plenty of traffic.
4. Make a sign board stating your destination.
5. Go to a suitable starting point, e.g. junction or roundabout.
6. Display your sign board.
7. Hold out your hand with thumb raised.
8. Make polite conversation with drivers who offer lifts.
9. Ask to be dropped where there is plenty of traffic.

Exercise 4

Read the following advertisement. Use the information given to write a short passage explaining hire purchase:

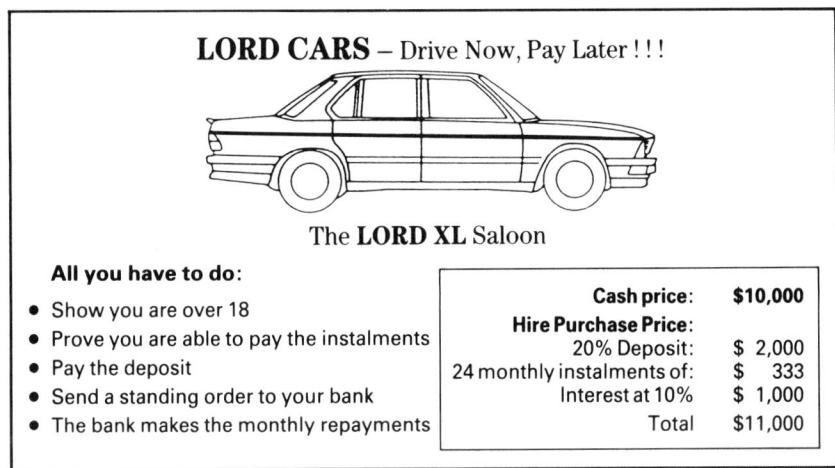

LORD CARS – Drive Now, Pay Later ! ! !

The **LORD XL** Saloon

All you have to do:

- Show you are over 18
- Prove you are able to pay the instalments
- Pay the deposit
- Send a standing order to your bank
- The bank makes the monthly repayments

Cash price:	**$10,000**
Hire Purchase Price:	
20% Deposit:	$ 2,000
24 monthly instalments of:	$ 333
Interest at 10%	$ 1,000
Total	$11,000

Exercise 5

Below is a set of instructions on procedure in case of fire. Use them as the basis for a written explanation of what to do when fire breaks out in an office block:

In case of fire:
(a) Break glass to sound alarm.
(b) Dial 999 on emergency telephone.
(c) Inform fire service of fire's location.
(d) Use the extinguisher provided.
(e) Close doors and windows.
(f) Leave the building by the nearest exit.
(g) Use stairs, not lifts.

Passive verbs

Study the following extract from an LCCI First Level Reading text:

> The Davy lamp, as it has always been known, consists of a hollow cylinder of wire gauze which surrounds the naked flame from an oil burner. The presence of an explosive gas is indicated by the burning of the fire damp in the interior of the gauze cylinder, the heat from which is conducted away with sufficient rapidity to prevent the flame inside the cylinder from spreading to the gas in the mine.

Note the way in which the process of the lamp's operation is described:

1. The presence of gas *is indicated by* the burning of fire damp.
2. The heat *is conducted away* to prevent the flame from spreading.

These sentences employ *passive* verb constructions, frequently used in describing processes. They delete a personal subject and give an impersonal, scientific style to the writing.

As we know, an *active sentence* in English places the *subject before the verb*, and the *object after the verb*:

SUBJECT (AGENT)	—————— VERB (ACTIVE) →OBJECT (ACTED UPON)
The burning of fire damp	indicates the presence of gas.
The gauze cylinder	conducts away the heat.

In sentence 1, agent and acted upon are reversed in the word order:

ACTED UPON ◄——— VERB (PASSIVE) — BY — AGENT
The presence of gas   is indicated   by   the burning of fire damp.

Note the addition of BY when the agent appears in a passive sentence.

In sentence 2, the agent has been omitted:

ACTED UPON —— VERB (PASSIVE) ◄——— AGENT
The heat   is conducted away . . .   (?)

Exercise 6

Below is a series of diagrams illustrating the waste disposal process. Use them, and the vocabulary given, to write a passage on keeping a city clean and tidy. Practise using *passive* constructions.

Vocabulary

Things: litter refuse waste rubbish garbage (American) trash (American)

bin container receptacle skip plastic bag bottle bank

operative worker employee vehicle lorry truck (American)

incinerator landfill underground

Actions: sweep dispose litter throw away recycle transport destroy
burn bury

Unit 7 NARRATIVE ───────────────────────────────

As part of an LCCI composition, you may wish to include a piece of *narrative*, such as:

1. History.
2. Anecdote.

History
Established facts from the past which contribute to the argument, e.g.:

How Sir Humphrey Davy Helped Coal Miners

Humphrey Davy *was* a carver's son who *had risen* to the rank of Professor of Chemistry. He *had been experimenting* with dangerous gases, and as a result of these experiments he *invented* the first safety lamp.

In this case, the narrative is explaining the history of the man himself and how he came to be in a position to help coal miners.

Verb tense

As we saw in the previous unit, a sequence of events can be indicated by *serial*, *numerical* or *chronological* markers. In narrative writing, the verb tense is also particularly important as an indicator of the sequence of events.

Look again at the extract above. The four *verbs* show how the facts relate to each other, as follows:

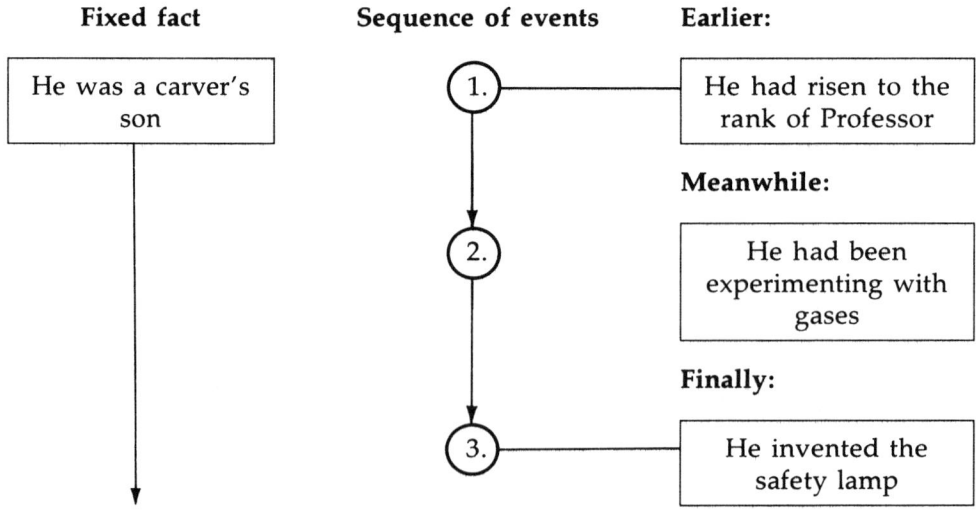

Fixed fact	Sequence of events	Earlier:
He was a carver's son	1.	He had risen to the rank of Professor
	2.	**Meanwhile:** He had been experimenting with gases
	3.	**Finally:** He invented the safety lamp

Exercise 1

Write a paragraph similar to the one on Sir Humphrey Davy, based on the following notes:

How Charles Dickens Drew Attention to the Poor

Charles Dickens — journalist from Kent
(become) a popular writer of fiction
(investigate) poverty in England
(write) the novel 'Hard Times'

Anecdote
Events from the writer's own experience, e.g.:

Life in Antarctica

Some years ago a colleague of mine **took part** in an Antarctic research project. He **had volunteered** to go south with the British Antarctic Survey. When **he had completed** the training and preliminary research he **left** for a two-year tour of duty. He **was to spend** the first winter in a base under the polar ice.

Exercise 2

Put into the correct sequence the events described above (the verbs are italicised):

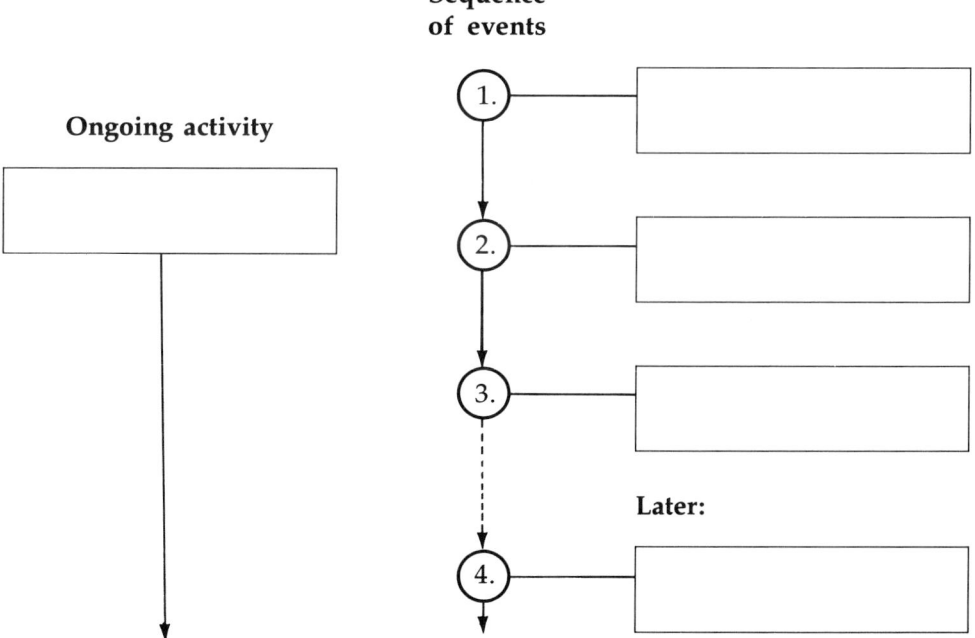

**Sequence
of events**

Ongoing activity

1.

2.

3.

Later:

4.

Note: 'was to'. Some forms which can be used in anticipating events after the time frame described in the narrative are:

(foreseen or unforeseen events)   was to, would
(planned events)   was going to

Note how the anecdote above begins 'some years ago'. It is common to introduce the elements in a narrative with expressions of time, e.g.:

> *In the middle of the eighteenth century* attention was once again drawn to Dudley's smelting process. *At that time* the total iron production of the country amounted to only 18,000 tons a year. Yet *by 1802* Great Britain produced 170,000 tons annually.

Some others are:

Once upon a time _____   One day _____
Last year _____   As _____
Some ⎫   By (the time) _____
Several ⎭ years ago _____   When I was young ⎫ _____
When _____   a child ⎭
During the holidays _____   On my first day at work _____
In the nineteenth century _____   During the Ice Age _____

Exercise 3

Fill the gaps as necessary, either with a time expression where you see (*TIME?*), or the correct tense of the VERB given:

Work for the Handicapped

____(a)____ (*TIME?*) there ____(b)____ (BE) an old soldier called John Thomas. He ____(c)____ (LOSE) an arm in the war and ____(d)____ (BE) unable to find a job after the war ____(e)____ (END).

____(f)____ (*TIME?*) he ____(g)____ (WALK) along the High Street and he ____(h)____ (MEET) his former commander. The Colonel ____(i)____ (ASK) what he ____(j)____ (DO) for a living, and Thomas ____(k)____ (REPLY) that he ____(l)____ (NOT WORK). The Colonel was surprised, and immediately ____(m)____ (OFFER) him a job as doorman at the hotel which he ____(n)____ (MANAGE), because Thomas ____(o)____ (BE) the smartest soldier in his regiment.

Writing questions

Write about 200 words on the following topics:

1. Important industrial developments in your part of the world in recent years.
2. The difficulties experienced in doing a particular job.
3. Your favourite form of transport.
4. At a sale.
5. The sort of work you enjoy doing.

Exercise 4   Industrial developments

Here are some details relating to industrial developments in the fictional state of Zahran. Use the information to practise the use of narrative in answering a question. Also practise using verbs in the *passive* (Unit 6).

Industrial Developments in the State of Zahran

Year	Event	Development
1930	Oil discovered	Rapid growth in economy
1935	Oil refinery opened	
1950	International airport opened	Improved worldwide communications
1960	Modern container port opened	
1975	Ship-repair yard opened	Growth of maritime sector
1980	First satellite-tracking station	Opening up of financial sector
1985	Stock exchange inaugurated	

Exercise 5   Difficulties in a job

Write an anecdote describing difficulties you have experienced. Practise the use of EXPRESSIONS OF TIME and PAST TENSES to set the scene and establish the sequence of events, e.g.:

It *was my first week* with a new company. I *had been placed* in the accounts department and I *had been learning* to operate the computer. *On my third day* the boss . . ., etc.

Exercise 6   My favourite form of transport

Answer the question using a combination of HISTORY and ANECDOTE, e.g.:

Aeroplanes

History	Anecdotes
First flight (Wright brothers) The first passenger planes The first passenger jets Jumbo jets and Concorde	My first flight as a passenger When I first went onto a flight deck When I first took the controls of a light aircraft When I bought my own aircraft

Exercise 7   At a sale

Answer this question with anecdotes of your own shopping experiences.

Exercise 8   The sort of work you enjoy doing

Answer with a combination of historical background to the work and your links with it, and anecdotal description of your experiences while doing it.

Exercise 9   My first day at work

Answer with a combination of sequence narrative and anecdote.

Exercise 10   Why I chose my present career

Answer with a combination of sequence narrative and cause and effect explanations.

Exercise 11   At a major sports event

Answer with a combination of sequence narrative and anecdote.

Exercise 12   How to enjoy work in my country/capital city

Answer with a combination of sequence narrative and anecdote.

SECOND LEVEL

Letter

QUESTION AND ANSWER FORMATS ―――――――――

In the Second Level Letter, there are two types of question:

1. Where you 'receive' a complete letter and are asked to reply to it.
2. Where you are given the specifications for a letter and are asked to write it.

Before attempting to answer either type of question, *it is important to understand and note all the instructions*.

Here is an example of a Second Level Letter question where you are asked to answer a letter received.

Write a correctly laid out reply, in 150–200 words, to the following letter, which has just been received by your company:

Ref: JP/TL/01   Point to Point Ltd
                                                         2 Eyre Street
                                                         Whitown
                                                         Whiltshire
                                                         WT1 2XY

Whitown Estate Agents
35 Rice Avenue
Whitown
Whiltshire
WT3 3VL
                                                         12 May 1990

Dear Sirs,

    I am hoping to open a shoe shop in Whitown town centre in the near future and I am looking for suitable freehold property. Could you, therefore, please send me details of any such properties that you have on your books selling between £140,000 and £150,000?
    Do you arrange mortgages on shop properties? If so, which building society do you represent? Do you accept monthly mortgage repayments at your office or do they have to be made directly to the building society?
    I am quite willing to call at your office to discuss my exact requirements with you if you think that this would be better than simply conducting business by correspondence. If so, would you please give me a date and time convenient to you?
    I look forward to receiving your reply.

                                            Yours faithfully,

                                            J. Point

                                            (signed) J. Point
                                            Managing Director

---

Formalities

You should be sure to apply all the information studied in First Level Letter on addresses, postcodes, salutations and complimentary closes. In addition, some Second Level Letter questions show the following:

Reference

As you are probably aware, most businesses employ a reference system to help them keep track of correspondence. Simply, the reference number consists of:

JP / TL / 01

1. The initials of the sender ————————┘
2. The initials of the typist ————————————┘
3. The sequence number of the letter ————————————┘

In your reply, you should quote the reference number after the receiver's address and before the salutation, as follows:

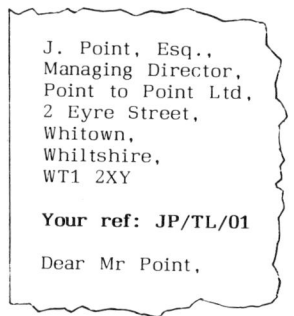

```
J. Point, Esq.,
Managing Director,
Point to Point Ltd,
2 Eyre Street,
Whitown,
Whiltshire,
WT1 2XY

Your ref: JP/TL/01

Dear Mr Point,
```

Position

In the original letter, Mr Point gave his title as Managing Director as follows:

(signed) J. Point
Managing Director

Please note the following:

1. As shown above under 'Reference', the title 'Managing Director' has been included in the *receiver's address* under his name.
2. In your reply, it is normally required that you include *your position* under your signature, e.g.:

J. Smith (Mrs)
Property Consultant

3. The word 'signed' is not necessary and only rarely used in special circumstances.

Salutation and close

It is important to note also that in the Second Level Letter, when you are answering a letter received, you are writing to a person whose name you know; thus, although Mr Point writes

> Dear Sirs,
>
> . . . .
>
> Yours faithfully,
>
> J. Point

you should reply

> Dear Mr Point,
>
> . . . .
>
> Yours sincerely,
>
> J. Smith (Mrs)

Marks will be lost if these conventions are not followed correctly.

Content

As shown in the example, Second Level Letter questions address not one but a number of points. It is important to read the letter carefully so as to identify and answer all the points raised.

Exercise 1

Look again at the letter from J. Point and answer the following:

First paragraph — MAIN POINT:
(a) What is he looking for?
(b) Why?
(c) What is the main thing he wants you to do?

Second paragraph — FURTHER DETAILS:
(d) What is the second question asked?
(e) What is the third?
(f) What is the fourth?

Third paragraph — PROPOSED MEETING:
(g) Do you think a meeting would be a good idea?
(h) Date?
(i) Time?

Note: This MAIN POINT—FURTHER DETAILS—PROPOSED MEETING arrangement is typical of Second Level Letter questions, but do not assume that *all* questions will follow that pattern.

Layouts — blocked or indented?

The letter from J. Point was laid out with INDENTED PARAGRAPHS and CLOSED PUNCTUATION, now commonest in *handwritten* letters:

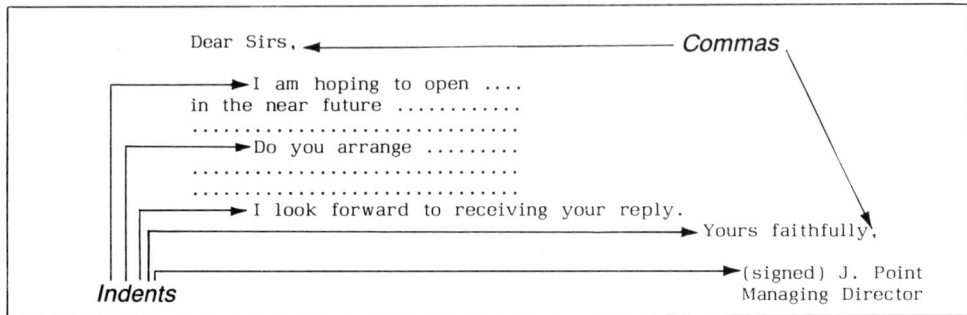

In presenting your reply, you have the option of using a similar indented layout, or the more modern BLOCK LAYOUT; this is now almost universal for *typed* and *printed* letters:

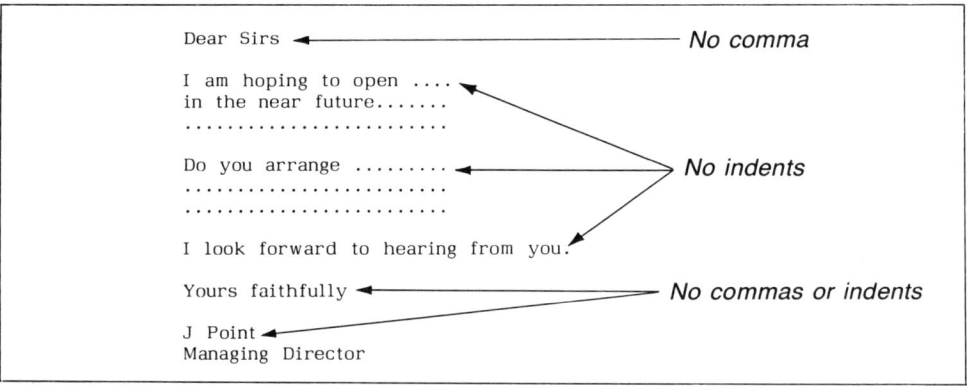

Note also that OPEN PUNCTUATION has been used with the block layout.

It is essential that letters written for the examination show a consistent approach, with **either** all blocked **or** all indented paragraphs, and all open or all closed punctuation. *A mixture of styles is not acceptable!* However, examiners will accept any of the variety of styles currently in use provided it is used correctly and consistently. This book shows examples of both for separate letters.

Exercise 2

Answer the letter from J. Point on page 123.

Writing a letter to specifications

Write a correctly laid out letter of between 150 and 200 words, for your company
(Broadbent Tools Ltd, Queen's Road, Barton, Yorkshire YK4 9BN) to the Sales Director
of Kerry Packing, King's Lane, Dursley, Lancashire LN6 3TY, asking for a catalogue
of their packagings and a price list. Point out that you are looking for someone to design
and supply packaging for your new line of do-it-yourself equipment, and that an associate
has recommended them. Ask for any other information you think appropriate. Add that
you would be interested in visiting their factory to view their process and facilities.

Exercise 3   Formalities

Complete the following:

(a) _____

(b) _____

_____

_____

(c) _____

(d) _____

(e) _____

(f) _____

(g) _____

Exercise 4   Content

Answer the following:

send catalogue   send price list   looking for supplier
    Kerry's recommended   additional questions   suggest meeting

Which points will you include in paragraph 1? (a) _____

(b) _____

paragraph 2? (c) _____

(d) _____

paragraph 3? (e) _____

paragraph 4? (f) _____

Exercise 5

Write the letter.

Unit 2 ANSWERING A SERIES OF QUESTIONS ———————

Here is a sample letter from a Second Level Letter question:

> Write a correctly laid out reply, in 150–200 words, to the following letter, which has just been received by your company:

J.L. Hill & Co. Ltd
Hill House
Carr Road
Tenhampton
Sussex
AL3 3ZA

18 March 1990

Super Travel
81 North Road
London
WC2 4BO

Dear Sirs

I am secretary of the above company's Employees' Social Club. Your agency has been recommended to me as one that provides excellent holidays at reasonable prices.

Would you please send me your brochures about skiing holidays in Switzerland in November and December this year? About forty members of our Social Club would like to spend part of their holidays this year skiing in a group. Do you give discounts for party bookings? As most of the party have not been skiing before, can instruction be provided for them? What is the latest date we have to notify you if we do decide to go on this holiday? Do your prices include insurance?

I should be grateful for answers to the above questions and any other relevant information as soon as possible.

Thank you in anticipation of your assistance.

Yours faithfully

Roger Smythe

Roger J Smythe

As you can see from the number of question marks in the second paragraph of the letter, the writer is looking for a lot of answers. However, most of the questions in this letter require 'yes' or 'no' answers, and the challenge in writing your reply is to express your short answers appropriately, using a variety of the sentence forms practised in the First Level Letter.

Comprehension

Exercise 1   Formalities

Answer the following questions:

(a) Who is the sender?
(b) In what capacity is he writing?
(c) On whose behalf is he writing?
(d) What is your position?
(e) Approximately when was the letter received? (This will affect the date of your reply.)
(f) How does he know about you?

You have been recommended

For the sake of good public relations, you may wish to refer to recommendations, etc., in your reply. There are several ways of doing this, e.g.:

We are I am	pleased glad	that we have been to have been	recommended	
		that your colleagues associates etc.		us

You may also wish to add a second sentence, e.g.:

We (always)	try to do our best to	provide the best service please our clients meet our customers' requirements etc.

Exercise 2   Your reply

Fill in the formalities:

(a) _____

J L Hill & Co Ltd
Carr Road
Tenhampton
Sussex
AL3 3ZA

Super Travel
81 North Road
London
WC2 4BO

(b) _____

(c) Dear _____

(d) Yours _____

(e) (Signed) _____

(f) _____

Exercise 3 Main point

Answer the following:

(a) What is the reason for writing?
(b) What does his group want to do?
(c) Where?
(d) When?
(e) How many of them?

Exercise 4 Additional points

Complete the questions:

(a) Do _____ ?
(b) Can _____ ?
(c) What _____ ?
(d) Is _____ ?

Sentence forms for answering questions and requests

For assistance with this it may help you to refer back to First Level Letter Unit 5. Obviously, it would be inappropriate to answer questions in a business letter with 'yes' and 'no', even though the questions themselves require only yes-no answers.

Exercise 5

Fill in the verbs, trying to use a different one each time:

Would you please send me your brochures ...?
We have pleasure in _____(a)_____ our brochures.
Do you give discounts?
We are happy to _____(b)_____ that discounts will be _____(c)_____.
Can instruction be provided?
We are pleased to _____(d)_____ that instruction is _____(e)_____.

What is the latest date we have to notify you?
I must _____(f)_____ that notification will be _____(g)_____ by (DATE).
Do your prices include insurance?
I _____(h)_____ to _____(i)_____ you that insurance is not _____(j)_____.

Exercise 6   Your reply: Body of the letter

Remember to group your points in PARAGRAPHS:

First paragraph (a) acknowledgement	Thank you _____
(b) recommendation	We _____
Second paragraph (c) brochures	We have pleasure _____
(d) discounts	Since your party _____
(e) instruction	Also, we are pleased _____
(f) notification	However, we shall _____
Third paragraph (g) insurance	Unfortunately, _____
Fourth paragraph (h) asking for reply	We look _____

Instructions for writing a letter

Here is an example of the type of question where you are given a set of specifications for writing a letter:

> Using between 150 and 200 words, write a letter for your company — J.S. Wallace & Co. Ltd, Wallace House, Eldon Road, Stock, Shropshire SO4 3UR — to the Headmaster of Hetley Secondary School, Hetley Road, Stock SO4 1TF saying how pleased your company has been in past years with youngsters from Hetley School who have started work in Wallace's office. These youngsters have been loyal, hard-working and efficient. Explain that two vacancies for office juniors have arisen and you are wondering if he can recommend any suitable pupils who will soon be leaving his school. Give details of the type of work envisaged.
> Lay out your letter correctly.

Comprehension

Exercise 7   Formalities

Answer the following:

(a) What is your company?
(b) What is your position in the company?
(c) To whom are you writing?
(d) How well do you know him?
(e) What will be the date of your letter?

Exercise 8   Content

Answer the following:

(a) What is the first thing you are going to say?
(b) Why?
(c) What is the main point of your letter?
(d) What vacancies?
(e) How many?

Exercise 9   Further details

Complete the following:

'Give details of the type of work envisaged'
What are the duties of an office junior?
Discuss and list examples, e.g.:

    making tea or coffee

(a) _____

(b) _____

(c) _____

(d) _____

Exercise 10

Complete the following letter:

(a) _____

(b) _____

_____

_____

_____

(c) _____

(d) _____

(e) Our company has been _____

(f) They have been _____

(g) I am writing to inform you that _____

(h) Perhaps you would be _____

(i) The sort of work we envisage _____

(j) If you require _____

(k) I look _____

(l) Yours _____
(your signature)

(m) _____

Unit 3 'ANY OTHER RELEVANT DETAILS WOULD BE APPRECIATED'

Adding details

In Unit 2, the questions posed in the letter received required simple 'yes' or 'no' answers. However, in some cases it is necessary to use imagination to provide additional details where these are requested.

Consider the following:

Your language school has just received the following letter. Write out a correctly laid out reply to it in 150–200 words:

Ref: JPL/BO/1A

Omega Oil Co. Ltd,
Lion House,
Bassett Road,
Eldon,
Yorkshire
CE2 8LL

4 July, 1990

The Principal,
Ford School of English,
Bridge Lane,
Dalton,
Essex
EX1 7BB

Dear Madam,

We are a company employing many nationalities in branches throughout the world. We wish to send some of our employees on language courses to improve their English for approximately six months to a year. A business colleague has recommended your school as being one of the best.

We envisage sending about forty employees a year on these courses and we will pay all fees and expenses. If you are interested in this proposal, please send us full details of the courses, such as term dates, fees and whether or not you can provide or find living accommodation for the students. Any other relevant details would be appreciated.

If it would assist, we could send our Personnel Manager to see you in the near future to discuss fully these proposals.

We look forward to your reply.

Yours faithfully,

James P. Long

James P. Long
UK Manager

Exercise 1   Formalities

Answer the following:

(a) Who is the sender?
(b) What is his position?
(c) Who does he work for?
(d) Who is the receiver?
(e) Is the receiver male or female?
(f) What is the reference?

Exercise 2

Complete the following:

```
                                                    Ford School of English
                                                    Bridge Lane
                                                    Dalton
         (a) _____                            Essex
                                                    EX1 7BB
                 Omega Oil Co. Ltd
                 Lion House
                 Bassett Road
                 Eldon
                 Yorkshire
                 CE2 8LL
                                                    (b) _____

         (c) _____ : _____

         (d) _____


         (e) _____
         (f) _____ *
         (g) _____
```

Note: The original salutation!

Content

Exercise 3   Main point

Answer the following:

(a) What do Omega want to do?
(b) With what aim in mind?

(c) Why is this necessary?
(d) How many?
(e) For how long?

Exercise 4 Information required

Complete the following:

(a) Are you _____ ?
(b) Send details of _____
(c)   dates of   _____
(d)   cost of   _____
(e)   whether   _____

Exercise 5 Second point

Complete the following:

(a) Would _____ ?
(b) When _____ ?

'Please send us full details such as terms, dates, fees ...'

It will be necessary here to invent the necessary details. For reference and revision, see First Level Letter Unit 6.

Exercise 6

Invent answers to the following:

(a) How long are the terms?
(b) Between what dates do they run?
(c) What is the fee for one student per term?
(d) What is the discounted fee for forty students?
(e) How much do you charge for a term's accommodation?

'Any other relevant details would be appreciated'

This is an opportunity for the writer to introduce some of his/her own ideas. What other information might the Principal add?

Exercise 7

Discuss and think of items to fill gaps (a)–(e). Note the construction 'for your information':

I have also included (a) _____ for your information.
                     (b) _____ which you may find helpful.
                     (c) _____ which you may find useful.
                     (d) _____ which may be of interest.
                     (e) _____ (etc.)

'If it would assist, we could send our Personnel Manager . . .'

Obviously, if you are serious about the Omega Oil proposal you will be prepared to meet their Personnel Manager. This part of the letter, then, is asking for an INVITATION.
    First you should indicate that you agree to a meeting, e.g.:

    We should be delighted to welcome your Personnel Manager to the school.

Then it would be a good idea to suggest a time or even a date, e.g.:

    I am available daily from 9 a.m. to noon.

OR:

    If it is convenient I suggest Monday July 20 at 9 a.m.

Exercise 8   Your reply

Complete the following:

First paragraph
(a) acknowledgement   Thank _____
(b) recommendation   I am _____

Second paragraph
(c) confirm interest   Your proposal _____
(d) details   The details _____
(e) dates   as follows:
(f) fees   Dates _____
(g) discount   Fees _____
                             Due to _____
                             a discount _____

Third paragraph	
(h) accommodation	I am pleased _____
(i) cost	The cost _____
(j) additional details	In addition, _____
Fourth paragraph	
(k) meeting	I should _____
(l) suggestion	May I _____
Fifth paragraph	
(m) ask for reply	I look _____

Instructions for writing a letter

Using 150–200 words, write a correctly laid out letter on behalf of your firm (R. Cullen & Co. Ltd, 2–12 Gilbert Street, Oak, Yorkshire AB1 3BA), to the editor of 'Dean Daily News', 140 Sullivan Street, Dean, Yorkshire PZ0 6LY, pointing out that your company will be opening a shop dealing in radio, television and hi-fi goods in Dean in the near future and asking him for his advertisement rates. State that you would like a two-page advertisement to announce the shop's opening and then you plan to take a half-page advertisement each Friday. Add any other information which you think may be necessary.

Comprehension

Exercise 9   Formalities

Answer the following:

(a) What is your company?
(b) What is your position?
(c) To whom are you writing?
(d) Is that a man or a woman?
(e) Do you know him/her?

Exercise 10   Content

Answer the following:

(a) What do you want to tell the editor?
(b) What do you want to ask?
(c) What is the first thing you want to buy?
(d) Then what?
(e) How often?

'Add any other information which you think may be necessary'

What else might the advertiser want to tell the editor?

Exercise 11

Discuss and think of further items of information, e.g.:

We already have artwork* from our last advertisement ...

(a) _____

(b) _____

(c) _____

(d) _____

(e) _____

*Artwork = design, graphics, lettering, etc.

Exercise 12

Write the letter.

Unit 4   A CHOICE OF ANSWERS

In some Second Level Letter questions you are given a choice as to how you will answer certain points in the letter, as in the following example:

> Your company has just received the following letter. Write a correctly laid out reply to it in 150—200 words:

Ref: LS/APM/1
                                                            A1 Furniture,
                                                            Spring House,
                                                            North Road,
                                                            Upsham,
                                                            Cheshire
                                                            LM2 3XX

                                                            24 November, 1990

J. Old,
Estate Agent,
121 Larkhill Crescent,
Adler,
Surrey
PS4 7YZ

Dear Sir,

As you are probably aware, we are one of the largest furniture retailers in the country with branches all over the United Kingdom.

We should like to open a shop in Adler in January next. We are looking for very large premises which will have space to display our goods to their best effect. The premises must be in one of the main streets of the town with adequate parking space for customers to leave their cars.

If you have any premises which you think may be suitable for our purpose, will you please notify us immediately? If not, will you please instigate a search for a suitable building?

We should like one of our senior representatives, Mr J.L. Johnson, to visit you next week to explain our requirements in more detail. If this is convenient, please let us know when he can call at your office.

We look forward to hearing from you before the end of this week.

Yours faithfully,

Leonard Smith

Leonard Smith
General Manager

Comprehension

Exercise 1 Formalities

Answer the following:

(a) Who is the sender?
(b) What is his status?
(c) Who are you?
(d) What is the reference?
(e) Approximately when was the letter received?

Exercise 2 Main point

Answer the following:

(a) What are A1 planning?
(b) Where exactly?

What does Leonard Smith want you to do?

Either (c)	_____
In which case you are to (d)	_____
Or (e)	_____

Exercise 3 Additional points

Answer the following:

(a) Can _____ ?
(b) When _____ ?

'If you have any premises ... if not ...'

You can decide which of these two options you will take in your reply. You should, however, bear in mind the content and fullness of your reply, and choose the option which offers most scope. Also, as in this case, you can use some of the information from the original letter in your reply:

> We are looking for *very large premises* which will have *space to display* our goods to their best effect. The premises must be in *one of the main streets* in town with *adequate parking space* for customers to leave their cars.

Exercise 4

Using the points italicised above, complete the following sentences from your reply:

I have pleasure in _____(a)_____ that we currently have available _____(b)_____ with _____(c)_____. The property is _____(d)_____, with _____(e)_____.

Note: More than one word is needed to fill these spaces.

Expanding the information

Writing as an estate agent, you should be aware of the need to make the property you have available sound attractive to the client.
   Consider this advertisement:

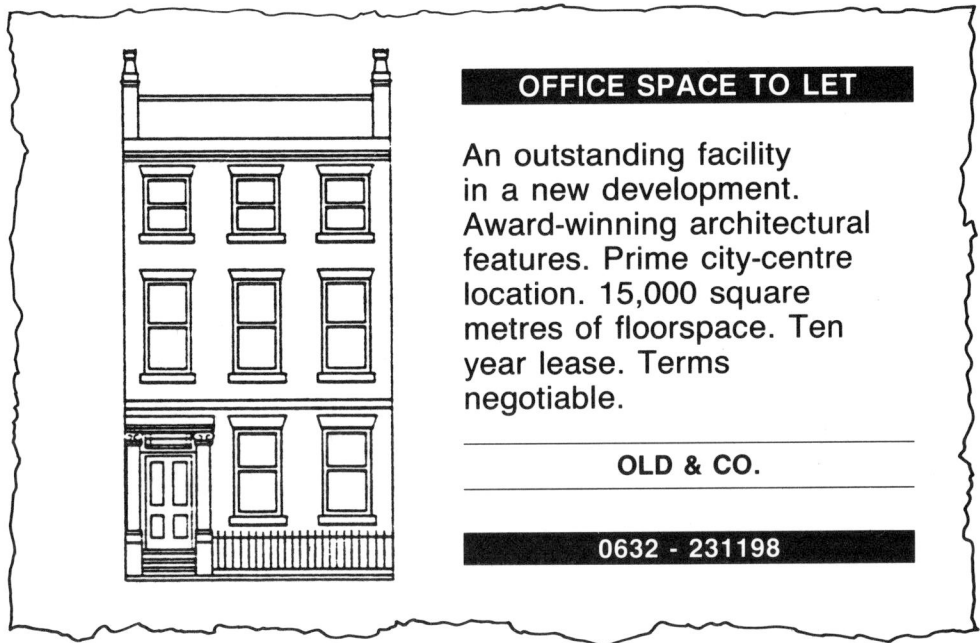

OFFICE SPACE TO LET

An outstanding facility in a new development. Award-winning architectural features. Prime city-centre location. 15,000 square metres of floorspace. Ten year lease. Terms negotiable.

OLD & CO.

0632 - 231198

Exercise 5

Adapt your description of a property which you have available, incorporating ideas from the above advertisement.

Exercise 6

Write your reply:

```
                                            (a) _____

                                                _____

    (b) _____


        _____


        _____
                                            (c) _____
    (d) _____ : _____

    (e) _____

        (f)  (acknowledgement) _____

    (g) (confirmation) _____

        (h)  (details) _____

            _____


        (i)  (meeting) _____


        (j)  (reply) _____

        (k) _____

        (l) _____
```

Instructions for writing a letter

Using 150–200 words, write a correctly laid out letter on behalf of your company (P. Drew & Co. Ltd, Drew House, Edgar Road, Pape, Perthshire L23 4XX), to Miss J. Short, Manageress of Office Staff Bureau, 120 Dean Avenue, Pape, Perthshire M30 5XY, asking if she would try to recruit three clerk/typists for your firm. Give essential details of the posts and the qualifications required of applicants. Add that you hope to make the appointments within a month and will pay the Bureau's fees when the successful applicants start work.

Comprehension

Exercise 7   Formalities

Answer the following:

(a) Who are you?   (d) Who is she?
(b) Who do you work for?   (e) What is the date?
(c) Who are you writing to?

Exercise 8   Main point

Answer the following:

(a) What are you asking her to do?   (d) When?
(b) What do you need exactly?   (e) What about payment?
(c) How many?

'Give essential details of the posts and the qualifications required'

Exercise 9

Posts: What exactly do clerk/typists do? Discuss and list examples, e.g.:

   copy typing

(a) _____
(b) _____
(c) _____
(d) _____
(e) _____

Qualifications: What do you think might be required? Discuss and list examples, e.g.:

   previous experience

(f) _____
(g) _____
(h) _____
(i) _____
(j) _____

Exercise 10

Write the letter.

Unit 5 CONFIRMING ARRANGEMENTS ————————————

In the following letter, we see a friendly approach from one executive to another. They are associates and so the tone of the letter is quite personal. Nevertheless, there is an element of urgency, even pressure in the request.

> Write a correctly laid out reply, in 150–200 words, to the following letter, which has just been received by your company:

Ref: JRK/MP/1A

Alpha Discs,
Pearl Road,
Sloane,
Derbyshire
SS1 5LP

2nd May, 1990

Mr J. Spinks,
Studio Manager,
Orange Recording Studio,
124 Rodham Road,
South Ham,
Sussex
OP0 1ST

Dear Mr Spinks,

I hope you are still keeping well and that business is prospering.

I'm writing to see if you can help me. On Monday, 3rd June I shall be having a visitor, Hiram B. Rogan, the Chief Executive of Bubble Recordings, USA. Mr Rogan is one of our best customers in the States and is coming over to see our working methods. I can arrange for him to see the technical side of making records but was wondering if you could invite him to your studio to see a recording being made, hopefully by a top singer or group. If you can help, perhaps you would let me know what day and time he should arrive, who will be recording and what time you would want him to leave so that we could arrange for him to be picked up by one of our cars. Mr Rogan will be in this country for three weeks.

By the way, I shall be sending you our autumn order within the next month or so.

I hope to hear from you soon.

Yours sincerely,

John R. King

John R. King
Managing Director

Exercise 1 Your reference

Your secretary is called Lucy Wood and your code for replies is '-B' after the serial number. Complete the following:

```
Derbyshire
SS1 5LP

Your ref: JRK/MP/1A
Our ref: _____

Dear _____
```

Exercise 2 Comprehension

Answer the following:

(a) Who is coming?
(b) What is his position?
(c) When is he expected?
(d) Why is he important?
(e) What does he want to do?
(f) What can Alpha arrange?
(g) How can you help?
(h) Why is there pressure on you to co-operate?

Personal touches

John King writes:

'I hope you are still keeping well and that business is prospering.'

In your acknowledgement you should return the compliment, e.g.:

Thank you for your letter of May 2nd. I am happy to say that I am keeping well and business was never better. I hope the same goes for you and Alpha.

'By the way . . .'

In referring to the autumn order, John King is putting subtle pressure on you to co-operate. In connecting the forthcoming order to the request through the use of 'by the way', he seems to be saying, 'We are good clients of yours; if you don't please our big American client, our business could be affected.' You can return the compliment by also referring to the order, as if to say, 'If we do this favour for you, we expect good business!', e.g.:

Our sales department is looking forward to receiving your order at your earliest convenience.

Exercise 3 Details

Prepare the following details for use in your reply:

Mr Rogan will be in Britain from _____(a)_____.

to _____(b)_____.

You will suggest he comes on   _____(c)_____.

at _____(d)_____.

The recording artist will be   _____(e)_____.

He will leave at approximately   _____(f)_____.

Exercise 4 Your reply

Write a letter on this pattern:

(a) _____

(b) _____   _____

_____   _____

_____

_____

(c) _____

(d) _____

(e) _____

(f) _____

(g) thanks

(h) pleasantries

(i) confirm

(j) artist and dates

(k) suggest day

(l) times

(m) order

(n) look forward*

(o) _____

(p) _____

(q) _____

Note: As you will be meeting Mr Rogan, it would be a good idea to say you were looking forward to this, rather than, for example, a letter.

Instructions for writing a letter

> Using 150–200 words, write a correctly laid out letter on behalf of your firm (Ukay Records, Scott House, Scott Road, London NW1N S22) to Singapore Audio, Connaught House, Raffles Square, Singapore 0825. Your company are distributors of hi-fi records and cassettes, your sales are running at over 2 million units a year and rising steadily, and you would like to extend your market to Singapore. You understand that Singapore Audio owns numerous outlets in Singapore and you would like to know if they would be interested in handling your products. If so you will send one of your directors to discuss the project. Ask for dates for a possible visit, and request any further information you think may be necessary.

Exercise 5   Formalities

Answer the following:

(a) What might be your position at Ukay?
(b) What will be your salutation when writing to a company?
(c) Your secretary's name is Pat Hay. What will be your reference?
(d) Who are you going to send?
(e) What is his/her position?

Exercise 6

Complete the following:

We are _____ (a) _____ .
At present _____ (b) _____ .
We should like to _____ (c) _____ .

We understand that _____ (d) _____ ,
and we _____ (e) _____ .
If _____ (f) _____ ,
we would be willing to send _____ (g) _____ ,
our _____ (h) _____ , to _____ (i) _____ .
This would not commit you in any way, but would give you an opportunity
to _____ (j) _____ .
If this is possible, kindly let us know _____ (k) _____
_____ and _____ (l) _____ .

Also, if you are interested in our proposal, we should be grateful if you
would _____ (m) _____ .

We _____ (n) _____ .

Exercise 7

Write the letter in full and correctly laid out.

Unit 6 COMPLAINTS ─────────────────────────

Consider the following:

Ref: TS/RJJ/42	Tasty Sweets, 1 Mell Street, Rodale, Essex PR2 3HH

The Manager,   29 June, 1990
Ace Confectionery Co. Ltd,
110 Comper Road,
Mellone,
Perthshire
AB3 8YZ

Dear Sir,

<u>Various Items of Confectionery, Invoice B8172</u>

I am writing to complain about the late delivery of the above order which arrived today, two weeks after your promised delivery date.

When I ordered these sweets I said it was essential that I received prompt delivery, because I had sold out of certain of my best selling lines — the result of your salesman failing to call on time. When I realised that delivery was delayed, I telephoned your office several times, only to be told that the consignment was on its way.

This delay has caused me great inconvenience and I have lost a great deal of business.

I cannot accept the possibility of this delay occurring again and I fail to understand how the consignment could have been 'on its way' for over a week. If you cannot reassure me about the reliability of your delivery dates, I shall have to seek an alternative supplier.

Yours faithfully,

R. J. James

R.J. JAMES

Subject line

'Various items of confectionery. Invoice B8172'

This is a useful method of stating clearly the subject matter of a letter, applicable not only to complaints but to any commercial correspondence, and particularly when the subject concerns ongoing business (as per the quoted invoice).

You may choose to include a subject line in your reply, e.g.:

Subject: Invoice B8172

Exercise 1 Formalities

Answer the following:

(a) Who sent the letter?
(b) What is his/her position?
(c) Who are you?
(d) What is the reference?
(e) What is the subject of the complaint?
(f) To which invoice does it relate?
(g) Which of (answers (d), (e) and (f)) will you include in your reply?

Exercise 2 Content

Answer the following:

(a) Why is the writer complaining?
      Which two factors compounded the problem? (b)
                                                                              (c)
(d) What has been the result of (answers (a), (b) and (c))?
(e) What are you being asked to do now?

Replying to complaints

There are at least two alternatives open to you in replying to a complaint:

1. You could dismiss the complaint with counter-arguments (it should, however,
    be borne in mind that this is not good for future business), e.g.:

    > Although our salesman was out of the area, you were informed of this
    > and asked to place your order well in advance. Also, despite the fact that
    > your order was received late, every effort was made to despatch your
    > consignment as quickly as possible . . .

2. On the other hand, in the interests of future business, it might be wiser to
    take a conciliatory line, apologising, making excuses and offering the
    appropriate assurances.

Apologies

May I/We	apologise				
I/We would like to	express	my	(sincere)		for . . .
I/We	extend	our	(profound)	apologies	
	offer				
Please accept					

Excuses

I	fail to cannot	understand how	X	(could have)	occurred happened etc.
I can only assume/suppose/imagine Obviously Presumably			Y	(must have)	forgotten overlooked omitted been damaged etc.

Assurances

		optional			
Please accept You have	my our	(personal)	guarantee assurance undertaking		
Let	me us	(personally)	assure guarantee	You	that ...
	I we	(can) (hasten)	promise reassure		

Exercise 3

Complete the beginning and ending of your reply:

(b) _____   (a) _____

    _____   _____

    _____   _____

Your ref: ____(d)____   (c) _____

Our ref: ____(e)____

Dear ____(f)____

                    Subject: ____(g)____

Yours _____(h)_____

_____(i)_____

_____(j)_____

Exercise 4

Fill in the blanks in the following:

Thank you for your letter of June 29th.

_____(a)_____ for the difficulties caused by the late delivery. _____(b)_____ why our salesman failed to call on time, but as a result of your complaint, which was one of several, the person concerned has been dismissed from the company. I hope that you will find our new representative more efficient and reliable. Also _____(c)_____ why our office staff gave you incorrect information on the progress of your consignment; _____(d)_____ that this was due to faulty paperwork by the same salesman. _____(e)_____ that every step has been taken to avoid this type of situation in future.

_____(f)_____ that problems of supply can be harmful to business, and by way of compensation I would like to offer you an introductory free sample of our new 'NUXO' line of confectionery bars. This product has performed well in major outlets, and _____(g)_____ will prove very popular with your customers.

Once again, _____(h)_____ for the inconvenience. You have my personal _____(i)_____ that our future deliveries will be as reliable as in the past. _____(j)_____ your order at your earliest convenience.

Exercise 5

Answer the letter in your own words.

Writing a letter from instructions

> Write a correctly laid out letter, in 150–200 words, to the manager of Acme Removals, 20–30 Andrews Road, Tonbridge, Kent TU4 3LG. You recently moved house and hired Acme to pack and transport your belongings. However, you found their staff rude, inefficient and uncooperative. Damage was caused both to items moved and to the fittings of your old house due to careless handling of large objects (specify), and some items were missing from the inventory. Ask what steps Acme are prepared to take to compensate you for the inconvenience and replace the lost and damaged items, and threaten further action if they fail to make good your loss.

Exercise 6 Specifying damage due to careless handling

Discuss in groups:

(a) What items might have been damaged?
(b) What damage might have been caused to the house?

Exercise 7   Steps to be taken

Discuss in groups:

(a) What could you ask Acme to do to compensate you?
(b) What steps could you threaten to take?

Exercise 8

Write the letter.

Unit 7 REVISION

Exercise 1

Your company has received the following letter. Write a correctly laid out reply in 150–200 words.

Oxford Brothers Ltd
94 Welton Road
Lock
Essex
GB1 3AJ

1 May, 1990

A. George & Co. Ltd
102–108 Milton Road
Pearl
Suffolk
MC33 8KL

Dear Sirs

Printing of Sales Catalogues

We are writing to you on the recommendation of Mr George Smart of Old & Co. Ltd of Lock to ask you to send us your price lists for printing sales catalogues in four colours. We are a mail order firm dealing in household goods and issue four catalogues a year, one every three months. On each occasion we shall need 400,000 catalogues, each of 80 pages.

The printers we have used till now have retired and closed their business. We must have our catalogues on time as delays would affect our business badly. Can you promise this? In addition to sending us your price lists, would you also send some samples of your printing work?

If you feel that you can cope with such a large order, we should like our publicity manager, Mr J.L. Rhode, to visit you to discuss arrangements. Would it be convenient for him to visit during the last week of this month?

I look forward to hearing from you soon.

Yours faithfully

Roger J. Oxford

Roger J. Oxford
Managing Director

Exercise 2

Write a correctly laid out letter of between 150 and 200 words for your company (Lambert Engineering, Bull Road, Hightown, Yorkshire HK2 2BG), to the Principal of Hightown College of Technology, High Street, Hightown, Yorkshire HK1 1FG, asking for a copy of his college prospectus. Point out that your company wishes to encourage staff to take up part-time study and to encourage this it is willing to pay the fees of anyone enrolling for a course which will be of benefit both to the company and to the person concerned. Add any information you think necessary.

Exercise 3

Your company has just received the following letter. Write a correctly laid out reply to it in 150–200 words:

Ref: GB/SL/45

White's Pharmaceuticals Ltd
Farford Road
Weston
WE4 6YH

The Manager
Picton Transport Ltd
Ashwood Industrial Area
North Weston
WE18 9BQ

4 June 1990

Dear Sir

Due to an upsurge in demand for one of our new products, our transport department is temporarily unable to meet our distribution requirements. I am writing to ask if you have any vehicles immediately available for sale or hire which could help alleviate our present transport difficulties.

Our existing transport fleet consists of ten light delivery vans, four medium lorries and two large articulated lorries for long distance deliveries. Since our total sales have now risen by fifty per cent, we need to increase our pool of vehicles by the same proportion.

I should be grateful if you would let us know as soon as possible what vehicles you have available, with full details of cost price and hire charges. As the present situation may prove to be temporary, we would prefer to lease with an option to buy at a discount at the end of the year. Please confirm if this would be possible. Also, do your hire charges include vehicle insurance, or is that the responsibility of the lessee?

I look forward to hearing from you at your earliest convenience.

Yours faithfully

G . Barnet

Geraldine Barnet (Mrs)
Transport Manager

Exercise 4

Write a correctly laid out letter of between 150 and 200 words on behalf of your company, Eastsea Oil Inc., of South Terminal, Eastsea, Essex EA12 7GN, to the Manager, Interlanguage Services Ltd, 3–5 High Street, Woodchester, Essex WC1 4BM. Explain that a group of refinery managers from an overseas country (give details as necessary) are currently studying your process methods, and they require English language training as soon as possible to improve their communication skills. Specify that a consultant with management experience will be required to conduct the training. Suggest that the course could be conducted either in your training centre or at Interlanguage. Ask for details of cost and duration. Add any other relevant information.

Exercise 5

Your company has received the following letter. Write a correctly laid out reply to it in 150–200 words.

---

1 April 1990

London Trading Co. Ltd,
9 Old City Wall,
London EC3 7YG

The Manager,
Global Travel Ltd,
5 Nightingale Square,
London W2 8UH

Ref: JS/JM/4

Dear Sir,

One of our directors, Mr Algernon Faure, will be undertaking a world sales tour in the autumn of this year. The journey will take in a number of countries in Europe, the Middle and Far East, Australia, North and South America, and we anticipate that the arrangements will be very complicated. You have been recommended to us as an agency which specialises in this type of business travel.

We should be most grateful if you could send us your brochures and any other material relevant to business travellers. Perhaps you could recommend one of the 'round-the-world' tickets which are now available from selected airlines; a list of these, with prices, would in any case be of interest to us. Also, do you deal with any particular hotel group, through which executive suites could be booked at a special price? If so, we would be interested in receiving details. It has come to our attention that there are certain cards which are available for business travellers and which ensure discounts on travel, accommodation, car hire, etc.; perhaps you would be kind enough to include details of these.

We look forward to hearing from you as soon as possible.

Yours faithfully,

James Smythe

James Smythe
Chief Administrator

Exercise 6

Write a letter, of between 150 to 200 words, on behalf of your company, A. Stringer & Co. Ltd, 30—38 Leven Road, Askford, Ayrshire YY3 3LM, to Mr J. James, the manager of your company's branch office at 94 Morgan Avenue, Nairobi, Kenya, East Africa. Inform Mr James that the Managing Director of the company, Mr Arthur Stringer, and his wife, will be visiting the Nairobi branch early next year on a combined business and holiday trip. Ask Mr James to tell you which month will be most suitable for the visit and if he will be able to book accommodation at a first-class hotel for three weeks for Mr and Mrs Stringer while they are in Nairobi. Bearing in mind that Mr and Mrs Stringer are elderly, suggestions for suitable holiday activities would be appreciated. State that you wish Mr James to arrange for Mr and Mrs Stringer to be met at the airport when they arrive in Nairobi.
    Lay out your letter correctly.

Exercise 7

Write a correctly laid out reply, in 150—200 words, to the letter opposite, which has just been received by your company.

Exercise 8

Write a correctly laid out letter of between 150 and 200 words to the Manager, Freepost Mail Order Company, Benford Commercial Park, East Benford, Kent KE15 3PF. You ordered some goods from the Freepost mail order catalogue (specify, giving an invoice number). On receiving the consignment, which arrived much later than the promised delivery date, you found that the goods were not as represented in the catalogue. Give all relevant details explaining your dissatisfaction. Explain that you are returning the goods and that you expect to be promptly reimbursed. Threaten to take appropriate steps if this is not done.

Popular Household Stores,
70— 76 High Street,
Lowford,
Lancashire
RS1 2AB

14 March 1990

L. Winter & Co. Ltd,
100—120 Range Road,
Boxham,
Northamptonshire
AL4 4MN

Dear Sirs,

I have been buying goods from you for resale in my shop for over fifteen years and have never had cause to complain until now.

Last Monday your van called with its monthly delivery of goods. I noticed that four of the packages containing your popular Ivy brand of cups and saucers appeared to be torn and damaged, and mentioned this to the driver who, by the way, was not the regular driver. He did not wish to listen to my comments and was very rude to me. When, later that day, I opened the packages, most of the contents were broken.

I am now out of stock of the Ivy brand and have customers waiting for it. I trust that you will look into the matter immediately and replace the broken cups and saucers as soon as possible.

I look forward to receiving your comments.

Yours faithfully,

John Smith

John Smith

Summary

Summaries

We give summaries every day of our lives without being aware of them. They do not occur only in examinations. If someone asks you to relate what someone else has said, or to give the gist of a book you have read, or the plot of a film or TV programme, you have to summarise in order to answer. A *written summary*, therefore, is merely employing the same skills on paper. The basic rules of summarisation are the same:

1. *Focus* on the matter to be summarised.
2. *Remember* as much as you can.
3. *Select* the important bits.
4. *Paraphrase* points in your own words.
5. Make sure they *link up* with each other.
6. *Adjust* to the correct length.
7. *Exclude* anything that does not add something important to the essentials.
8. *Include* everything that is needed to explain the essentials.

Title

If you are focusing properly on the subject, you should find it easy to give it a title, and this is asked for in the 'English for Commerce' Second Level Examination. DO NOT LEAVE IT OUT because not only does it earn a few marks but it also helps you to decide what is important for your summary. You should therefore think of a title *before* you start your summary, not just at the end.

Exercise 1 Oral practice in pairs

(a) Give a spoken summary of the fire/emergency procedure in your building.
(b) Summarise a novel or story you have recently read.
(c) Look at today's/this week's newspaper headlines. Summarise as best you can the most important chain of events in a recent news story.

(d) Relate the essentials of a recent film or TV programme.
(e) Summarise the life story of some famous person.

Oral summaries

What did you notice about the oral summaries?

Did you forget some important detail which left your partner confused, or caused you to go back and explain some part of the story?
Did your partner have to interrupt you for clarification?
Did you get half-way through a sentence and have to start again?
Did you have to keep asking your partner whether he or she was following what you were saying?

Clearly the summarising process requires careful thought and some degree of planning to ensure clarity and coherence.
Remember the basic rule in EIGHT STAGES:
Focus Remember Select Paraphrase Link Adjust Exclude Include

Written summaries

In a *written summary* you cannot clarify things as an afterthought, and there is no partner to let you know how badly you are doing it. It is therefore important to have a clear procedure so that you can get it right first time. Question 2 in 'English for Commerce' Second Level aims at giving you the necessary training for this, not so that you can pass examinations but so that you can communicate concisely and effectively in the office.

The LCCI summary

The text to be summarised consists of about 400 words of *expository prose*. It will consist of the following:

1. Stating facts.
2. Drawing conclusions.
3. Urging arguments.
4. Expressing opinions.

Cohesion

All these four elements will be related by the DISCOURSE MARKERS we have already discussed in First Level Reading Unit 4. The passage is therefore COHERENT − its elements are all linked − and a good summary will reflect this by showing the same logical relationships between the points as in the original. (An informal oral summary would probably not do this, but writing it down gives you time to think.)

Length

You are asked to reduce the passage to not more than 120 words, which means the correct length should fall between about 100 and 120 words.

Through the following units we shall examine in detail the various skills which go together to perfect the summary-writing technique. In the meantime, here are some ideas for summary practice:

Exercise 2

Take the main front page article in one of today's newspapers and summarise it to a third of its length.

Exercise 3

Take the leading article in one of today's newspapers and summarise it to a third of its length.

Exercise 4

Take the rules of a game or sport and summarise them to one third of their length.

Unit 2 FOCUS

Topic structure

As discussed in the previous unit, after reading carefully the text to be summarised, the next step is to FOCUS on the main ideas.

The types of text you are likely to be asked to summarise consist of what we have called *expository prose*. This kind of writing serves to clarify and explain facts, ideas, arguments and opinions, and it does so by employing a logical pattern according to which the information is presented and whereby the objective, to 'persuade' the reader, is achieved. This logical pattern is the topic structure. Each paragraph contains a *topic sentence*, supported by various other information which the author introduces to strengthen the argument.

We might, for example, find a text whose underlying structure looks something like this:

Title	**Dental Care**
Topic 1	Dental care is important (supporting information)
Topic 2	You should go to the dentist regularly (supporting information)
Topic 3	You should keep your teeth clean (supporting information)
Topic 4	Bad teeth cause other problems (supporting information)
Topic 5	You can avoid dental problems (supporting information)

However, in such a concise form the text would not seem very interesting or persuasive, and we would normally expect to find the topic sentences supported by additional information such as, for example, the following:

Dental care is important. The modern diet tends to be rich in sugars and fats. Teeth are vulnerable to decay if not properly looked after.
You should go to the dentist regularly. As in all matters of health, prevention is better than cure. Six-monthly check-ups can help you avoid painful treatment.
You should keep your teeth clean. Brushing twice a day can keep teeth healthy. Eating apples and carrots is also advisable.
Bad teeth cause other problems. Gum disease is a painful side effect. Bad teeth are also socially disadvantageous.
You can avoid dental problems. Who wants false teeth? All you have to do is follow these simple rules.

As you can see from this example, supporting information consists of illustrations, examples, analogies, etc., which enrich the text but can be excluded if necessary for the purposes of summary writing. If you were asked to summarise the above passage to one third of its length, *it would be sufficient to include only the topic sentences.*

Finally, it should be noted that the topic sentence of a paragraph is *frequently, though by no means always, the opening sentence.*

Carefully read the following passage, which contains about 400 words. Then, using your own words as far as possible, write a summary of it in not more than 120 words. Finally, supply a title for your summary.

The manager must depend, to a greater or lesser extent, on one or more of the staff to take supervisory roles, and oversee the day-to-day working of the section. Clearly, there must be as good a relationship as possible between the manager and supervisor and, while this can be an excellent opportunity to create and maintain effective communication, there are sometimes problems.

The supervisor is sometimes known as an assistant manager, or under-manager, and has an area of responsibility which in many ways parallels that of the manager. Like the manager he (or she) is often under pressure from above and from below, and has to keep contact with other supervisors, perhaps in other departments, and thus has a 'sideways' pressure also.

More than anything else, the supervisor has to have such information as will enable him to carry out the duties effectively. He needs to feel that he is in the manager's confidence, and that he has been given all the relevant information, together with an opportunity to discuss aspects of the work with the manager. There are managers who fail to recognise fully the importance of information sharing, or who do not always take the trouble to explain fully what is required of the supervisor.

In addition to the delegation of duties, the manager has the problem of having to assess just how much of the information he possesses should be passed on to the supervisor. Some managers, alas, try to bolster up their own position by a secrecy which they suppose adds to their status. Others rely on a telephone conversation, or at best a memo, which they naively believe will be fully understood.

It is not always easy for the manager to decide what information is essential to the supervisor; on the whole it may be better to give too much information than too little, but the manager also has to ensure that what is passed on is understood.

Somehow or other, the manager must try to find an opportunity to discuss with the supervisor(s) just what is required for a particular day or week. Some organisations have set up a daily or weekly 'briefing session', during which not only can up-to-the-minute information as it affects the supervisor be given, but the supervisor has the opportunity to question or comment, so that the manager has a better idea of the difficulties which any individual may feel or anticipate.

Exercise 1

Supply a title for your summary. Which of the following is most appropriate?

(a) Delegating
(b) The Under-Manager
(c) Day-to-day Working
(d) The Supervisor
(e) Office Machines

Exercise 2

First paragraph, topic sentence: which of the following would you select?

(a) The manager must depend on the staff.
(b) The manager must oversee the day-to-day working.
(c) The manager must depend on his supervisors.

Exercise 3

First paragraph, second point:

(a) There are sometimes problems.
(b) Their relationship is important.
(c) There are excellent opportunities.

Exercise 4

Second paragraph, topic sentence:

(a) The supervisor is sometimes known as the assistant manager.
(b) The supervisor is sometimes known as the under-manager.
(c) The supervisor's situation parallels the manager's.

Exercise 5

Second paragraph, second point:

(a) The supervisor is often under pressure.
(b) The supervisor is in contact with others.
(c) The supervisor has sideways pressure.

Exercise 6

Third paragraph, topic sentence:

(a) The supervisor needs proper information.
(b) The supervisor has to carry out duties.
(c) The supervisor must be effective.

Exercise 7

Third paragraph, second point:

(a) Confidence is important.
(b) Discussion is important.
(c) Managers fail to recognise important things.

Exercise 8

Fourth paragraph, topic sentence:

(a) Managers have more to do than delegate duties.
(b) Managers have problems assessing supervisors.
(c) Managers have to inform supervisors appropriately.

Exercise 9

Fifth paragraph, topic sentence:

(a) It is not always easy for managers to decide.
(b) Information is essential to the supervisor.
(c) Managers should ensure supervisors understand the information they receive.

Exercise 10

Final paragraph, topic sentence:

(a) The manager must try to find opportunities.
(b) The manager must discuss requirements with supervisors.
(c) Managers must find out what is required for a day or week.

Exercise 11

Final paragraph, second point:

(a) Some organisations have set up daily or weekly briefing sessions.
(b) Up-to-the-minute information affects supervisors.
(c) Briefings provide an opportunity for updating and feedback between manager and supervisor.

Exercise 12

Put together your answers to Exercises 2–11 in the form of a continuous paragraph under your title from Exercise 1.

Unit 3   SELECTING INFORMATION

Supporting information

Summarising means reproducing a message in a shorter form, preserving the essence of the original but discarding inessential information. We have seen how the topic structure of the original provides a skeleton for the summary. In order to reproduce the message as fully as possible, it will usually be necessary to select from the original *some* of the SUPPORTING INFORMATION. Supporting information usually consists of the following:

Amplification

Further explanation, expansion or restatement of the topic sentence. To take an example from the text summarised in Unit 2:

> *The supervisor has to have such information as will enable him to carry out his duties effectively.* He needs to feel that he is in the manager's confidence, and that he has been given all the relevant information, together with an opportunity to discuss aspects of the work with the manager.

In this instance, the topic sentence (italic type) opens the paragraph, and the second sentence reinforces the point by illustrating various aspects of the main idea, *the need to provide information* (sharing confidences, holding discussions) as well as repeating the main concept, *relevant information*:

(Sentence 1): He needs such information as will enable him to carry out his duties.

That means (sentence 2): Discussion and relevant information.

Exemplification

In many cases, the main point is supported by examples. To take a further extract from the previous unit:

> *Somehow or other the manager must try to find an opportunity to discuss with the supervisor(s) just what is required* for a particular day or week. Some organisations have set up a daily or weekly 'briefing session' ...

Here, having cited a particular problem as the main point in the topic sentence, the author goes on to mention an example of how the problem can be solved:

(Sentence 1): Discussions are needed.

For example (sentence 2): Briefing sessions.

Analogy

A further form of supporting information is the use of analogy, whereby the point is strengthened by means of a comparison or parallel situation, e.g.:

> The supervisor is sometimes known as an assistant manager or under-manager, and has an area of *responsibility which in many ways parallels that of the manager.*

The main point is that the supervisor's position shares similarities with the manager's. The reinforcing information is that the title is sometimes analogous to the duties:

AS with the name (sometimes),
SO with the duties.

Carefully read the following passage, then write a summary of it in not more than 120 words:

> Do-it-yourself is for the handy homeowner, not the busy executive. Smart managers have learned that they can get more work done by delegating to others.
>
> Delegating gives you added hours for such true managerial functions as planning and controlling. It also helps you develop those working under you. There is no better way to get your subordinates producing at their highest capacity.
>
> In addition, when you delegate you create the person or persons who can step into your shoes in the event of your illness, an accident, or just the taking of a worry-free vacation. If you are a man on the way up in a large organisation, delegating will help you prepare the person who will succeed you.
>
> The first step is the hardest for most businessmen. They must make the decisions to let others do some of their work and it isn't easy to let go. The successful leader is one who is willing to accept and support decisions made and actions taken by those under him.
>
> First, it is wise to understand the true meaning of delegation. When you delegate authority to another, you don't surrender your rights and responsibilities to others. You remain accountable for whatever is done.
>
> Let's look at some of the things you must do and consider when you want to improve your skill at delegation.
>
> One key factor is that you must know the capabilities of those to whom you will delegate responsibility. This knowledge of each person should include their training, interests, likes and dislikes, and their capabilities for advancement.
>
> Second, give all facts about his responsibilities to the person to whom you delegate authority. Provide him with a clear picture about what he is to do and how he should do it. Tell him how much authority he will have.
>
> Make certain that those working under you understand and agree to meet certain work standards. They should know what is to be done, by when, and to what specifications. A good way to achieve this goal is to help them set the standards.
>
> Smooth the pathway for your subordinates by telling all others affected by the new authority of your assistants of these changes. You must also impress upon your assistants the importance of earning the respect of others.

Exercise 1

Choose a title for your summary from the following:

(a) Smart Managers.
(b) Handy Homeowners.
(c) Staff Development.
(d) Delegating.
(e) Do-It-Yourself.

Exercise 2 Paragraph 1

Note the topic structure of the paragraph:

Sentence 1. Analogy.
Sentence 2. Main point.

Make a note of the main idea in your own words:

_____

Exercise 3 Paragraph 2

Topic structure:

Sentence 1. Point 1.
Sentence 2. Point 2.
Sentence 3. Amplification.

Note the main ideas:

1. _____

2. _____

Exercise 4 Paragraph 3

Topic structure:

Sentence 1. Main point + Exemplification.
Sentence 2. Exemplification continued.

Note the main idea:

_____

Exercise 5

Repeat the above procedure for the seven remaining paragraphs.

Sample summary

By noting the main ideas, you might have produced a summary rather like this:

Delegating

Managers can achieve more by delegating, which allows time for planning, controlling and staff development.
Delegating can also help you train others to take over from you ____(a)____.
Successful leaders encourage their subordinates, (although) ____(b)____.
In delegating, you remain responsible.
To improve delegating skill, know the capacities _____(c)_____
of your assistants. Ensure they have all the necessary information __(d)__.
Lay down clear standards, and make sure everyone understands the situation.
Also, emphasise that your assistants need to win respect.   (75 words)

As you can see, the main ideas alone, as reproduced here, amount to only seventy-five words − rather more than half the total required. There is room to add some SUPPORTING INFORMATION, selected from the AMPLIFICATIONS, EXAMPLES and ANALOGIES used in the original.

The blanks marked (a)−(d) above suggest points at which supporting material might usefully be introduced:

(a) We might add EXAMPLES to clarify this point.
(b) We might AMPLIFY this point with CONTRASTING information.
(c) We might AMPLIFY.
(d) We might EXEMPLIFY.

Exercise 6

Select supporting information for the purposes noted under (a)−(d) above, and add to the summary to produce a total of not more than 120 words.

Unit 4   PARAPHRASING ———————————————————

The instructions for the LCCI Second Level Summary question require that you answer *using your own words as far as possible*. To meet this requirement, you have to PARAPHRASE the original. *Marks will be lost for lifting whole sentences from the original text and this is a frequent cause of failure in the examination.* However, although students should not reproduce large chunks of the original passage, they will not lose marks for occasionally using the same words if those are the shortest and most natural way of expressing the meaning; e.g. if the original has 'often', use 'often' and not 'in a great number of instances'.

Paraphrasing, in the sense of replacing the author's words with your own, takes place at three levels; yet it is important to remember that all are inter-dependent:

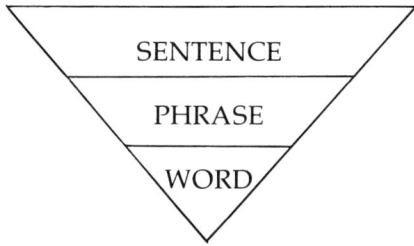

In order to paraphrase successfully, you have to understand the original correctly. Without paying attention to the CONTEXT, it is easy to employ a paraphrase which is incorrect. For example, to take a sentence from the text summarised in Unit 2:

The manager must depend on his staff.

You could paraphrase 'depend' in a number of ways, but not all would be correct, e.g.:

The manager must rely on his staff.
*The manager must hang on his staff.
*The manager must be determined by his staff.

The first sentence is the correct one in this case. For this reason, it is not enough to simply take the most obvious replacement for a word when paraphrasing; remember that you always have to consider the context. You are reproducing *meaning*, not translating *words*.

Condensing

Paraphrasing also contributes to the summarising process in that it is frequently possible to do the following:

1. Condense a PHRASE into a single word, e.g.:

in a great number of instances = often
highly complex and challenging = difficult
at the present moment in time = now

2. Condense a long and complex SENTENCE into a much shorter one:

On balance it was considered preferable not only to have the items produced at the main factory, but also to have them packaged there.   (24 words)

They decided to produce and package the goods at the main factory.

(12 words)

Consider the following text:

Modern industries need a great many things in addition to their prime raw materials — machinery of different types, power and labour to work them, transport to get the finished products to market, and it may quite well happen that it pays to carry the raw materials over long distances in order to avoid transporting machinery, fuel or workers. The businessman wants to produce his goods as economically as he can and get them to the purchaser in the cheapest and most convenient way. It would be a very remarkable coincidence if he found a particular spot, advantageous from every point of view, with basic materials, power, transport, labour and markets. He has to balance advantage against disadvantage and make up his mind whether, for example, it is better to have the expense of carrying his raw materials a long way in order to be near his market for the finished goods or save the carriage on raw materials but have to meet the extra cost of transporting his finished goods. As circumstances change, so do the different factors affecting this calculation.

In the early years of this century there would have been some excuse for confusing a map of the coalfields with one showing industrial concentrations, for the two were so closely connected. Nowadays, however, such confusion would be unlikely, for the emphasis of industrial development has changed greatly. Until the First World War the large majority of manufacturing industries relied on steam for their power, and this made heavy demands on coal. As coal is a bulky article and expensive to carry, it generally paid to settle the factory on or near the coalfields and bring all the other necessary materials there, rather than the other way round. When, however, electricity began to replace steam as the chief motive force, this concentration on the coalfields was no longer so essential for, although electricity is usually generated from coal in this country, it can be carried long distances with comparative ease and cheapness. This allowed industries to give greater weight to other factors when deciding their location, and it happens that the type of goods with which our manufacturing industries are now mainly concerned induces producers to gravitate to other areas than the coalfields, if their power can be equally well provided.

Paraphrasing

Let us now practise the paraphrasing operation sentence by sentence, carrying out substitutions at word, phrase and sentence level:

First sentence

> Modern industries need a great many things in addition to their prime raw materials — machinery of different types, power and labour to work them, transport to get the finished products to market, and it may quite well happen that it pays to carry the raw materials over long distances in order to avoid transporting machinery, fuel or workers.   (58 words)

WORD–WORD

modern	— today
need	— require
machinery	— equipment
transport	— carry
fuel	— power, fuels
labour	— workers, staff

} (interchangeable in most contexts)

PHRASE–WORD
  labour to work them — workers

PHRASE–PHRASE

in addition to	— as well as
transport to get the finished product to the market	— distribution facilities
it may quite well happen	— it may be
in order to avoid	— (rather) than

SENTENCE SHORTENING
This results from the above and from changes in the sentence structure e.g.:
Inverted phrase structure:

(A) Modern industries need a great many things *in addition to* (B) prime raw materials ...

becomes:

As well as (B) raw materials, (A) industries today need ...

RESULT
As well as raw materials, industries today require equipment, fuel, workers and distribution facilities, and it may be easier to transport raw materials than machines, labour and fuels.   (28 words)

Second sentence

> The businessman wants to produce his goods as economically as he can and get them to the purchaser in the cheapest and most convenient way.
>
> (25 words)

WORD–WORD

The businessman — businessmen, businesses
wants — seeks, wishes
economically — cost-effectively, cheaply

PHRASE–WORD

get (them) to the purchaser — distribute (them)

PHRASE–PHRASE

in the cheapest and most convenient way (ADJECTIVE + NOUN)
= as efficiently as possible (ADVERB)

SENTENCE SHORTENING
Condensing the superlatives:

... produce his goods *as economically as he can* and get them to the purchaser *in the cheapest and most convenient way*.

becomes:

... produce goods as cost-effectively and distribute them as efficiently as possible.

RESULT

Businesses seek to produce goods as cost-effectively and distribute them as efficiently as possible. (13 words)

Exercise 1 Guided paraphrase

A summary of the text is reproduced below. Your task is to fill the gaps with suitable paraphrases of the original. This will involve the following:

1. A thorough understanding of the text.
2. Careful attention to context.
3. Good vocabulary resources.

The number of lines in the gaps indicates the number of missing words from the model summary.

(Title) _____(a)_____

As well as raw materials, businesses today require equipment, fuel, workers and distribution facilities, and it may be easier to transport raw materials than machines, labour and fuels. Businesses seek to produce goods as cost-effectively and distribute as efficiently as possible. _____(b)_____ are rare, and the business-man has to _____(c)_____ of transporting raw materials or products. A _____(d)_____ ago the _____(e)_____ and the _____(f)_____ _____(g)_____ because most industries _____(h)_____ on steam power, which _____(i)_____ of coal. However, as steam was _____(j)_____, which is _____(k)_____ easy to transport, other _____(l)_____ _____(m)_____ the _____(n)_____ of industries.

(105 words)

Exercise 2

Summarise the following text in not more than 120 words, paying special attention to paraphrasing. Provide a title.

Relationships with colleagues is probably one of the most difficult problems with which the junior worker is faced. For one thing, there is always a certain element of competition between staff for promotion, and this can lead to all kinds of suspicion of the motives of fellow workers. The ambitious drive of some people can make them very difficult to work with. It can be very disturbing, for example, to discover that one's mistakes are being relayed to the 'higher-ups' by colleagues who are seeking to benefit themselves by that method. Unfortunately, human nature being what it is, this kind of situation does happen, and when it is discovered, the relationships within an organisation can be seriously impaired. This is not an easy situation to deal with because there is little defence against an accusation which is justifiable. The fact that we are all prone to error is no real defence. What irritates and frustrates us the most is that we have been betrayed by those with whom we work, and once the resentment and suspicion get to work, our 'communicability' is lessened because we become more guarded and less than frank with our colleagues.

Perhaps we should look at a couple of the main motives which make the promotion seeker what he is.

The first motive, not unnaturally, is the desire to earn more money. Most of us never seem to have enough money anyway, and it is not unreasonable to want more. The age we live in places a high value on the possession of money and what it can buy, so the urge to increase our income is very strong in most of us.

The second motive behind promotion seeking is what we loosely called 'status'. This is closely linked with money, of course, but is based on the belief that the higher up the ladder we climb, the more we receive the satisfactions of respect and authority. We may certainly acquire a measure of power and authority, but respect is another matter. Respect depends more on the nature and personality of a person than on his position in an organisation.

It is important to recognise the efforts, even among junior staff, to acquire both money and status and to be aware of the kind of threat they create to human relationships at this level.

Unit 5   LINKING POINTS ──────────────────────────

As discussed in First Level Reading Unit 4, the points in a text are linked by the discourse markers, which reflect the logical structure of the argument. Concepts are also linked by reference words (First Level Reading Unit 2), as well as by the functions of exemplification, amplification and analogy (Summary Unit 3). The effect of all the above is to give the text COHESION, so that all points fit together and the argument develops logically. A good summary should reflect this coherent structure.

Consider text A:

Text A

Anything which indicates what you can or cannot do in certain situations is a policy. It does not have to be written. It may not even have been stated explicitly. But if there is an understanding 'that this is the way we do things round here', then there is a policy.

For example, one business may lay down that 'company salary levels should be at the upper quartile of the range of salaries paid for comparable jobs elsewhere'. This is quite clear, although salary administrators can get bogged down in defining what is comparable and what is not.

Another business may have a salary structure which has developed in a more haphazard way. There may have been a general understanding that the company is prepared to pay above the going rate to get and to keep good quality staff, but nothing so precise as the upper quartile has been defined and nothing has been written down.

Both these companies have salary policies. Which of them has the best policy? There is only one answer to this question. The one that works. A clearly defined, almost rigid policy, quoting the upper quartile is fine if people find out what the upper quartile is and try their best to match it; otherwise it is useless. A policy of paying above the going rate is great if that is what happens, and as long as the application of the policy is consistent between different jobs and different parts of the company. Inconsistency is, of course, the danger of ill-defined policies, just as undue restraint of judgement and initiative is the danger of a policy which is too rigid.

When faced with a crisis or difficult decision it is helpful to have a guide. Consequently it is essential to let people know what they can and cannot do when they are running a business or department.

A direct selling business will tell its agents in the field what they can do − they are to sell direct to housewives who are broadly in the middle income group. It will also tell them what they must not do − perhaps it is not the firm's policy to go in for high-pressure selling.

A retail store will tell its buyers what it wants them to do − perhaps to achieve a three times mark-up on the cost of the goods they purchase. It will also tell them what it does not want them to do − in this case not to sacrifice the firm's reputation for quality in the pursuit of low-cost merchandise.

Exercise 1   Focus

Complete the following skeleton of main ideas:

TITLE _____

A policy is a   _____
    ↑   _____
⎧ For example _____
⎪   ↑
⎨   ↑
⎪ Another   _____
⎩   _____

↳ Both   _____
Which   _____?
(Answer 1)   _____
otherwise _____
(Answer 2)   _____
as long as _____

When   _____
Consequently _____
    ↓
(Example 1) _____
    ↓
(Example 2) _____
    _____

Exercise 2

Paraphrase the condensed version of Text A on the next page.

Note: Try to paraphrase the links if possible, e.g.:

A rigid policy must be followed through *otherwise* it is useless.

becomes:

Unless it is followed through, a rigid policy is useless.

Anything which indicates what you can do in a situation is a policy. For example, one business may lay down salary levels in the range of salaries for comparable jobs, although administrators can get bogged down. Another may have a salary structure which is haphazard. There may be a general understanding to pay above the going rate but nothing precise and nothing written. Both have policies. Which is the best? A clearly-defined policy is fine if people find out and try to match comparable levels, otherwise it is useless. A policy of paying above the going rate is great if that happens, and as long as the application is consistent.

When faced with a difficult decision it is helpful to have a guide. Consequently it is essential to let people know what they can do when running a business or department. A direct selling business will tell its agents whom they are to sell to − housewives − and what they must not do − perhaps high-pressure selling. A retail store will tell its buyers what it wants − high mark-up − and does not want − to sacrifice the firm's reputation.   (190 words)

Exercise 3

Reduce the above to 120 words. If your **paraphrased** version is still more than 120 words in length, exclude any information which is not essential.

Exercise 4   Guided summary

Complete the following in 120 words:

_____

A policy indicates _____
One company's policy, for example _____
whereas another company _____
A successful policy _____
Fixed policies _____ unless _____
Similarly, a tacit agreement _____ only if _____
Policies are useful for _____
It is therefore important to _____
Different companies will have different policies: _____

Exercise 5

Carefully read Text B (overleaf), which contains about 400 words. Then, *using your own words as far as possible*, write a summary of it in not more than 120 words. Supply a *title* for your summary, and pay particular attention to the *links between ideas*.

Text B

Selling by mail order originated in the United States of America as a solution to the problems of customers who lived far away from the nearest shop. The shop-window for the mail-order firm is its catalogue, which is expensive to produce and to distribute but which presents the customer with a very wide range of goods attractively advertised. Unlike stock in some shops, it does not need dusting or rearranging more often than once a year and there is no chance of the clothes and fabrics displayed becoming shop-soiled or faded. Thus it is in many ways a very satisfactory shop window.

Not all mail-order firms issue catalogues. Very successful businesses worth millions of pounds have been set up using newspaper advertisements. This type of advertisement can be seen in any popular newspaper, particularly on Saturdays.

In Great Britain, where shops are plentiful, it might seem unnecessary to have mail-order firms at all, but they offer one attraction which most shops do not offer, and that is hire-purchase of non-durable goods. Many families are glad to spread their payments for clothing, footwear, soft furnishings, linoleum, etc., over a period.

The usual period of credit in Great Britain is 20 weeks, in which case the weekly repayments amount to five pence in the pound. If the customer sends her payments regularly, she soon becomes a credit-worthy customer and entitled to re-order at any time. Whatever is unpaid from the previous order is added to the price of a new article, and the total is paid for over the next 19 weeks. In this way the housewife is always in debt but always able to order more goods if required.

Two things are required if this system is to work satisfactorily for all parties: the goods must be of high quality and value for money, and bad debts must be kept to a minimum. Some mail-order firms establish nationwide links by having housewives who act as agents. These housewives collect the weekly payments from their friends who are customers and remit them to Head Office weekly in return for a commission of about 10 per cent. This reduces the bad debts but, of course, managers of such types of business expect a higher rate of bad debts than ordinary shops.

The mail-order business is an example of the elimination of the retailer by the wholesaler.

Unit 6 STYLE AND ATTITUDE ——————————————

In preparing a summary, it is necessary to take account of the author's STYLE of presentation, and ATTITUDE to the subject matter, both of which influence the processes of selection and paraphrasing.

Style

As noted in Unit 3, analogy is one of the categories of supporting information; some authors use a relatively high proportion of ANALOGY and SIMILE, as well as REPETITION, much of which is redundant (i.e. adds nothing essential to the main idea) and can thus be excluded. Other stylistic devices which the summary writer will usually wish to exclude from the summary are as follows:

Irony
Writing something inappropriate in the context so as to add force to the argument, e.g.:

> The Luddites destroyed all Horsfall's new looms, which was *somewhat inconsiderate* of them.

The choice of words gives no indication of the hostility of the situation.

Euphemism
The use of mild words and expressions in place of harsher but more appropriate ones, e.g.:

> The Wall Street crash was *rather upsetting* to many investors.

This is a major understatement, as many of those involved were in fact driven to suicide!

Metaphor
The use of words to indicate something other than their literal meaning, e.g.:

> Grand Universal Stores *steamrollered* all their opposition in the High Street.

Here the image of a large and heavy road-making machine is used to express the force of a business success.

Idiom
Groups of words often used together as a well-known saying, e.g.:

> It's *just a matter of time* before the company goes bankrupt.

This common idiom is used to indicate inevitability; the bankruptcy is inevitable, the only question being when.

Negatives
These can be confusing when they are used in certain stylistic devices to achieve emphasis, e.g.:

> *By no means the least* of their problems was the growing militancy of the trade unions.

A quick glance at the above sentence might leave a careless reader believing that union activity *was* the least of their problems. However, 'by no means' is another way of saying 'not'. Moreover, 'not the least' is an idiomatic way of saying 'one of the greatest'. Thus the real meaning of the sentence becomes:

> One of their greatest problems was the growing militancy of the trade unions.

Consider also:

> I couldn't agree more (= I agree strongly)

Attitude

On the other hand, the attitude to the subject matter expressed by the author is a useful guide to the importance of the various concepts in the text.

Categorical statements

> Before opening a business it is *essential* to prepare a business plan.
> The manager *must* keep his supervisors well informed.

The information expressed in such categorical statements will usually be essential to the summary.

Emphasis

> *It cannot be too strongly stated that* smoking is bad for the health.

In this case, the summary writer may wish to reflect the strength of the author's view in the summary.

Degrees of certainty

> probably / possibly
> might   / will certainly
> could   / should
> ought to / must
> etc.

It is important that these are not misrepresented or confused by the summary writer (see the Second Level Writing section, Unit 5).

Consider text A:

Text A

The first rule in filing is 'Don't let it accumulate.' Good filing is generally recognised as an indispensable aid to efficiency. Bad filing means chaos. Gone are the days when things can be left to the memory. Modern conditions of business and industry demand that there should be quick and easy access to all available information and an effective system of filing is the best means of securing and maintaining this objective. No matter if the system is simple or complex, if it is no more than a quick reference card index or, at the other extreme, an expensive installation, filing is imperative, it has got to be effective and it has got to be up to date — speed of access has to be the keynote. How else could Scotland Yard identify a fingerprint among millions at a moment's notice? It is done because a system has been devised that is foolproof; and yet neglect by any one member of the team involved can ruin the whole operation. Filing may be humdrum and uninspiring, but it must be done.

Whatever the filing requirement, there has got to be a system and that system must be the most sensible one to suit the purpose of the office. You, as a secretary, may be made responsible for your own filing. Apart from organisations having a vast central filing system which is maintained by staff specially engaged for filing, you need to operate your own filing system for day-to-day matters mainly concerning yourself and your immediate boss; beware of the consequences when he suddenly asks for some document which he knows you should have if you lamely admit that you can't find it. Don't be surprised if he thinks you may be incompetent in other ways, too.

Many secretaries, knowing full well what is required of them, devise their own filing system to suit their own requirements or the specific demands or vagaries of their own job. You should do likewise. Think in terms of an easily accessible filing system for each part of your work. It needn't be involved or difficult; the simpler the system, the better, and this is especially so during periods of holiday or sickness, when somebody else will have to stand in for you and her attitude — and possibly through her the attitude of some of your fellow-workers — could be that, if your filing system is so complicated that only you can find your way through it, you might be a rather secretive person in other respects too.

Analysis

Line 1	The first rule	— EMPHASIS 'The first' here indicates not 'one in a series' but 'the most important'.
Line 2	indispensable	— CATEGORICAL STATEMENT
Line 2	Gone are the days	— IDIOM (*paraphrase or exclude*)
Line 4	demand	— EMPHASIS A strong word for 'require'.
Line 6	No matter	
Line 6	no more	— EMPHASIS The negatives are used to stress that the form and scale of the system are arbitrary.

Line 8	Imperative	– CATEGORICAL STATEMENT
Line 9	How else could	– ANALOGY (*exclude*)
	Scotland Yard . . .?	
Line 11	ruin	– EMPHASIS
		Strong word for 'harm'.
Line 12	must be done	– CATEGORICAL STATEMENT
Line 15	vast	– EMPHASIS
		A slight overstatement, used to highlight the contrast between a personal and an institutional filing system.
Line 18	beware	
Line 19	lamely	– METAPHOR (*exclude*)
		The author illustrates the importance of good filing to perceived efficiency with an imaginary scenario of a rather frightening boss ('beware' suggests fear) and an inadequate secretary ('lame' suggests 'incapable').
Line 21	knowing full well	– IDIOM + EMPHASIS
		Here the use of the idiom serves to strengthen the argument that making a filing system is the knowledgeable thing to do.

Exercise 1   Guided summary

Fill the gaps in the following, paying particular attention to *attitude markers*:

TITLE _____(a)_____

It is ____(b)____ that good filing is ____(c)____ to business efficiency. The contemporary commercial scene ____(d)____ for readily accessible information, and a good filing system is the ____(e)____ way of achieving this. The system ____(f)____ be a simple card index or a complex information centre, but it ____(g)____ be both fast and efficient, which means that all involved ____(h)____ play their part in keeping it updated.

The system ____(i)____ be adapted to the needs of the office. A secretary ____(j)____ have a personal filing system independent of the organisation's central system, and this ____(k)____ reflect the secretary's competence. A simple system is often ____(l)____, especially when others take over. A complicated system ____(m)____ suggest to others a secretive personality.

(120 words)

Exercise 2

Summarise Text B in not more than 120 words, and supply a title.

Text B

Advertising exists to sell goods and services. Some people feel strongly that it should not be necessary to *sell* things: produce a better article and the world will rush to buy it. In practice, however, it is impossible to co-ordinate production and demand exactly, because selling and price are the buffers between them. When demand exceeds production selling is unnecessary; when production exceeds demand you have no choice but to sell — or waste the product.

The mass-selling of popular goods and services, promoted by advertising, performs several useful functions here. It helps manufacturers stabilise and predict their production schedules; and advertising informs consumers about the products available and goes a long way to guarantee their quality.

Nobody claims that the production of goods and services is the most admirable of all human activities. Certainly nobody has ever been so foolish as to claim that all the good things in life are solely to be found in advertisements. Advertising affects only a small part of our lives. In the United Kingdom there is virtually no advertising concerned with law and order, public health, income tax, education, country rambles, science or the arts. Advertising is a small industry in the United Kingdom, with less than 16,000 people employed in agencies (about as many as work in one medium-sized industrial company), and with only about £60 million spent on the production and placing of advertisements. Most areas of our lives are in no way affected by advertising. Yet it is surely foolish to argue that those areas where advertising is involved — cars, cosmetics, chocolate, clothes — give no pleasure or are totally unimportant.

Man's relationship with material objects is an extremely complex one. Watch a baby, just a few months old, grab at objects of which it likes the look or feel. Try to take away the scrap of paper or old sock upon which it has temporarily become fixated and you will suffer screams of righteous fury not dissimilar from those I make myself when I cannot have a car or painting that I have set my heart upon. Experimental psychologists have shown that babies react quite differently to people and to things and gain great pleasure from both. Anthropologists, students of mankind, seeking a way to distinguish man from other animals, defined him as a tool-making animal, not a thinking, speaking or a cello-playing animal. Materialism, the involvement of human beings with material objects, is part of us. Advertising is its most obvious and most public manifestation.

Unit 7   REVIEW ──────────────────────

Worked example

Below is an example of how the procedures analysed in the preceding units can be realistically applied within the context of the LCCI examination. There are, of course, a variety of ways in which you can arrive at the same result, and your teacher may have other suggestions. However, if you at least follow the procedure outlined below, you will find that summarisation gets easier.

Summary method

You should do the summary in the following five stages, taking about forty minutes:

1. *Read* the passage *several times, underlining* what you think are the *main points* and *marking* by some personal *code* the *main divisions* in the passage.
2. Jot down in your answer booklet in *note* form a *skeleton* of the original passage. Think of a *title*.
3. *Link up* the notes into *continuous prose* and *count the words*.
4. *Cross out the notes* and sketches and proceed to *write the final version,* adding or subtracting matter to fit the *120 words* allowed.
5. *Check over* what you have written for spelling and punctuation errors and to *ensure that nothing important has been left out and nothing new or irrelevant has been put in.*

Carefully read Text A, which contains about 400 words. Then *using your own words as far as possible,* write a summary of it in not more than 120 words. Finally, supply an appropriate title for your summary.

Text A

The care needed to be taken in the actual selection of an office machine is as great as that of the consideration to mechanise in the first place. The type of machine required can be decided only after the work to be done on it has been carefully analysed. It is, therefore, absolutely essential to investigate each operation in the procedure or procedures thoroughly in order that the right machine may be chosen for the task in hand. Other areas of possible mechanisation should also be considered so that a possible extension of the use of the machine can be noted for the future. Hence, where this is relevant, a machine capable of adaptation or programming for other work must be selected.

It should be noted that the majority of manufacturers are only too willing to give full information on the scope of their machines, and most of them have a consultancy service to advise potential customers. In addition, some of the simpler equipment can be borrowed on demonstration loan to ascertain the benefits that will accrue from its acquisition. Some machines such as electric typewriters, standard typewriters and calculating machines are freely available on this basis.

However, it must be remembered that the primary aim of a manufacturer is to sell and he may not bring to the client's attention any shortcomings the equipment might have. In addition, some claims as to the versatility of a machine may be rather optimistic so far as speed or convenience in carrying out operations, other than the principal ones, are concerned. Hence, it is essential that equivalent machines of different makes be thoroughly investigated from all points of view before a final choice is made. If at all possible, a friendly word with some other users may be advantageous in securing information as to a particular machine's performance and reliability.

The pre-sales and after-sales service of the various manufacturers is also a very important aspect in the selection of a machine. Before the sale the manufacturer should be prepared to aid and guide the purchaser in advising on the precise equipment best suited to the client's problems, on the necessary procedural changes in the work affected, and to make suggestions for expanding the use of the machine into other areas of work.

Where necessary, after the order is placed and before delivery is made, facilities for training operating staff should be provided. (30 marks)

Stage 1 Focus, select — underline the main ideas and code the others

The care needed to be taken in the actual selection of an office machine is (as great as) that of the consideration to mechanise in the first place. The type of machine required can be decided cat. only after the work to be done on it has been carefully analysed. It is, therefore, absolutely essential to investigate each operation cat. in the procedure (or procedures) thoroughly in order that the right machine may be chosen for the task in hand. Other areas of possible mechanisation should also be considered so that a possible extension of the use of the machine can be noted for the future. Hence, where this is relevant, a machine capable ∴ of adaptation or programming for other work must be selected. cat.

? It should be noted that the majority of manufacturers are only too willing to give full information on the scope of their machines, and most of them have a consultancy service to advise potential customers. In addition, some of the simpler equipment can be borrowed on demonstration loan to ascertain the benefits that will accrue from its acquisition. Some machines (such as) electric typewriters, standard typewriters and calculating machines are freely available on this basis.

O.K. but

However, it must be remembered that the primary aim of a manufacturer is to sell and he may not bring to the client's attention any shortcomings the equipment might have. In addition, some claims as to the versatility of a machine may ? be rather optimistic so far as speed or convenience in carrying out operations, other than the principal ones, are concerned. ∴ Hence, it is essential that equivalent machines of different makes cat. be thoroughly investigated from all points of view before a final choice is made. If at all possible, a friendly word with some other users may be advantageous in securing information as to a particular machine's performance and reliability.

e.g. The pre-sales and after-sales service of the various manufacturers is also a very important aspect in the selection cat. of a machine. Before the sale the manufacturer should be prepared to aid and guide the purchaser in advising on the precise equipment best suited to the client's problems, on the necessary procedural changes in the work affected, and to make suggestions for expanding the use of the machine into other areas of work.

Where necessary, after the order is placed and before ? delivery is made, facilities for training operating staff should be provided.

simile - delete

overspecific - delete

irony

examples - delete

euphemism/irony

examples of presales service

example of after sales service ?

CODE
Note the use of a simple code of signs, e.g.:

∴	= therefore	cat.	= categorical statement
∵	= because	?	= meaning not clear
↔	= connected	e.g.	= example
( ) *	= can be deleted	▭	= essential

Note: Some teachers or invigilators do not let candidates write on the question papers because they intend to use them afterwards for teaching purposes. This puts candidates at a disadvantage. The LCCI assumes students will be free to write on their papers as above.

Stage 2   Skeleton

Office machinery
Selection office machine − needs care.
Analyse work to be done first.
∴ Investigate each operation.
Is it suitable for task?

Also, investigate other uses to extend its range.
Where relevant, choose extendable model.

Beware manufacturers! They provide info, offer consultancy service and loan demo but exaggerate versatility and hide defects.

∴ Get comparison with equivalent machines from other sources.
Consult other users − performance/reliability.

Pre- and after-sales service important.
↓
advice on equipment, procedures, extending
↓
Train staff.

Stage 3 First draft

Choosing office machinery
An office machine should be selected with great care only after an analysis of the work it will be required to do and investigation of each operation to ensure it is right for the task it has been selected for and perhaps suitable for extension to other tasks. A model that has potential for expansion should be chosen. Manufacturers will provide abundant information, consultancy and sometimes demonstration loans before sales but conceal defects and are over-optimistic about the versatility of their machine beyond the basic tasks they are designed for. Therefore comparative quotations from several manufacturers should be obtained and other users consulted. Pre- and after-sales service is very important, the first providing advice on equipment, office procedural changes and the extension of the machine to other work. Between ordering and delivery staff should be trained (by the manufacturer?).

(140 words – *reduce*)

Stage 4 Reduce to 120 words

Choosing a New Machine for the Office
An office machine should be chosen with care and only after analysis of its intended work-load and detailed operations to ensure it is the right one for its primary job and has potential for extension elsewhere. Manufacturers provide abundant information, consultancy and, sometimes, a demonstration loan facility before sale but they frequently conceal the machine's shortcomings and exaggerate its versatility beyond its basic role. Therefore comparative quotations from several manufacturers must be obtained and other users consulted. Pre- and after-sales service is very important. The first provides advice on equipment, on changes in office procedures entailed, and on the machine's use in other spheres. Between your ordering and taking delivery, the manufacturer should also arrange to train staff on it.

(120 words)

Exercise 1

Carefully read Text B, which contains about 400 words. Then *using your own words as far as possible*, summarise it in not more than 120 words. Finally, supply a title for your summary.

Text B

The ship is by far the largest vehicle which has ever been devised by man, and its cargo-carrying capacity is greater than that of any other single transport unit. Oil tankers capable of carrying 250,000 tonnes of petroleum crude oils or by-products are, in fact, being built today. As compared with the motor vehicle or even the railway train, the cargo space available on the modern ship is enormous, and developments in shipbuilding technique are constantly increasing the cargo space in relation to the total capacity of the ship. The vessel can be operated with a relatively limited crew, whilst its permanent way is provided freely by Nature. Consequently, goods can be transported more cheaply by this method than by any other. Furthermore, competitive conditions normally prevailing in the shipping industry operate to keep these charges down to a minimum, which benefits the trader in the freight charges which he pays on his goods. At the same time, it may create difficulties for those engaged in the industry and invite action to restrain the competitive struggle.

Two developments since the Second World War have been the complete change-over from coal-burning to oil-burning vessels and a trend towards ship 'specialisation'. The latter has been due mainly to a heavy demand for the sea carriage of mineral ores and other bulk commodities, and economy in operation has resulted in the design and construction of ships capable of carrying maximum tonnage of cargoes consistent with accessibility to loading and discharging berths, coupled with availability and regularity of flow of the 'specialist' traffic. Most of these ships are designed to permit easy loading and discharging by mechanised means. The transfer from coal to oil as a fuel for propulsion in ships has had an effect on the mining industry of this country. Formerly a large amount of coal was supplied annually for bunkering ships and maintaining coaling stations all over the world. The maintenance of stocks at these stations provided outward cargoes for a considerable tonnage of tramp ships.

The facilities afforded by shipping firms may be classified according to the type of carrying function which they perform — namely, the conveyance of passengers and of merchandise. This classification is not, however, a particularly good one, since there is no clear line of distinction between the vessels engaged in these two types of traffic.

Exercise 2

Summarise Text C in not more than 120 words and supply a title.

Text C

The distinguishing feature of a department store is that it is really a collection of shops all under the same roof, each department dealing in a particular branch of retail trade. Very large premises are required, and these are frequently almost palatial in design and occupy central sites in the main shopping centres. At one time it would probably have been true to say that department stores were single-unit shops without branches. At the present time, however, some firms operate department stores in a limited number of large cities. In addition, there has been a tendency for department stores to amalgamate, possibly to secure greater economies in buying. Since the stores usually continue to do business under their old names — on account of the goodwill appertaining to them — the ordinary shopper generally does not know whether two department stores which appear to be competing against one another are in fact competitors or really different sections of the same firm.

Since the overhead expenses of this type of retail business are very great, a large turnover is essential, and so these shops are to be found only in large cities which serve as shopping centres for wide areas. As is only to be expected, most of them in Great Britain are located in London, but examples — though usually smaller than those in the capital — are to be found in Leeds, Manchester, Birmingham, Edinburgh and other large cities, each of which attracts customers from a wide area, known as its 'shopping hinterland'. Their development has been assisted by recent improvements in road transport as a result of which it has become possible for greater numbers of people in the surrounding districts to do their shopping in these large cities.

Department stores had their origin in France, the first being Bon Marché, which was established in 1852. They are well established in that country and in the United States. In England many of them developed out of drapery businesses, and in many of the smaller ones the drapery department is still the main centre of business. In their early years, especially, one of their attractions was that they charged lower prices than did the independent traders who in those days offered their customers the maximum amount of service and personal attention and in consequence had to charge a high price for the goods they sold.

Writing

Unit 1 INTRODUCTION

Second Level Writing tests your ability to express your thoughts in writing over several paragraphs in a clear and interesting way. Although it is a free and open-ended form of writing, the following ground rules should be followed:

Before you start:

Preparation:

Execution:

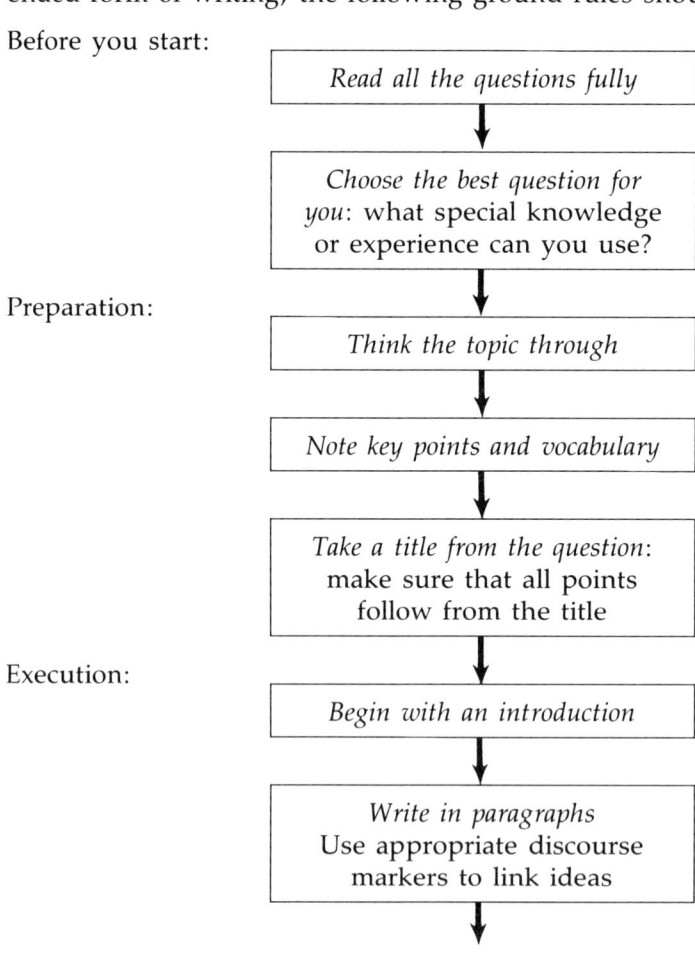

Read all the questions fully

Choose the best question for you: what special knowledge or experience can you use?

Think the topic through

Note key points and vocabulary

Take a title from the question: make sure that all points follow from the title

Begin with an introduction

Write in paragraphs Use appropriate discourse markers to link ideas

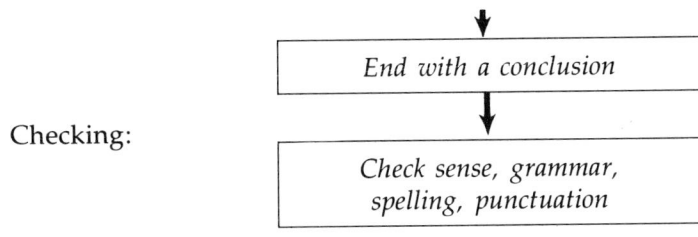

End with a conclusion

Checking:

Check sense, grammar,
spelling, punctuation

Note: Leave adequate time for all these stages!

Here are some examples of Second Level Writing questions:

Write a composition of approximately 300 words on the following:

1. Discuss some of the essential points that should be considered before opening a shop.
2. How can a government help its country's exporters?
3. Put the case either for or against cars being banned from city centres.
4. What do you think should be done to tackle the drug problem in your country?
5. How do you think the shops of the twenty-first century may differ from those of today?

Understanding the questions

Exercise 1

State which question refers to:

(a) toxic exhaust fumes
(b) illegal use of toxic substances
(c) planning a retail outlet
(d) retailing in the future
(e) selling goods abroad

Exercise 2

Decide for which question you might write about the following:

(a) duties and tariffs
(b) market research
(c) pedestrian precincts and park-and-ride schemes
(d) home shopping and automation
(e) customs and police search laws

Title

A title is essential for a complete piece of writing. Whereas in First Level Writing the same wording as the question could in most cases be used as a title, in Second Level Writing you have to form a suitable title from the key words in the question.
  So, if you were answering the following question:

What do you think are the best methods of tackling inflation?

You could take either the key words themselves:

Tackling Inflation   (Note the use of capital letters)

or a longer title:

The Best Methods of Tackling Inflation

There are no absolutely *right* titles, but some are better than others and they would be completely *wrong* if they gave no indication of what is to follow!

Vocabulary

Exercise 3

Place the following assorted items under the appropriate headings:

addicts	automation	buses	business plan
customers	credit cards	dealers	detectives
education	hypermarkets	licences	market research
parking	pollution	ports	product range
robots	shipping	subsidies	taxis

Helping exporters	Opening a shop	Banning cars	The drug problem	21st-century shops

Exercise 4

Discuss and add as many more items as possible to each column.

Exercise 5 Key points

Study the following points and list them in the appropriate column; add any further points:

increased use of public transport . . . danger to pedestrians . . . shortage of parking spaces . . . inconvenience of leaving the car . . . danger of crime on public transport . . . walking in bad weather . . . use of the car as a mobile office . . . cancer risk from exhaust fumes . . . pride of car ownership . . . sitting in traffic jams for two hours per day . . . revenue from parking fines

Cars in City Centres

For	Against

Exercise 6 Tackling the drug problem

Consider the two lists. Think of what could be done by the INSTITUTIONS in the left hand column, in relation to the AREAS OF ACTION in the right hand column:

Institutions | Areas of Action

Institutions	Areas of Action
the police	advertisements
schools	undercover detectives
television	laws and penalties
the community	educational programmes
newspapers	detection equipment
courts	stop-and-search rights
airports and ports	public co-operation
doctors	international liaison

Exercise 7

Discuss and add more items to each column.

Visualising the topic

It is often helpful to sketch out, in the form of a chart, table or diagram, the topics and arguments to be used in writing a composition, e.g.:

How do you think shops of the twenty-first century may differ from those of today?

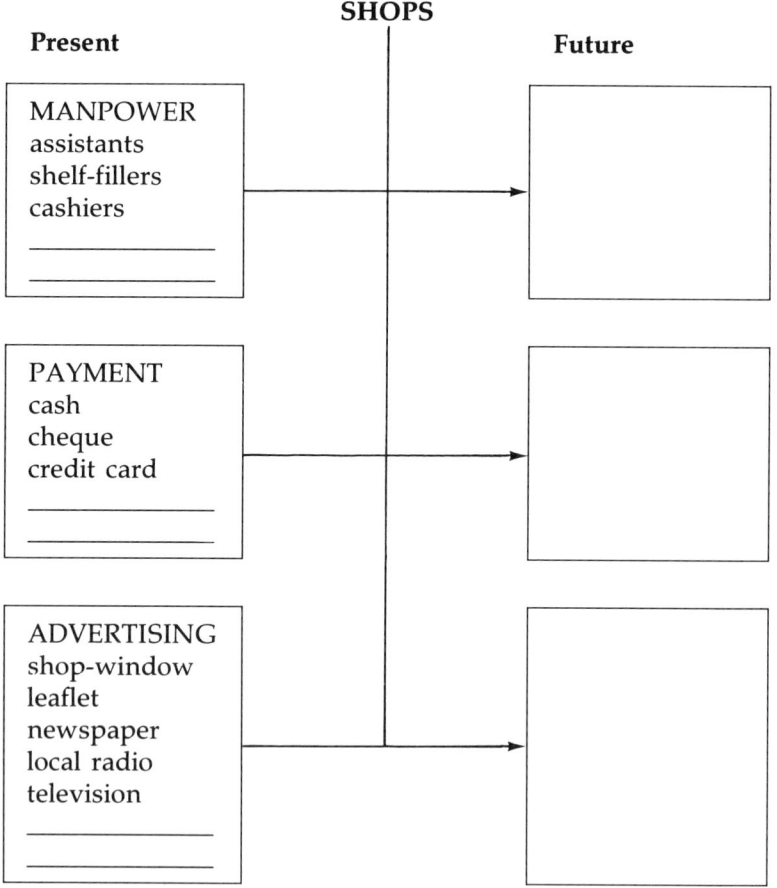

SHOPS

Present   **Future**

MANPOWER
assistants
shelf-fillers
cashiers

PAYMENT
cash
cheque
credit card

ADVERTISING
shop-window
leaflet
newspaper
local radio
television

Exercise 8

Add more items to the PRESENT side of the diagram.

Exercise 9

Write what you think will be the twenty-first century equivalent on the FUTURE side of the diagram.

Introduction

Consider the following introductions:

1. Do-it-yourself is for the handy homeowner, not the busy manager. Smart managers have learned that they can get more work done by delegating to others.
2. Good filing is generally recognised as an indispensable aid to efficiency.
3. Modern industries need a great many things in addition to their prime raw materials — machinery of different types, power and labour to work them, transport to get the finished products to market ...
4. Anything which indicates what you can or cannot do in certain situations is a policy.
5. Relationships with colleagues is probably one of the most difficult problems with which the junior worker is faced.
6. Selling by mail order originated in the United States of America as a solution to the problems of customers who lived far away from the nearest shop.

Exercise 10

Match the above introductions with the following titles:

(a) Policies   (d) Delegating
(b) The Location of Industries   (e) Promotion
(c) Mail Order   (f) Filing

Exercise 11

Decide which of the above introductions employs the following:

(a) generalisation   (d) a definition
(b) background narrative   (e) hypothesis*
(c) exemplification   (f) an illustration

*An assumption for the sake of argument

Exercise 12

Select one of the Writing Questions 1–5 above and write a composition of approximately 300 words, following the answer plan.

Unit 2 DEFINITIONS ────────────────────────────

When writing a composition, it is often appropriate to begin by defining your terms. Consider the following example:

Company Policy

Anything which indicates what you can or cannot do in a certain situation is a policy. It does not have to be written. It may not even have been stated explicitly. But if there is an understanding 'that this is the way we do things round here', then there is a policy.

In the above example, the first sentence constitutes a clear definition of the key term 'policy'. Sentences 2 and 3 amplify the definition by adding more information, and the last sentence summarises the rest of the paragraph by restating the definition in the form of an 'if-then' sentence.

Exercise 1

Below are a number of terms taken at random from Second Level Writing questions. Match the terms to the definitions given:

Trade unions   Nationalisation   Inflation   Barter
Sole trader   Commodities   Insurance   Economy

(a) Trade by the direct exchange of goods without using money or other medium of exchange.
(b) The act of bringing land, industries and trade under the control and ownership of the nation.
(c) Any useful article or substance, especially foodstuffs and raw materials.
(d) An organised system for the production, distribution and consumption of the needs of society.
(e) Associations of employees formed to improve conditions of employment by means of collective bargaining.
(f)   A rise in the general level of prices caused by an excess of demand over supply and linked to an increase in the supply of money.
(g) Someone who owns their* own business, manages its affairs, provides the capital and bears all the risk.
(h) The practice of sharing among many persons risks to life and property that would normally be suffered by only a few.

*See the grammatical note on this phenomenon in First Level Reading Unit 2.

Exercise 2

Here are some more terms taken at random from Second Level Writing questions. Supply definitions:

(a) ambition _____

(b) nuclear weapons _____

(c) disarmament _____

(d) the generation gap _____

(e) credit cards _____

(f) zoos _____

(g) flexitime _____

(h) job sharing _____

Note: A definition should be the same part of speech as the thing defined, i.e. a noun should be defined by a noun or a noun phrase, and an adverb by another adverb or adverbial phrase.

Writing questions

Write about 300 words on the following topics:

1. Give your views on the nationalisation of industry.
2. Discuss some of the problems that may arise in a country if the majority of its population is concentrated in urban areas.
3. Indicate, with reasons, the kinds of insurance essential for a large business enterprise.
4. Make suggestions as to how the so-called 'generation gap' can be overcome.
5. Give your views on monopolies.
6. Discuss how consumers can be protected against unscrupulous retailers.

Using definitions in compositions

Definitions can be used as the topic sentences of paragraphs with various forms of reinforcement and expansion.

Definition + amplification
As we saw in the example at the start of the unit, the definition can be expanded by the addition of information, e.g.:

> Nationalisation is action by a government to bring land and industries under the control and ownership of the nation. This can result in a fiscal (government) monopoly, or in a situation whereby the government is in competition with private suppliers.

Definition + qualification
The definition is qualified by exclusions, provisions, etc.:

> The generation gap is usually considered to be the incompatibility in ideas and lifestyle between elderly and young people, although changes in popular culture and the so-called 'grey revolution' are gradually narrowing the differences between the two groups.

Definition + classification
Classification often occurs either as part of a definition, or in addition to a definition, e.g.:

> Rates are a form of taxation levied by a local authority to fund local services. A new variety of rate is the poll tax, which is based not on land value but on occupancy.

Note the construction:

> X is a kind/form/class/type/variety of . . .

Exercise 3

From the following list, form ten pairs of words linked by classification. Put the individual term on the left and the class to which it belongs on the right, e.g.:

> (individual) cotton − fabric (class)

metal	bucket	book	centipede	trawler
lorry	tool	platinum	garment	pump
ship	insect	waistcoat	machine	dictionary
hoe	garage	container	vehicle	structure

Exercise 4

As above, form ten pairs from the following lists:

Individual		Class	
accountancy	duty	crime	penalty
calculator	electricity	currency	profession
catering	fine	device	service
coinage	fraud	document	surcharge
contract	secretary	employee	utility

Exercise 5

For each of the 20 pairs of words, write a definition similar to the following:

Cotton is a type of fabric which is used for making shirts and bed sheets.

Exercise 6

Study the following definitions and, using your own words as far as possible, transform them into a short composition by completing the outline below:

Authorised dealership	One given official permission to trade in a given commodity.
Guarantee	A promise by the supplier that an article sold is of good quality and that any fault for which the supplier is responsible will be made good within a given period.
List price	A retail price to the consumer fixed by the manufacturer and published in a list.
Recommended price	The prices which the manufacturer advises the retailer to charge.
Sale or return	An agreement which allows a buyer to return goods within a stated or reasonable time.
Trade Descriptions Act	A law which makes it an offence to give a false description of goods offered for sale.
Warranty	A statement by the seller that goods are fit for the purposes for which they are sold.

Protecting the Consumer

The _____ is always at risk from unscrupulous _____, but there are various steps which can be taken to protect the _____. One of these is _____ (define + amplify/qualify/classify).
Another measure which serves to _____ is _____ (define, etc.).
Some countries have introduced laws which _____ (define, etc.).
In addition, there should be _____ (define, etc.).
Retailers should be made to provide _____ (define, etc.).

Exercise 7

Below are definitions of four different types of monopoly. Use the definitions as the basis of your arguments for answering the following question:

Give your views on monopolies.

Pure monopoly	A market situation in which there is only one supplier of a commodity and therefore no competition.
Fiscal monopoly	A monopoly held by the state for the production and sale of certain commodities in order to obtain maximum revenue e.g. salt, tobacco.
Natural monopoly	A monopoly which exists because the entire demand for a given product can be met by one producer operating on the smallest viable commercial scale.
Public monopoly	A monopoly which belongs to the government by law, usually a public service, e.g. mail.

Exercise 8

Discuss some of the problems that may arise in a country if the majority of its population is concentrated in urban areas.

Useful terms:

urban	built up, town or city areas
ring development	tendency of cities to grow outwards; prosperous suburbs are built, leaving central areas to run to slums
slums	dirty, overcrowded housing areas of high crime rate

Complete the following:

(Title) _____

Although the term 'urban areas' is becoming synonymous with social problems, this has not always been the case. Urban areas are _____ (definition). However, these can be _____ (amplification/ qualification/classification).

The concept of urban ring development is particularly linked to social problems.

_____

(Continue with your own views)

Introducing definitions

There are numerous words, signs or expressions that are used to signal a definition:

i.e. . . .   that is . . .   that is to say . . .   we mean . . .   by which I mean . . .
viz. . . .   broadly . . .   roughly . . .   − . . . −   sometimes defined as . . .
' . . . . '   , ... ,

Here are some examples using these signs or expressions:

1. The lecture was about defoliation, *i.e.* the process of killing off the leaves of trees and other vegetation.
2. He complained about cynics, *that is*, people who know the price of everything and the value of nothing.
3. The danger of inflation − unhealthy growth in the money supply − is greater than ever before.
4. The scientist demonstrated osmosis, *sometimes defined as* the process of transfer from areas of high saturation to areas of low saturation.
5. When we speak of the market being saturated, *we mean* it cannot absorb any more goods.
6. The paratroopers took to 'yomping', marching over long distances carrying all they needed on their backs.

Exercise 9

Practise these constructions with the definitions given in Exercises 6, 7 and 8.

Exercise 10

Answer in full one of the Writing Questions 1−6 above.

Unit 3　COMPARISON ────────────────────────────

To say what something is like, or what it is unlike, often reveals things about it which we would otherwise not notice. It gives us a new and fresh look at the subject. Comparison, therefore, can serve a number of functions in an argument.
　Consider the following:

Supervisors

The manager must depend, to a **greater or lesser** extent, on one or more of the staff to take supervisory roles. Clearly, there must be **as** good a relationship **as** possible between the manager and the supervisor.

　The supervisor is sometimes known as an assistant manager, or under-manager, and has an area of responsibility **which in many ways parallels** that of the manager. **Like** the manager, he or she is often under pressure from above and below. But a supervisor who is **as soft as butter** is bound to fail, because a section without leadership is **like a headless monster. 'If you can't stand the heat, keep out of the kitchen'** is good advice to a faint-hearted would-be supervisor.

Explicit comparison

> *Like* the manager, the supervisor is often under pressure from above and from below.

> Commerce, *like* all other human activities, is not static but dynamic.

Note also:

> The supervisor *resembles* the manager *in that* . . .
> 　　　　　　　　　*is similar to*
> The supervisor is *as* pressurised *as* the manager.

Negative comparison (contrast — see First Level Writing, Unit 5)

> *Unlike* stock in shop-windows, a mail order catalogue does not need dusting.

> Direct mailing is *not as* effective *as* door-to-door selling.

Simile

> An efficient company is *like* a well-oiled machine.

The similarity between a company and a machine is figurative, suggesting smooth operation and parts fitting together harmoniously.

Analogy

> Do-it-yourself is for the handy homeowner, not the busy executive. Smart managers have learned that they can get more work done by delegating to others.

As in the case of simile, the point is made by comparison with a situation which is not obviously similar, but whose parallels serve to reinforce the point.

Emphasis

Combinations of comparative and superlative forms and 'as ... as possible' constructions lend emphasis to the argument, e.g.:

> There is *no better way than* delegating to get your subordinates working at their highest capacity.

> *More than anything else,* the supervisor has to have such information as will enable him to carry out his duties effectively.

> *The simpler* the system, *the better.*

> The businessman wants to produce his goods *as economically as he can* and get them to the purchaser in *the cheapest and most convenient* way.

Writing questions

Write about 300 words on the following:
1. Outline some ways by which you think that employer–employee relations could be improved.
2. Discuss the advantages and disadvantages of a shorter working week.
3. What part do you think the state should play in assisting people to lead happy and satisfying lives?
4. Modern music trends.
5. It has been said that life without ambition is not worth living. Give your views on this statement.

Exercise 1   Employer–employee relations

Study the table overleaf:

(a) Discuss and fill the gaps comparing past and present conditions.
(b) Complete the third column with your suggestions for future improvement.

	Past	Present	Future
Working week	Up to 6 days or more	_____	?
Hours per day	_____	As few as 6	
Holidays	A few days per year at best	_____	
Rewards	_____	Salaries, shares, bonuses, benefits	
Worker participation in management decisions	Nil	_____	
Conditions	Unhealthy	_____	

Exercise 2   A shorter working week means . . .

Discuss, and add more items under the axis below:

Less   **More**

◄ — — — — — — — — — | — — — — — — — — — ►

productivity   leisure
time on the job   time with the family

_____   _____
_____   _____
_____   _____
_____   _____

Exercise 3   Life without ambition

Life without ambition is like a boat without a rudder.

This is an example of a 'simile', a comparison between two things which are not actually similar other than in a 'figurative' sense.

Think of some items to complete the following similes:

(a) _____ like a cat with the cream.
(b) _____ like a headless monster.
(c) _____ like a fish out of water.
(d) _____ like a dose of salts.
(e) _____ like a dream come true.

(f) _____ like a man with no arms.
(g) _____ like a bird.
(h) _____ like a thief in the night.
(i) _____ like the sun shining through the clouds.
(j) _____ like a knight in shining armour.

Exercise 4   Modern music trends

Discuss and make observations comparing modern music trends with music in the past, according to the following criteria:

Criterion	Past	Present	Trend
(a) Instruments			
(b) Volume level			
(c) Compositional complexity			
(d) Lyrics (words)			
(e) Styles of entertainers			
(f) Recording techniques			
(g) Recording media (tape, etc.)			
(h) Domestic equipment			
(i) Marketing techniques			
(j) Use of other media (radio, TV)			

Exercise 5   What part should the state play in assisting people to live happy and satisfying lives?

Fill the gaps in the following passage:

_____(a)_____

_____(b)_____ the state aims to make people _____(c)_____ productive, _____(d)_____ it should seek to make their lives happier and _____(e)_____ satisfying. _____(f)_____ a well-oiled machine works _____(g)_____ efficiently, _____(h)_____ a contented individual operates _____(i)_____ effectively.

It is a medical fact that a person who is happy is much _____(j)_____ likely to take sick leave _____(k)_____ one who is depressed, and _____(l)_____ in the proverb, all work and no play makes Jack a dull boy. _____(m)_____ leisure time and _____(n)_____ facilities are therefore the first step towards improving the quality of life.

_____(o)_____ the ancients with their amphitheatres, the state should provide cultural and sporting venues to cater for the needs of the populace. The theatre should be _____(p)_____ accessible to the modern man-in-the-street _____(q)_____ it was to his Athenian counterpart, and modern spectator sports such as football play a role _____(r)_____ that of the gladiators in ancient Rome.

_____(s)_____ leisure time and recreational facilities are available, _____(t)_____ the people will be, and there can never be _____(u)_____ in the way of sporting facilities or public entertainment available. '_____(v)_____ you sow, _____(w)_____ shall you reap'. A state can only expect _____(x)_____ much from its people _____(y)_____ it is prepared to invest in their wellbeing. _____(z)_____, a grateful people is more likely to exert efforts to support the state.

Exercise 6

Answer one of the Writing Questions 1–5 above.

Unit 4 CAUSE AND EFFECT

An important part of the argument in a piece of writing involves explaining the CAUSE or EFFECT of facts presented by the writer.
  Emphasis can be placed on the cause or the effect:

CAUSE	*Because of* . (x) . , . (y) .
EFFECT	. (x) ., *as a result* . (y) .

Here are some examples of expressions of CAUSE and EFFECT in use:

Cause

1. Introducing the point:

   Because of the tendency of pigeons to fly back to the same place, they have been used as a means of communication since antiquity.

2. Following the point:

   The encroachment of viewing on activities other than listening to the radio and cinema going has been broadly impartial. *This is because* each viewer tends to reduce the time he gives to activities which matter to him least.

Other ways of expressing cause

NOUNS — (x is) a cause of ⎫
                 a reason for ⎬ (y)
                 a factor in   ⎭

CONJUNCTIONS — (x) because ⎫
                          since ⎬ (y)
                          as   ⎭

VERBS — (x) causes ⎫
                 leads to   ⎪
                 brings about ⎬ (y)
                 creates   ⎪
                 results in   ⎪
                 produces   ⎭

Exercise 1

Can you add any more ways of expressing CAUSE?

_____

_____

_____

Exercise 2

Invert Example 2 above, so that the CAUSE introduces the point.

Effect

1. Introducing the point:

> *As a result of* experiments with dangerous gases, Sir Humphrey Davy invented the first safety lamp.

2. Following the point:

> Before the commencement of the nineteenth century, coal itself was employed for the purpose of propping the roofs of coal mines. *As a result* only sixty per cent of the produce of each mine was raised above the ground.

Other ways of expressing effect

NOUNS — (y is) a result
an outcome
a consequence   of (x)
an effect

ADJECTIVE — (y is) due to   (x)

ADVERBS — (x) therefore
hence   (y)
consequently

VERBS — (y) results
stems   from (x)
arises

Exercise 3

Can you add more ways of expressing EFFECT?

_____

_____

_____

Exercise 4

Invert Example 2 above so that the expression of EFFECT introduces the point.

Writing questions

> Write about 300 words on each of the following:
>
> 1. Inflation.
> 2. Labour-saving devices.
> 3. The contribution of reading to success and/or happiness in life.
> 4. The qualities to which you would attach most importance if you were interviewing a candidate for a business appointment.

Exercise 5   Inflation

Some notes on the causes of inflation are given below. Use them as the basis for a composition consisting of four short paragraphs. Practise using EXEMPLIFYING discourse markers (see First Level Writing, Unit 3).
  Begin your composition as follows:

The Causes of Inflation

There are four major theories on the causes of inflation ...

Theory	Cause
Quantitative	Wage payments, shopping and saving habits become unstable in relation to each other.
Keynesian	People try to buy more goods and services than can be supplied.
Cost-push	Workers try to take higher wages, and businessmen more profit, than their output permits.
Structural	The gap between imports and exports in a country leads to a fall in the international value of its currency.

Exercise 6 Labour-saving devices

Below is a list of labour-saving devices in the home and in the office. In the EFFECT column, make notes on how these devices save labour, e.g.:

Vacuum cleaner	No need for manual sweeping with dustpan and brush. Dust collected more efficiently.

Use your notes as a basis for a composition on labour-saving devices.

Device	Effect
HOME microwave oven dishwasher washing machine tumble-drier lawnmower food mixer	
OFFICE word processor intercom fax machine computer photocopier	

Exercise 7 Reading, success and happiness

What is the contribution of reading to success and happiness? Think about this question carefully, and DISCUSS IN GROUPS if possible. Do success and happiness necessarily go together? Might reading lead to one and not the other?

Below are two tables on how reading contributes to success and happiness respectively. Use your notes from your consideration and/or discussion of the question to add to the list of REASONS and RESULTS in each table.

Use the notes from the completed tables as the basis for a composition.

The contribution of reading to success in life	
Reason	**Result**
Source of information on any subject	More knowledge is available to enrich work and other interests
_____	_____
_____	_____
_____	_____

The contribution of reading to happiness in life	
Reason	**Result**
A world of fantasy can be found in fiction	The reader can escape from the dull reality of life
_____	_____
_____	_____
_____	_____

Exercise 8   The qualities to which you would attach most importance if you were interviewing a candidate for a business appointment

Discuss, then list the important qualities.

WRITE a composition EXPLAINING your choice of qualities; practise expressions of cause and effect, e.g.:

Team spirit *stems from* gamesmanship on the playing field and *leads to* better collaboration.

Unit 5 POSSIBILITY AND LIKELIHOOD _____

Consider the following:

The loud and overbearing characters of some people *can* make them very difficult to work with, and *it is unlikely* that there *could* be an office without its share of personality clashes. *It is* however *possible* to avoid these dangers, and *probably* the best advice is hear all, see all and say nothing — if you *are capable*! Unfortunately, gossip *can* be a major source of entertainment, and it *may* be difficult for some people to keep to themselves all the information they *might* have heard.

Perhaps ...
Possibly ...
Probably ...

It is	impossible unlikely	to/that
	improbable	that

Something	can could may might	happen

Ability

to be	able enabled	to do	something
	capable	of doing	

Writing questions

Write about 300 words on the following:

1. What do you think could be done to ease the worsening traffic congestion on the roads as car ownership increases?
2. Could there be life on other planets?
3. How do you think world peace could be achieved?
4. How can mankind prevent the extinction of endangered species?
5. What can be done to prevent further damage to the environment?

Exercise 1   Traffic congestion

Discuss the following and decide how they could contribute to the reduction of traffic congestion:

working from home − computers
                       data links
                       fax machines
                       other telecommunications
   improved railways
   improved motorways
   improved public transport in cities − surface
                                            underground
   heavy vehicle restrictions
   city centre airports − helicopters
                            vertical take-off aircraft

Others: _____

_____

_____

Exercise 2

Write the composition.

Exercise 3   Life on other planets

Study the following information about stars and planets:

The solar system

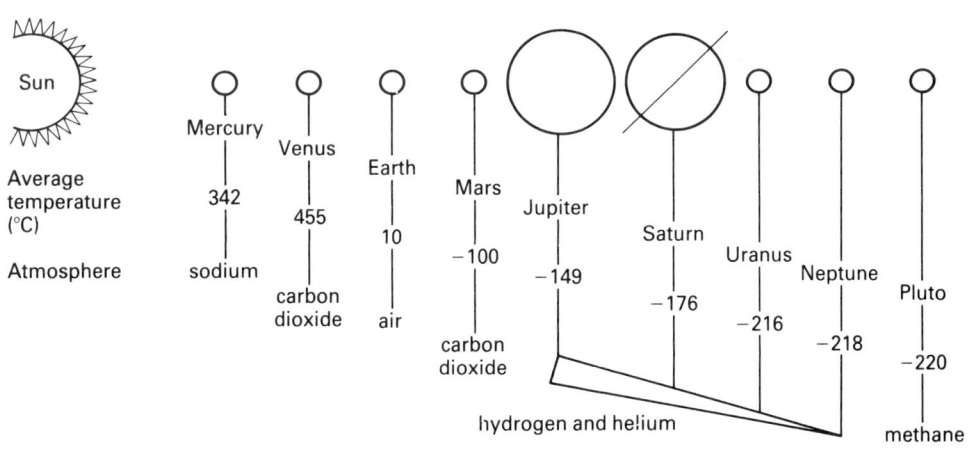

Continued overleaf

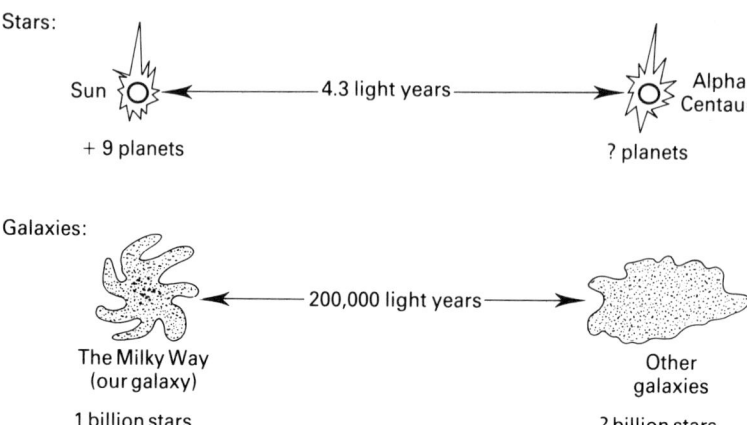

Stars:

Sun + 9 planets ← 4.3 light years → Alpha Centauri ? planets

Galaxies:

The Milky Way (our galaxy) ← 200,000 light years → Other galaxies

1 billion stars
? billion planets

? billion stars
? billion planets

Exercise 4

Discuss and write a composition.

Exercise 5   World peace

Consider the table below. Discuss each of the criteria and decide what could be done in relation to them to aid the cause of world peace:

Criteria	Suggestions
The United Nations	
Language	
Third World debt	
Trade competition	
Arms control	
Ideological systems	
Racial conflict	
Colonialism	
Nationalism	
Religion	
Additions? *Human nature*	

Exercise 6

Write the composition.

Exercise 7   Endangered species

Here are some examples of endangered species. Study and discuss the table. Use a dictionary to check any unfamiliar terms. Decide what you think could be done to save them.

Species	Why endangered	Measures
Tiger	Hunting for sport Destruction of environment	
Leopard	Killed by poachers for skin (used in coats)	
Elephant	Shot by poachers for tusks (ivory)	
Rhinoceros	Shot by poachers for horn (believed in Far East to be an aphrodisiac)	
Giant panda	Environment disturbed by mankind – harm to food supply	
Whale	Hunted for food and oil products despite world bans on hunting	

Exercise 8

Write a composition outlining your suggestions.

Exercise 9   Damage to the environment

Study and discuss the following report:

> By the end of the twenty-first century, mankind itself will be close to extinction. The rain forests will have been cleared, and soil microbes will produce vast quantities of carbon dioxide from the decaying soil, adding to that already placed in the atmosphere by the burning of fossil fuels. Due to the overfishing of the oceans, an oversupply of dead plankton will give off sulphur and methane gases, assisting aerosol gases in the depletion of the ozone layer. As a result of the damage to the atmosphere and global overheating, floods and famine will have decimated the earth's population.

Exercise 10

Write a composition outlining what could be done now to prevent such a scenario.

Unit 6   OBLIGATION AND NECESSITY ─────────────

There are some things that we ought to do because they are morally right or
expected by convention, good manners or common sense; these are obligations.
There are other things from which we have no escape and which we must do
out of necessity, e.g. breathing. When giving instructions or guidance it is common
to express obligations as if they were necessities. Contrast the following:

Obligation

When speaking on the telephone the operator *should* always try to sound
friendly and helpful. She *should* listen to, and show an interest in, what the
caller has to say. A medium to low-pitched voice *is preferable* and consonants
should be emphasised. She *should* learn to recognise all who use the telephone
within the organisation, and familiarity with the organisation's work *is
desirable*. Personnel officers *ought to* be aware of these requirements when
recruiting staff. Finally, companies *owe it to* themselves to install an efficient
telephone system.

One	should (not)			
	ought (not)			
	owes it has a duty an obligation	(to someone)	to	do something

Note also:

It is preferable
　　　desirable　　　to . . .

Necessity

At some stage, businessmen *have to* make the decision to let others do some
of their work. At this point, *it is necessary* to understand the true meaning
of delegation. You *must* know the capabilities of those to whom you delegate,
and you *have to* give them all the facts. *It is essential* that those working under
you understand and agree to meet your standards. You *must* also impress
upon your assistants the *need to* earn the respect of others.

One	must (not)		do something
	has does not have needs	to	
	need not		

Note also:

It is necessary
        essential   to . . .
        vital
        etc.

Advisability

Anyone thinking of opening his own shop for the first time *would be well advised* to gain experience by taking a job in the trade.

It is	advisable wise	to do something
One would be	well advised sensible etc.	

Writing questions

Write about 300 words on the following:

1. What advice would you give to a person wishing to set up as a sole trader?
2. Suggest ways in which the general public can help the police in their fight against crime.
3. Do you think that housing should be provided by local councils or by private enterprise, or a combination of both? Give reasons for your answer.
4. Discuss the circumstances in which you think that government subsidies should be given to assist industry.
5. What do you think is the greatest problem facing your country today? How do you think it could be overcome?

Exercise 1   Advice to a sole trader

Definition: a sole trader is one who owns his own business, manages its affairs, provides the capital and bears all the risk.

There follows a list of various courses of action open to a person wishing to become a sole trader.

(a) Discuss.
(b) Decide how necessary they are.
(c) Write a composition based on your conclusions.

Options:

(i)   Obtain a business plan.
(ii) Employ a market research consultant.
(iii) Find suitable premises.
(iv) Decide on a suitable product.
(v)   Hire an accountant.
(vi) Go to university to study business management.
(vii) Lie to your bank manager to obtain a loan.
(viii) Work for another sole trader for some time.
(ix) Make sure you understand what is involved.
(x)   Talk to experienced sole traders.

Exercise 2   The general public and the police

Consider the following newspaper report:

DONCHESTER EVENING ECHO — Monday July 3rd 1997

Have-a-go Hero Killer Lynched

Three men tonight face trial accused of the murder of a man who had earlier stabbed a brave passer-by following an attempted robbery in South Donchester yesterday.

Mr James Long of Brabham, South Donchester, went to the aid of pensioner Mrs Nellie Dean when Reginald Nail, an escaped convict, tried to snatch her handbag. Mr Long tried to perform a citizen's arrest on Nail but was fatally stabbed during the struggle. Later yesterday, a group from the South Donchester Neighbourhood Watch organisation caught Nail and gave him a severe beating, as a result of which he died later in hospital.

The Prime Minister today sternly criticised what he called 'vigilante groups', saying that the law would not tolerate kangaroo courts and lynch mobs.

(a) Make sure you understand the meaning of the following terms: use a dictionary if necessary:

citizens' arrest   kangaroo court
lynching   have-a-go hero
neighbourhood watch scheme   vigilante

(b) Discuss the article: decide to what extent the above concepts are advisable or necessary.

(c) Consider the following areas. Discuss and decide what should be done by the public to help the police:

SECURITY	home	car
EDUCATION	in schools	in the home
CO-OPERATION	giving information or evidence	active involvement of bystanders
SELF-HELP	community protection groups	carrying personal weapons

(d) Use your conclusions as the basis of your composition.

Exercise 3   Who should provide housing?

Fill the gaps; notice how many require 'would' or 'should':

_____ (a) _____

It goes without saying that every citizen ____(b)____ be provided with adequate housing. How that housing is provided is, however, a matter of debate. It is ____(c)____ that local councils provide a certain amount of housing for emergency cases of sudden homelessness. On the other hand, contractors ____(d)____ keep their workers busy and their businesses active. In any case, a choice between public and private sectors ____(e)____ be available.

In the past occupiers of council housing ____(f)____ pay rent and ____(g)____ not purchase their property outright. Anyone who wanted to own their own place ____(h)____ buy from a contractor. However, many people nowadays believe that council tenants ____(i)____ be given the option to buy their houses.

Of course, there will always be a demand for larger, more prestigious houses which local councils ____(j)____ provide. It ____(k)____ be possible, and is indeed ____(l)____, to cater for all requirements by providing a mixed market. One point which ____(m)____ be made, however, is that building standards ____(n)____ be carefully supervised. If ____(o)____, contractors ____(p)____ be supervised by local authority engineers, and quality ____(q)____ thus be controlled.

Exercise 4   Government subsidies to industry

Consider the following industries.

(a) Discuss whether you think they should under any circumstances be given government subsidies.
(b) Complete the table.
(c) Use it as the basis for a composition.

Industry	Should subsidy be given?	Under what circumstances?
Farming Fishing Arms manufacture Car manufacture Banking Insurance Arts and crafts Chemicals Nuclear power Mining		

Exercise 5   Your country's major problem

This is a particularly fertile subject for discussion, ideal for group work.

(a) Note that you are being asked about one problem – the greatest one. Discuss and decide what the greatest problem is. If it is not possible to reach a consensus, let each student decided for himself or herself on the basis of the discussion.
(b) Taking the following matrix as an outline, list some steps that should be taken to solve the problem.
(c) Use your conclusions as the basis for your composition.

Sector	Solution: We should ...
Religion Politics Society Government Industry Trade Environment	

Unit 7 CONDITION AND HYPOTHESIS

We often have to imagine states of affairs that may or may not exist, and draw conclusions about what might happen purely on the basis of supposition. Moreover, our suppositions about hypothetical events usually depend on conditions, thus:

> The threat of nuclear war *might* disappear completely *if* the superpowers can continue their present policies.

> Pay Policy
> A policy of paying above the going rate is fine *if* that is what happens and *as long as* the application of the policy is consistent, but *unless* you can ensure absolute fairness the policy is worthless. For example, *if* one employee *were to* divulge that he or she had received preferential treatment, the policy *would be* seen not as an incentive but as a cause of division. *So long as* confidentiality is maintained, high incentives can be effective, but *if* it happens that too much information is shared between employees, you are faced with a formula for disaster. *No matter* what you say to placate the disaffected, suspicions *will* persist. *In case of* pay policy problems, it *would be* wise to go to arbitration, *provided* no immediate solution is at hand, *otherwise* you face a long and bitter struggle. *If* our company *had* realised this fact, we *would have* avoided the confrontation of 1990 and the ensuing strike *would not have* taken place, *whether or not* the cash was available and *even though* the militants were restless.

Condition

If So long as As long as Provided Providing	anything new nothing something that the best what we hope the worst this event	happens occurs	the matter our problem the case this predicament the crisis	will	be resolved go away evaporate vanish diminish solve itself
Should		happen occur			

In case In the event that	something what we fear the worst	happens occurs	prepare for a disappointment think of another plan you will need a lawyer
Should	a disaster that nothing	happen occur	secure your bank account you had better book a flight you should phone your agent

It	anything like that such a thing an accident something	were to should chanced to	happen occur befall	I he she you	could lose your job would be left alone might lose a lot of money would be pleased
	a miracle a disaster what you predict what she says	befell happened occurred		we they	could retire rich would die happy might live to regret it

Negative conditions

    No matter what happens, this will be the result.
    Unless this happens, that will be the result.
    This had better happen, *otherwise* that will be the result.
    However much you protest, the plan will go ahead.
    Whatever the outcome, our firm will be the loser.

Condition and contrast

    Even $\begin{array}{l}\textit{if}\\\textit{though}\end{array}$ something happens, this will be the result.
    Whether or not something happens, this will be the result.

Exercise 1

Complete the following:

(a) If we are sick, _____
(b) If I had seen the other car, _____
(c) If I had the money, _____
(d) If you are not careful, _____
(e) If I were the boss, _____
(f) If he does not hurry up, _____
(g) If we had been warned, _____
(h) If the cap fits, _____
(i) If I had three wishes, _____
(j) If only he had realised, _____

Note: The comma is required when the conditional clause comes before the main clause, but vice versa it is omitted, e.g.:

    If winter comes, the sheep will starve.
    The sheep will starve if winter comes.

Writing questions

Write about 300 words on the following:

1. It has been said that the wholesaler is superfluous in the chain of production and that his disappearance would enable goods to be sold at lower prices than at present. Give your views on this.
2. If you were compelled to leave your country, which other country would you choose to live in, and why? How would you go about building a new life there?
3. A friend of yours will be starting work soon and has asked you whether or not you think it is advisable to join a trade union. What advice would you give this friend?
4. Is there any decision you have made concerning your education or career which you regret? What changes would you have made in your life if you had known what you know now?
5. If you had the power, what would you change to make the world a better place?

Exercise 2 The wholesaler

What would the economic system be like without wholesalers? Consider the following factors:

prices	distribution	communication
availability	advertising	marketing
perishable goods	mail order	competition

Others: _____   _____   _____

What would be the advantages if there were no wholesalers? What would be the disadvantages?
   Discuss and write the composition.

Exercise 3 If you were compelled to leave your country ...

Discuss the following and write the composition:

(a) Where would you choose to live?
    Why?
(b) How would you set about building a new life?
    Money
    Language
    Job
    Home
    Social life
    Family, etc.

Exercise 4 Joining a trade union

Base your advice to your friend on the following considerations. Make sure you know the meanings of the following terms: use a dictionary if necessary:

	If you are in a trade union ...	If you are not in a trade union ...
'closed shop' pay negotiations unfair treatment strikes picketing 'blacklegs' OTHER FACTORS?		

Exercise 5 'If I had known ...'

Complete the following:

(Title) _____

Few people can maintain with honesty that _____.

In my own experience, there are several decisions _____.

One which springs readily to mind is _____.

If I had known then what I know now, _____.

Another _____ (continue)

Exercise 6 Making the world a better place

Discuss the following:

(a) If there were one thing you could change, what would it be? Why?
(b) If you had sweeping powers, what would you change in the following areas?:
    Religion
    Politics
    Economy
    Energy
    Technology
    The environment

Other potential areas of improvement: _____

_____

Write the composition; here is a possible outline:

_____

If there were only one thing in the world I could change, it would be ____.

I feel this is necessary because _____.

If on the other hand I had sweeping powers to change the world, I would
_____ .
Firstly, _____ .
The reason is _____ .
Secondly, _____ .
This is due to _____ .
In addition, _____ .
As a result of this _____ .
Finally, _____ .
In this way, _____ .

Appendix 1
Examination Technique

Any good examination will measure accurately the candidates' levels of language whether or not they are familiar with the tests and regardless of whether they are experienced in taking examinations. The London Chamber's examiners are careful to ensure that candidates are not tripped up by obscure or complicated instructions and they do not set traps for candidates to fall into. There are no 'trick' questions! On the contrary, they do everything possible to ensure that candidates show what they *can* do rather than what they can*not* do. Even at the marking stage they will make allowances if they feel a candidate has been misled or confused by something on the examination paper.

Nevertheless, they must reach a judgement in the end as to whether candidates have made the best possible use of the opportunities the examination paper offers them. Not all candidates do this. Too many candidates see an examination as a threat rather than as an opportunity. They have a short time to show what they have learnt on a course lasting months or even years. Their future may depend on how well or how badly they do this. This leads some candidates to panic. If they knew how many of their fellow candidates felt the same way, they would be more relaxed. So the following hints are intended to give candidates a more positive attitude to taking 'English for Commerce', and British examinations in general, and to ensure that they make the best of the opportunities offered.

Timing

1. Note how long you have to do the paper and then work out how long you will need to spend on each question.
2. Allow about ten minutes at the beginning to read over the question rubrics (instructions) and another ten minutes at the end to review what you have written.
3. Allow more time for the questions that carry more marks.
4. Do not leave the examination room early. Make full use of the time for checking and improvements.

Choosing

1. Choose which questions you are going to answer and the order in which you are going to answer them.
2. Do the questions that carry most marks first.
3. If all questions carry equal marks, do the easiest ones first.

Reading

1. Before you start answering a question, *re*-read the rubric carefully and make sure you understand what you have to do. Read it as many times as you need for this, as many candidates throw away marks by careless reading of the question.
2. Do not assume it is a repetition of some task or question you have practised in class, however similar it may seem. It will usually be different if you look at the details.
3. Where the question gives you data for your answer, ensure that you make full use of that data. It is there for your benefit.
4. Pay attention to the little words in the rubric, e.g.: either/or; both/and; for/against; before/after; all/some; few/many, etc.

Thinking

1. Think about your answer before you start writing.
2. Jot down your thoughts on the paper and work them into a plan if extended writing is required.
3. Make the plan on the answer booklet itself and cross it through. It will give the examiner an idea of what you intended to write in case you do not have time to finish.
4. Good writing has a beginning, a middle and an end so your plan should reflect this. Most reports, essays, memos and letters start with an introduction, then make a series of points related to the introduction and lead to a conclusion deriving from the points. This is reflected in paragraphing.
5. Do not be afraid to use your own ideas and your own experience to answer questions.
6. Your thinking should be concrete rather than abstract, clear rather than vague; and do not make it so complicated that you cannot express it in English. Keep it simple and within the bounds of what you know you can write. Examiners are assessing your English, not your brains.

Writing

1. Start writing only when you have a good idea of what you want to say and arrange your ideas into *paragraphs*.

2. Do not change your mind half way through a question and decide to do another one instead. There will probably not be time to finish another one.

3. Write as well, as quickly and as clearly as you can, remembering that native speakers also make slips of the pen or spelling errors, especially when they are in a hurry.

4. Leave time to read over what you have written at the end to eliminate such errors. Do not be afraid to cross something out and replace it with something better. Examiners are assessing your English, not your calligraphy (handwriting).

5. Even if you could write more, do not go over the time you have allotted for the question. You can always add more at the end of the examination if you find you have time to spare. Additions should be neat and clearly marked for insertion in the proper place.

6. Make sure you write an answer to every question demanded of you. You can gain no marks for questions that are not even begun!

7. Do not write more on any question than the marks are worth. You cannot gain more than full marks!

8. Write leaving enough space between lines for you to insert additions and corrections clearly. If your handwriting is big, write on alternate lines.

9. Do not waste time copying whole questions from the question paper on to the answer book if it is not asked for, but give the minimum referencing needed for the examiner to know which question you are answering.

10. If you are asked to answer in a 'full sentence' and/or 'using your own words' make sure you do so. If not, a brief but adequate answer will be accepted.

11. Do not 'lift' portions of the question unaltered and reproduce them in your answer as this is heavily penalised.

12. On the other hand, if asked to quote or identify words in a passage, make sure you do so.

13. Make sure you distinguish between questions that require you to use your imagination or personal experience, and those which require you to stick to the facts or passage given on the question paper.

Checking

1. Check each answer after you have written it and make any corrections it may need. Cross out mistakes neatly but completely. Do not enclose them in brackets.

2. Check all the answers at the end of the examination in the ten minutes you have allotted.

3. Your vocabulary, spelling and grammar may be shaky but the question paper itself may provide you with models of these which you can use for guidance without merely 'lifting'. Use these models to the full.

4. Re-read all the rubrics. If you find you have overlooked something that was

required in the rubric, now is the time to carry out repairs. A few additional sentences may be all that is needed to bring your answer back on target.

5. If you are asked to give examples, make sure you do. Now is the time to supply them if you have forgotten them, or to add to what you have already given.

6. Make sure each question is properly numbered and that you have supplied all the details required on the front of the answer book.

In conclusion, it should be said that while examination technique alone will not turn a weak candidate into a strong one, it is frequently the case that lack of it ruins the chances of candidates likely to pass. Therefore, candidates approaching the examination should bear in mind the six commandments outlined above:

Time
Choose
Read
Think
Write
Check

Appendix 2   Answer Key

UNIT 1   Address, Date, Salutation and Close

Exercise 1

(a) Jack
(b) 2 Elm Avenue, Southend SS4 7BD
(c) We don't know
(d) P.O. Box No. 82, New Place, Liverpool L69 3HS
(e) Dr D. Black, Principal
(f) Assistant Manager, Claims
(g) No
(h) 66 Grimshaw Gardens, Folkestone, Kent CT20 2PY
(i) No
(j) Jack and Jill

Exercise 2

(a) Letter 1
(b) Letter 2
(c) Letter 3

Exercise 3

(a) Dear Sir
(b) Yours faithfully
(c) Dear Dr Black
(d) Yours sincerely
(e) Dear Jill

Exercise 4

(a) Dear Bill – Yours sincerely/Best wishes/etc.
(b) Dear Mr Willis – Yours sincerely
(c) Dear Sir – Yours faithfully
(d) Dear Marge – Yours sincerely/Love/etc.
(e) Dear Sir – Yours faithfully

Exercise 5

General Dealers Ltd
Mill Lane
London EC1 2BF

The Station Master
British Railways
Little Chippings
Buckinghamshire
MK18 9OL

(date − today's)

Dear Sir

Yours faithfully

_____

Ronald Wrigley

Exercise 6

29 Oak End Lane
Bradford
BD5 4RG

Miss Rosie Lee
The Nook Inn
Ingleton
Derby DE7 8ME

(date − today's)

Dear Rosie

Love
Ben

Exercise 7

149 Great North Road
Motherwell
ML2 2WA

Arthur Pointer, Manager
Gerry's Building Supplies
Grimes Street
Gloucester
GL2 6YH

(date − today's)

Dear Mr Pointer

Yours sincerely

_____

Walter Wimborne

Exercise 8

(a) Dear Sir or Madam
(b) Dear Sir or Madam
(c) Dear Ms Jones

(d) Dear Sir
(e) Dear Mrs Lang

Exercise 9

(a) Date
(b) Sender's address
(c) Receiver's address

(d) Salutation
(e) Complimentary close
(f) Signature

UNIT 2   Addresses

Exercise 1

1. The addressee
2. The name of the company
3. The number and street

4. The town or city
5. The postcode

Exercise 2

(a) Oak End Community Centre
(b) In Step Ltd
(c) Adventure Safaris Ltd
(d) Prudent & Provident
(e) The Farchester Echo

(f) Brite Interiors
(g) Greenhill Lodge
(h) Newfont Council
(i) Sandford Athletic
(j) Greys Instruments Ltd

Exercise 3

(a) the secretary
(b) the manager
(c) the manager
(d) the manager
(e) the editor

(f) the manager
(g) the warden
(h) the chief clerk
(i) the secretary
(j) the manager

Exercise 4

Leicester LE7 4RG
Swansea SA4 1EB
Liverpool L17 4JG
London SE5 2RU
Edinburgh EH3 9YW
Birmingham B4 6DA
Tunbridge Wells TN3 7YD
Southampton SP9 5BE
Slough SL6 3QL
Hemel Hempstead HP2 4RG

Exercise 5

(a) 8	(b) 4	(c) 10	(d) 1	(e) 9
(f) 7	(g) 3	(h) 6	(i) 2	(j) 5

Exercise 6

(a) 2   (b) 3   (c) 10

Exercise 7

(a) Little Essex Street   (c) Western Road
(b) Grimston Gardens   (d) Holborn Circus

Exercise 8

(a) The Old Town Jail
(b) Falcon House
(c) Springfield
(d) Hexagon House
(e) The Foreign and Commonwealth Office

Exercise 9

THE STUDENT

UNIT 3   Reasons for Writing

Exercise 1

(a) about/that/you/for   (f) about
(b) that   (g) for
(c) about/that   (h) that/you
(d) you   (i) you
(e) you   (j) for/about

Exercise 2

(a) apply   (f) ask
(b) apologise   (g) confirm
(c) thank   (h) inquire
(d) inform   (i) complain
(e) invite   (j) request

Exercise 3

THE STUDENT

Exercise 4

(e.g.) (a) seeing
       (b) receiving
       (c) visiting

(d) meeting
(e) (etc.)

Exercise 5

(e.g.) (a) brochure
       (b) prospectus
       (c) report

(d) memo
(e) postcard
(f) (etc.)

Exercise 6

(a) explanation
(b) advice
(c) application
(d) thanks
(e) confirmation

(f) request
(g) warning
(h) information
(i) inquiry
(j) quotation

Exercise 7

(a) With reference to your complaint ...
(b) With reference to your application ...
(c) With reference to your request ...
(d) With reference to your inquiry ...
(e) Thank you for your suggestion ...
(f) Thank you for the information ...
(g) Thank you for the invitation ...
(h) Thank you for the confirmation ...
(i) Thank you for the explanation ...
(j) With reference to your advice ...

Exercise 8

(a) Thank you for confirming the arrangements for the fair.
(b) Thank you for informing me of your opinions on the subject.
(c) Thank you for inquiring about the facilities we provide.
(d) Thank you for advising me that my book is ready for collection.
(e) Thank you for inviting me to the reception for Professor Stern.

Exercise 9

(a) Dear Mr Grey,
     Thank you for your letter of October 10th applying for the post of beverage operative.
(b) Dear Mr Coleridge,
     Thank you for your letter of June 6th inviting me to the annual Lord Byron Evening.
(c) Dear Sir,
     Thank you for your letter of 3rd March confirming my travel arrangements.

Exercise 10

THE STUDENT

UNIT 4   Letters of Request

Exercise 1

We should be grateful if you could explain the delay in the shipment expected on May 1st. You might call us on the above number to save time, otherwise it would be appreciated if you could reply by return.

Exercise 2

(a) would
(b) could/would
(c) would
(d) would

(e) could/would
(f) would
(g) would
(h) could/would

Exercise 3

THE STUDENT

Exercise 4

THE STUDENT

Exercise 5

THE STUDENT

UNIT 5   Additional Requests and Replying to Requests

Exercise 1

(a) also
(b) further
(c) besides
(d) additional
(e) as well as

Exercise 2

(Suggested order, subject to discussion):

1. (d) (most polite)
2. (a)
3. (b)
4. (e)
5. (c)
6. (f) (least polite)

Exercise 3

THE STUDENT

Exercise 4

THE STUDENT

Exercise 5

THE STUDENT

Exercise 6

THE STUDENT

Exercise 7

THE STUDENT

Exercise 8

THE STUDENT

Exercise 9

THE STUDENT

UNIT 6   Further Details

Exercise 1

(a) On Saturday, March 31st, at 2.30 p.m.
(b) On Thursday, April 4th, at 9.35 a.m.
(c) On Wednesday, July 6th, at noon (midday)
(d) On Sunday, October 19th, at midnight
(e) On Monday, January 31st, at 7.15 p.m.

Exercise 2

THE STUDENT

Exercise 3

(a) in	(b) on
(c) from − to	(d) at (in)
(e) (no preposition)	(f) at (in)
(g) at	(h) to
(i) by	(j) to

Exercise 4

THE STUDENT

Exercise 5

THE STUDENT

Exercise 6

THE STUDENT

Exercise 7

THE STUDENT

Exercise 8

THE STUDENT

Exercise 9

THE STUDENT

Exercise 10

THE STUDENT

UNIT 7 Review

Exercise 1

(a) (number, road)	(b) (London postcode)
(c) (number, road)	(d) Madam
(e) faithfully	(f) (name)
(g) (date)	(h) (number, road)
(i) (town, postcode)	(j) faithfully
(k) (date)	(l) (town)
(m) Mr Rich	(n) sincerely
(o) (signature)	(p) (number, road)
(q) (number, road)	(r) Dr Benn
(s) Yours sincerely	(t) signature

Exercise 2

(a) for	(b) your
(c) (date)	(d) reference
(e) application	(f) regret
(g) inform	(h) Thank
(i) for	(j) sincerely
(k) Madam	(l) writing
(m) inform	(n) enclose
(o) further	(p) please
(q) forward	(r) receiving
(s) earliest	(t) convenience

Exercise 3

THE STUDENT

Exercise 4

I would be grateful if you could explain the incident at the Polo Club last Saturday, although I should be surprised if there could be an acceptable explanation. You might also consider writing to the committee to ask if they would consider a hearing, since otherwise your membership could be revoked.

Exercise 5

THE STUDENT

FIRST LEVEL READING ————————————————————————————

UNIT 1   Understanding Vocabulary

Exercise 1

(a) otherwise
(b) conditions
(c) altogether
(d) acquire
(e) principal

(f) means
(g) delights
(h) consume
(i) maintain
(j) superseded

Exercise 2

(a) distractions
(b) difficult
(c) general
(d) acquire
(e) many

(f) more
(g) maintain
(h) pleasure
(i) altogether
(j) successive

Exercise 3

(a) replaced/taken the place of
(b) main/most important
(c) diversions/activities which take away people's attention
(d) distract/take away
(e) following/coming later

Exercise 4

(a) appearance
(b) consumption
(c) diversion
(d) acquisition
(e) delight

(f) maintenance
(g) encroach
(h) supersession
(i) please
(j) gift

Exercise 5

THE STUDENT

Exercise 6

THE STUDENT

Exercise 7

THE STUDENT

Exercise 8

(a) party
(b) crowd
(c) ice
(d) slush
(e) steam

(f) jars
(g) machines
(h) apparatus
(i) nets

Exercise 9

(a) sea creatures/organisms of the ocean
(b) penguins
(c) parts of the ship
(d) deck

(e) occupation
(f) technician
(g) seaman
(h) sightseer

Exercise 10

(a) inhospitable/harsh
(b) protected
(c) very small

(d) empty/unfit to live in
(e) friendly/gregarious

Exercise 11

THE STUDENT

Exercise 12

(a) beginning
(c) exploit
(e) famous
(g) situation
(i) Continent
(k) bulletins
(m) extremely
(o) financiers
(q) organised
(s) telegraph

(b) century
(d) pigeon's
(f) news
(h) pigeons
(j) result
(l) engage
(n) transactions
(p) newspaper
(r) carrier
(t) networks

Exercise 13

THE STUDENT

Exercise 14

(a) during	(b) before
(c) completely	(d) still
(e) whose	(f) Since
(g) yet	(h) first
(i) new	(j) certain
(k) same	(l) ingenious
(m) Thus	(n) along
(o) return	(p) as
(q) so	(r) that
(s) safely	(t) themselves

Exercise 15

THE STUDENT

UNIT 2   Understanding Reference

Exercise 1

(a) people who use a car
(b) (other) people who travel by train
(c) a country
(d) of the country
(e) the train travellers

Exercise 2

(a) of this year
(b) = when
(c) the thing
(d) the author
(e) the author
(f) the thing
(g) the author's
(h) the author and his wife

Exercise 3

(a) (propaganda) as defined in the previous sentence
(b) people
(c) people
(d) a person
(e) propaganda
(f) those who use propaganda (propagandists)
(g) when propaganda is not bad
(h) propaganda as described in the previous sentence
(i) most people
(j) idea

Exercise 4

(a) a coalminer
(b) miners
(c) by explosion
(d) a young Cornishman
(e) 'fire damp'

(f) Davy
(g) discoveries
(h) Davy's
(i) inventions
(j) the safety lamp

Exercise 5

(a) some people
(b) reading
(c) the habit
(d) people
(e) of reading
(f) others
(g) to indulge the inclination and cultivate the capacity
(h) the others
(i) to indulge the inclination ..., etc.
(j) the others

Exercise 6

(a) It
(d) it
(g) so
(j) this
(m) such
(p) they

(b) which/that
(e) himself/themselves
(h) who
(k) they
(n) its
(q) they

(c) this
(f) he/they
(i) their
(l) they
(o) it

Exercise 7

(a) it
(d) our
(g) their
(j) their
(m) Thus
(p) that
(s) ourselves

(b) this
(e) their
(h) this
(k) their
(n) its
(q) this
(t) our

(c) which
(f) their
(i) their
(l) others
(o) those
(r) we

UNIT 3   Skimming and Scanning

Exercise 1

(a) (iii)
(b) (ii)
(c) (ii)

Exercise 2

(a) #3   (b) #1   (c) none   (d) #2   (e) #1

Exercise 3

(a) Paragraph 1, sentence 3: 'Aeroplanes ...'
(b) Paragraph 2, sentence 4: 'Members ...'
(c) Paragraph 3, sentence 3: 'Those who ...'
(d) Paragraph 2, sentence 3: 'Fruit ...'
(e) Paragraph 1, sentence 4: 'Even without ...'

Exercise 4

(e.g.):
(a) He was a novelist/writer.
(b) Its ability to travel at twenty miles per hour.
(c) They can make in a day a journey which once took weeks.
(d) They become lazy.
(e) People become anxious, nervous and lose the power to relax.

Exercise 5

(a) (i)
(b) (iii)

Exercise 6

(a) #3   (b) #5   (c) #1   (d) #4   (e) #2

Exercise 7

(a) Paragraph 2, sentence 3: 'For a small ...'
(b) Paragraph 4, sentence 4: 'That cost me ...'
(c) Paragraph 5, sentence 3: 'I have both an ...'
(d) Paragraph 2, sentence 5: 'At no cost ...'
(e) Paragraph 2, sentence 1: 'If neither your ...'
(f) Paragraph 3, sentence 3: 'At a second ...'
(g) Paragraph 4, sentence 2: 'I am nearly ...'
(h) Paragraph 5, sentence 2: 'I love beautiful ...'

Exercise 8

(a) his twenty-fifth wedding anniversary
(b) at eleven o'clock
(c) those who are merely interested
(d)   (i) they feel that Christie's is unapproachable
      (ii) they are reluctant to change their minds
(e)   (i) he loves beautiful things
      (ii) he is interested in people
      (iii) he is curious

UNIT 4   Discourse Markers

Exercise 1

(a) In addition
(b) and/as well as
(c) as well as
(d) furthermore/moreover
(e) too

(f) besides/too
(g) also
(h) moreover
(i) nor
(j) either

Exercise 2

(a) Although
(b) yet
(c) but
(d) However
(e) Nevertheless

(f) whereas
(g) However
(h) while
(i) still
(j) though

Exercise 3

(a) Owing to
(b) Since
(c) as

(d) thanks to
(e) due to
(f) for

Exercise 4

(a) As a result
(b) therefore
(c) consequently

(d) hence
(e) thus

Exercise 5

(a) unless
(b) where
(c) provided
(d) Whether

(e) when
(f) When
(g) If

Exercise 6

(a) so that
(b) to
(c) so as to

(d) with a view to
(e) intending
(f) with the intention of

Exercise 7

(a) the accountant was unavailable.
(b) the match will be postponed.
(c) local unemployment has risen.
(d) long-term mining.
(e) removing the need to carry cash.

(f) protect society against rising violence.
(g) it received a large refund of taxes.
(h) a wealthy buyer can be found.
(i) nobody answered the telephone.
(j) he was a rich man on his release seven years later.

Exercise 8

(a) On the other hand
(b) while
(c) and
(d) If

(e) because
(f) so
(g) Moreover

Exercise 9

(a) however
(d) On the other hand
(g) Moreover
(j) if

(b) although
(e) and
(h) otherwise

(c) therefore
(f) if
(i) and

Exercise 10

Correct order: 1. (c), 2. (e), 3. (a), 4. (d), 5. (b)

Exercise 11

(a) Since
(d) As/Since
(g) and
(j) and

(b) but
(e) Since/As
(h) As a result/Therefore

(c) Nevertheless
(f) As/Since
(i) so that

UNIT 5 Prediction

Exercise 1

(a) (ii)
(b) (iii)
(c) (i)

Exercise 2

(a) (ii)
(b) (iii)
(c) (i)

Exercise 3

(e.g.):
(a) History of coal use
(b) Description of the difficulties
(c) Details of the discovery
(d) The man and his experiments
(e) Description of the lamp and its use

Exercise 4

(a)	as	(b)	it	(c)	of	(d)	which
(e)	by	(f)	which	(g)	with	(h)	from
(i)	to	(j)	in				

Exercise 5

(a) astonishing
(b) rapidity
(c) countless
(d) commencement
(e) contrivances

Exercise 6

(a) cost-effective
(b) used in place of
(c) vocation/occupation
(d) vulnerable/put at risk
(e) prone to burn or explode

Exercise 7

(a) heating
(b) iron smelting
(c) to prevent it collapsing
(d) coal
(e) only 60 per cent of production was raised above ground
(f) timber
(g) all the coal could then be raised
(h) fire damp
(i) it was highly inflammable and explosive
(j) wood carver
(k) Penzance
(l) Professor of Chemistry
(m) fire damp
(n) the Davy lamp
(o) 1815
(p) it increased the safety of coalmining

Exercise 8

(a)	F	(b)	T	(c)	F	(d)	T	(e)	F
(f)	T	(g)	F	(h)	T	(i)	F	(j)	F

UNIT 6   Inference

Exercise 1

(e.g.): ostensibly, happily, to my surprise, sadly, naturally, inevitably, etc., etc.

Exercise 2

THE STUDENT

Exercise 3

(e.g.):

good − excellent	bad − appalling
hot − blistering	cold − icy
large − enormous	small − microscopic
loud − ear-splitting	quiet − inaudible
tall − gigantic	old − ancient
pretty − exquisite	ugly − repulsive
funny − hilarious	silly − preposterous
unusual − bizarre	difficult − impossible
unpleasant − horrific	frightened − terrified
expensive − exorbitant	valuable − priceless

Exercise 4

(a) probably   (b) Undoubtedly   (c) naturally
(d) Fortunately   (e) conclusively   (f) extraordinary

Exercise 5

(a) backward   (b) pragmatic   (c) progressive
(d) excessive   (e) workforce

Exercise 6

(a) 'Parliament itself' (line 14)
(b) 'The impetus ... was extraordinary' (lines 22−23)
(c) 'the rich mines of England' (line 3)
(d) 'The Romans established iron works' (line 4)
(e) 'the total ... amounted to only ...' (lines 23−24)

Exercise 7

(e.g.):
(a) It is more useful than any other metal.
(b) It is relatively difficult to manufacture.
(c) It happened later than could be expected.
(d) The Britons were slow to follow the Romans' example.
(e) Wood was plentiful in southern England.
(f) Wood was the only available fuel for the iron trade.
(g) Country gentlemen had to balance the demand for wood from both iron and shipping industries.
(h) Parliament disapproved of the demands made on timber resources by the iron trade.
(i) This would have been an extreme solution.
(j) Dudley's process revolutionised the iron trade.

Exercise 8

(a)	timber	(b)	imitate	(c)	purely
(d)	feasibility	(e)	prosperity	(f)	elapsed
(g)	abundance	(h)	contemplated	(i)	established
(j)	disfavour				

Exercise 9

(a) driven/made to act
(b) critical/of central importance
(c) cure/solution to the problem
(d) hostility/unreasoned opposition
(e) boost/input of energy

Exercise 10

(a) a mineral
(b) of the Britons
(c) Great Britain
(d) the places where wood was found
(e) of the iron trade
(f) of the country gentlemen
(g) being hesitant to sell their timber for smelting
(h) Parliament
(i) Dudley's
(j) as a result of Dudley's process
(k) in the middle of the eighteenth century
(l) Great Britain

Exercise 11

(a) the Romans
(b) from Sweden
(c) in the south
(d) because it used too much timber
(e) because it was needed for shipping
(f) it disapproved of its timber consumption
(g) because it preferred to use timber for shipping
(h) because Dudley's process substituted coal for wood
(i) because of the prejudice of the workers
(j) after the mid-eighteenth century

UNIT 7   Review

Exercise 1

(c)

Exercise 2

(a)	object	(b)	rival	(c)	evolved
(d)	fixed	(e)	devoted	(f)	substitute

Exercise 3

(a) stadium   (b) amphitheatre
(c) fans   (d) enthusiasts
(e) match   (f) ritual battle

Exercise 4

(a) ceremonial/imitation/feigned
(b) blown up/full of air
(c) smartness/precision
(d) position
(e) famous people/stars

Exercise 5

(a) association football
(b) 'that it began as a ritual battle'
(c) the ritual battle
(d) a game
(e) the 1950s
(f) millions of devoted supporters
(g) going to a stadium to watch one's heroes
(h) many football enthusiasts

Exercise 6

(a) soccer
(b) as a ritual battle between rival villages
(c) in Britain
(d) an inflated pig's bladder
(e) after the 1950s

Exercise 7

(a) F   (b) T   (c) F   (d) F   (e) F   (f) T

Exercise 8

(b)

Exercise 9

(f)

Exercise 10

(h)

Exercise 11

(k)

Exercise 12

(a) fantasy   (b) unwary   (c) caution
(d) eliminated (e) irresistible

Exercise 13

(a) people who buy things
(b) ways of doing something
(c) happening/about to happen
(d) buying, selling and paying/exchanges
(e) gadget/machine

Exercise 14

(a) However   (b) but   (c) and
(d) On the other hand (e) However   (f) Thus

Exercise 15

(a) Agencies to help those who overspend on credit cards.
(b) Because credit cards make it so easy to overspend that many people are in that situation.
(c) It is safer.
(d) It can be slow.
(e) They are sent in the form of a voucher.
(f) It sends transaction details instantly.
(g) By a device which decodes the magnetic strip.
(h) They instantly adjust the cardholder's bank balance.

Exercise 16

(a) sceptical   (b) more secure   (c) intolerable
(d) excessive   (e) more acceptable

FIRST LEVEL WRITING ——————————————————————

UNIT 1 Choosing a Topic

Exercise 1

(a) 4   (b) 5   (c) 6   (d) 2   (e) 3   (f) 1

Exercise 2

(a) 3   (b) 4   (c) 5   (d) 6   (e) 1   (f) 2

Exercises 3–14

THE STUDENT

UNIT 2   Sentence, Paragraph, Text

Exercises 1 and 2

(a) Railways helped to change people's habits by enabling them to move about much more.
(b) Gentlemen themselves regarded the destruction of trees with disfavour.
(c) Neither your dress nor your manners are clearly unacceptable.
(d) Sales begin at eleven o'clock precisely.
(e) The Davy lamp, as it has always been known, saved the lives of many miners.
(f) 'It is the early bird that catches the worm.'
(g) In propaganda some facts are distorted, while others are concealed.
(h) Two boys travelled in Antarctica.
(i) These adventurous boys were then aged sixteen.
(j) Since Roy worked as an ordinary seaman, he had to swab the decks.

Exercise 3

When I was doing my homework last night I was stuck on some questions. First I asked my father the date of Waterloo. He said he couldn't remember. Then I asked him the formula for pi. He answered he had no idea. I said I hoped he didn't mind my asking. He replied that if one never asks, one never learns.

Exercise 4

There are a number of factors which should be taken into account when buying a dog. The first is breed or type. Some dogs are bred for domestic life as pets, whereas others are suited only for an outdoor existence. The foxhound is a good example of a dog which is almost impossible to house train. If left at home alone it will destroy clothing, furniture and any other items it can get its teeth into. Its proper place is running with the pack.

Exercise 5

Paragraph 1: (d) + (f) + (b)
Paragraph 2: (g) + (a)
Paragraph 3: (c) + (e)

Exercise 6

THE STUDENT

Exercise 7

(a) contrasting points
(b) giving examples
(c) telling a story
(d) making generalisations

Exercise 8

(a) suggested title: Good Salesmanship
(b) THE STUDENT
(c) THE STUDENT

Exercises 9 and 10

THE STUDENT

UNIT 3   Giving Examples

Exercise 1

1. Twentieth-century man can communicate quickly and easily:
   (a) aeroplanes fly hundreds of miles per hour;
   (b) trains are nearly as fast;
   (c) telecommunications are global.
2. Speed brings many advantages:
   (a) journeys take hours instead of weeks;
   (b) perishable goods can be shipped long distances.
3. There are also disadvantages:
   (a) car users become lazy;
   (b) train passengers see little of the countryside.

Exercises 2–5

THE STUDENT

Exercise 6

In the toolshed I found an old, rickety lawn-mower; five rusty nails; a thick, heavy hammer; a tube of Join, the best glue available; a spade; and a fork borrowed from my neighbour, Joe Payne.

Exercise 7

In the lift were: Fred, the lift attendant; two salesmen; the Managing Director, Roger Clive; his secretary, Ruth Wedge; Harry, the Chief Accountant; and Harry's dog, Rover.

Exercises 8 and 9

THE STUDENT

UNIT 4   Generalisation and Generic Terms

Exercise 1

(a) no(ne)	(b) few	(c) a few	(d) some
(e) a minority	(f) many	(g) the majority	(h) most
(i) almost all	(j) all		

Exercise 2

(a) never	(b) rarely	(c) seldom	(d) occasionally
(e) sometimes		(f) frequently	
(g)(h) usually/normally		(i)(j) without fail/always	

Exercise 3

(a) 2	(b) 1	(c) 5	(d) 4	(e) 3	(f) 4
(g) 4	(h) 3	(i) 1	(j) 3	(k) 1	(l) 2

Exercise 4

(a) 4	(b) 1	(c) 5	(d) 2	(e) 3	(f) 5
(g) 3		(h) people 4, time 5			(i) 2

Exercises 5—11

THE STUDENT

UNIT 5   Contrasting Information

Exercises 1—4

THE STUDENT

UNIT 6   Process

Exercise 1

1. Go through the door.
2. Pass the desk.
3. Proceed up the stairs.
4. Locate the auction rooms.
5. Buy a catalogue.
6. Inspect the items.
7. Take a seat.

Exercises 2—6

THE STUDENT

UNIT 7   Narrative

Exercise 1

Charles Dickens was a journalist from Kent who had become a popular writer of fiction. He had been investigating poverty in England, and as a result of these investigations he wrote the novel 'Hard Times'.

Exercise 2

1. He had volunteered. (Ongoing activity: he was taking part.)
2. He did the training and preliminary research.
3. He left.
(Later . . .):
4. He spent the winter under the ice.

Exercise 3

(a) Once	(b) was	(c) had lost
(d) was/had been	(e) ended	(f) One day
(g) was walking	(h) met	(i) asked
(j) was doing	(k) replied	(l) was not working
(m) offered	(n) managed	(o) had been

Exercises 4–12

THE STUDENT

SECOND LEVEL LETTER ——————————————————————

UNIT 1   Question and Answer Formats

Exercise 1

(a) a freehold property
(b) to open a shoe shop
(c) send details of suitable properties
(d) Do you arrange mortgages?
(e) Which building society do you represent?
(f) Are mortgage payments made to you or directly to the building society?
(g) THE STUDENT
(h) THE STUDENT
(i) THE STUDENT

Exercise 2

THE STUDENT

Exercise 3

(a) Broadbent Tools Ltd
     Queens Road
     Barton
     Yorkshire YK4 9BN

(b) The Sales Director
    Kerry Packing
    King's Lane
    Dursley
    Lancashire LN6 3TY

(c) (today's date)

(d) Dear Sir

(e) Yours faithfully
(f) (name)
(g) (title)

Exercise 4

(a) You are looking for a packaging designer and supplier.
(b) Kerry have been recommended by an associate.
(c) You would be grateful for their catalogue ...
(d) ... and price list.
(e) (Ask for any other information.)
(f) Express interest in a visit.

Exercise 5

THE STUDENT

UNIT 2   Answering a Series of Questions

Exercise 1

(a) Roger J. Smythe
(b) secretary of the J.L. Hill & Co. social club
(c) the social club members
(d) ? (Director? Manager?)
(e) approximately March 20th–25th
(f) You have been recommended

Exercise 2

(a) Roger J. Smythe
(b) (Date – around March 20th–25th)
(c) Mr Smythe
(d) sincerely
(e) (name)
(f) (title)

Exercise 3

(a) To arrange a holiday
(b) Go skiing
(c) Switzerland
(d) November–December 1990
(e) About forty

Exercise 4

(a) ... you give discounts for party bookings?
(b) ... ski instruction be provided?
(c) ... is the latest date by which notification is required?
(d) ... insurance included in your prices?

Exercise 5

(a)	enclosing	(b)	confirm	(c)	available
(d)	affirm	(e)	provided	(f)	point out
(g)	required	(h)	regret	(i)	inform
(j)	included				

Exercise 6

THE STUDENT (see also Exercise 5)

Exercise 7

(a) J.S. Wallace & Co. Ltd
(b) ? (Personnel Director? Training Manager?)
(c) The Headmaster, Hetley Secondary School
(d) Your company and the school have had previous contact.
(e) (today's)

Exercise 8

(a) Your company has successfully employed former pupils of Hetley School.
(b) They have been loyal, hard-working and efficient.
(c) You have vacancies to fill.
(d) Office juniors.
(e) Two.

Exercises 9 and 10

THE STUDENT

UNIT 3   'Any Other Relevant Details Would Be Appreciated'

Exercise 1

(a) James P. Long
(b) UK Manager
(c) Omega Oil Co. Ltd
(d) The Principal, Ford School of English
(e) Female
(f) JPL/BO/1A

Exercise 2

(a) James P. Long, UK Manager
(b) (today's date)
(c) Your ref: JPL/BO/1A
(d) Dear Mr Long
(e) Yours sincerely
(f) (a woman's name)
(g) Principal

Exercise 3

(a) Send employees on a language course.
(b) To improve their English.
(c) They employ many nationalities.
(d) About forty.
(e) Approximately six months.

Exercise 4

(a) interested?
(b) courses
(c) terms
(d) fees
(e) accommodation can be provided

Exercise 5

(a) ... you like to meet our Personnel Manager?
(b) ... could he come to see you?

Exercises 6–8

THE STUDENT

Exercise 9

(a) R. Cullen & Co. Ltd
(b) ? (Marketing Director? Advertising Manager?)
(c) The Editor, 'Dean Daily News'
(d) A man
(e) No

Exercise 10

(a) You are opening a shop.
(b) Advertisement rates.
(c) A two-page advertisement.
(d) A half-page advertisement.
(e) Every Friday.

Exercises 11–12

THE STUDENT

UNIT 4   A Choice of Answers

Exercise 1

(a) Leonard Smith
(b) General Manager
(c) J. Old
(d) LS/APM/1
(e) approximately 26th–30th November 1990

Exercise 2

(a) to open a new branch
(b) in Adler town centre
(c) select suitable premises from your list
(d) notify him immediately
(e) start looking for suitable premises

Exercise 3

(a) . . . one of our senior representatives visit you?
(b) . . . can he come?

Exercise 4

(a) confirming
(b) a suitable property
(c) ample space for displaying goods
(d) located on Adler High Street
(e) a large car park at the rear

Exercises 5 and 6

THE STUDENT

Exercise 7

(a) ? (Personnel Manager?)
(b) P. Drew & Co. Ltd
(c) Miss J. Short
(d) The Manageress, Office Staff Bureau
(e) (today's)

Exercise 8

(a) try to recruit some staff for you
(b) clerk/typists
(c) three
(d) within a month
(e) to be made when the recruits start work

Exercises 9 and 10

THE STUDENT

UNIT 5   Confirming Arrangements

Exercise 1

JS/LW/1B

Exercise 2

(a) Hiram B. Rogan
(b) Chief Executive, Bubble Recordings, USA
(c) Monday, 3rd June
(d) He is one of the best American clients of Alpha Discs.
(e) He wants to see a studio recording being made.
(f) For him to see the technical side of record production.
(g) You can let him see the artistic side.
(h) Because you do a lot of business with Alpha Discs.

Exercise 3

(a) 3rd June
(b) 24th June
(c) THE STUDENT
(d) THE STUDENT
(e) THE STUDENT
(f) THE STUDENT

Exercise 4

THE STUDENT

Exercise 5

(a) ? (Managing Director? Marketing Director?)
(b) Dear Sirs
(c) THE STUDENT
(d) THE STUDENT
(e) THE STUDENT

Exercises 6 and 7

THE STUDENT

UNIT 6   Complaints

Exercise 1

(a) R.J. James
(b) ? (Proprietor?)
(c) The Manager, Ace Confectionery Co. Ltd
(d) TS/RJJ/42
(e) Various Items of Confectionery
(f) B8172
(g) Possibly all

Exercise 2

(a) Because a promised delivery was late.
(b) A salesman had failed to call, causing Tasty Sweets to sell out of popular lines.

(c) R.J. James had been assured by your company that the delivery was on its way.
(d) Inconvenience and lost business.
(e) Assure R.J. James that it will not happen again.

Exercise 3

(a) Ace Confectionery Co. Ltd
110 Comper Road
Mellone
Perthshire AB3 8YZ

(b) R.J. James
Tasty Sweets
1 Mell Street
Rodale
Essex PR2 3HH

(c) 6 July 1990

(d) Your ref: TS/RJJ/42
(e) Our ref: (e.g.) AB/CD/1

(f) Dear R.J. James

(g) Subject: Various Items of Confectionery.

Invoice B8172

(h) Yours sincerely
(i) (name)
(j) Manager

Exercise 4

(a) I would like to express my/our sincere apologies
(b) I cannot understand
(c) I fail to understand
(d) I can only assume
(e) However you have my assurance
(f) I can well appreciate
(g) I hope
(h) we apologise
(i) guarantee
(j) We look forward to receiving

Exercises 5—8

THE STUDENT

UNIT 7   Revision

Exercises 1—8

THE STUDENT

SECOND LEVEL SUMMARY ────────────────────────────

UNIT 1   Introduction

Exercises 1–4

THE STUDENT

UNIT 2   Focus

Exercise 1

(d)

Exercise 2

(c)

Exercise 3

(b)

Exercise 4

(c)

Exercise 5

(a)

Exercise 6

(a)

Exercise 7

(b)

Exercise 8

(c)

Exercise 9

(c)

Exercise 10

(b)

Exercise 11

(c)

Exercise 12

THE STUDENT

UNIT 3   Selecting Information

Exercise 1

(d)

Exercises 2−6

THE STUDENT

UNIT 4   Paraphrasing

Exercises 1 and 2

THE STUDENT

UNIT 5   Linking Points

Exercises 1−5

THE STUDENT

UNIT 6   Style and Attitude

Exercises 1 and 2

THE STUDENT

UNIT 7   Review

Exercises 1 and 2

THE STUDENT

SECOND LEVEL WRITING ────────────────────────

UNIT 1   Introduction

Exercise 1

(a) 3   (b) 4   (c) 1   (d) 5   (e) 2

Exercise 2

(a) 2   (b) 1   (c) 3   (d) 5   (e) 4

Exercises 3–9

THE STUDENT

Exercise 10

(a) 4   (b) 3   (c) 6   (d) 1   (e) 5   (f) 2

Exercise 11

(a) 4   (b) 6   (c) 3   (d) 4   (e) 5   (f) 1

Exercise 12

THE STUDENT

UNIT 2   Definitions

Exercise 1

(a) Barter   (b) Nationalisation   (c) Commodities
(d) Economy   (e) Trade Unions   (f) Inflation
(g) Sole trader   (h) Insurance

Exercise 2

THE STUDENT

Exercise 3

bucket   – container   centipede – insect
trawler   – ship   lorry   – vehicle
platinum – metal   pump   – machine
waistcoat – garment   dictionary – book
hoe   – tool   garage   – structure

Exercise 4

accountancy – profession
calculator   – device
catering   – service
coinage   – currency
contract   – document
duty   – surcharge
electricity – utility
fine   – penalty
fraud   – crime
secretary   – employee

Exercises 5–10

THE STUDENT

UNIT 3 Comparison

Exercises 1–4

THE STUDENT

Exercise 5

(a) (e.g.): The Role of the State in Improving the Quality of Life
(b) The more (Just as)
(c) more
(d) the more (so)
(e) more
(f) As
(g) more
(h) so
(i) more
(j) less
(k) than
(l) as
(m) More
(n) more/better
(o) Like
(p) as
(q) as
(r) like/similar to
(s) The more
(t) the happier
(u) too much
(v) As
(w) so
(x) as
(y) as
(z) Moreover

Exercise 6

THE STUDENT

UNIT 4 Cause and Effect

Exercise 1

THE STUDENT

Exercise 2

Because/Since/As each viewer tends to reduce the time he gives to activities which matter to him least, the encroachment of viewing on activities other than listening to the radio and cinema going has been broadly impartial.

Exercise 3

THE STUDENT

Exercise 4

Before the commencement of the nineteenth century, only sixty per cent of the coal produced was raised above the ground. *This was due to* the use of coal for propping the roofs of coalmines.

Exercises 5–8

THE STUDENT

UNIT 5   Possibility and Likelihood

Exercises 1—10

THE STUDENT

UNIT 6   Obligation and Necessity

Exercises 1 and 2

THE STUDENT

Exercise 3

(e.g.):

(a) Council Housing	(b) should/must/has to
(c) necessary/required/obligatory	(d) have to/need to
(e) should	(f) had to
(g) could	(h) had to
(i) should	(j) need not
(k) should	(l) preferable
(m) should	(n) should
(o) possible	(p) should
(q) could	

Exercises 4 and 5

THE STUDENT

UNIT 7   Condition and Hypothesis

Exercises 1—6

THE STUDENT